Caitlín R. Kiernan

CRITICAL EXPLORATIONS IN SCIENCE FICTION AND FANTASY
(a series edited by Donald E. Palumbo and C.W. Sullivan III)

Earlier Works: www.mcfarlandpub.com

Recent Works: 52 *Michael Moorcock: Fiction, Fantasy and the World's Pain* (Mark Scroggins, 2016)

53 *The Last Midnight: Essays on Apocalyptic Narratives in Millennial Media* (ed. Leisa A. Clark, Amanda Firestone, Mary F. Pharr, 2016)

54 *The Science Fiction Mythmakers: Religion, Science and Philosophy in Wells, Clarke, Dick and Herbert* (Jennifer Simkins, 2016)

55 *Gender and the Quest in British Science Fiction Television: An Analysis of Doctor Who, Blake's 7, Red Dwarf and Torchwood* (Tom Powers, 2016)

56 *Saving the World Through Science Fiction: James Gunn, Writer, Teacher and Scholar* (Michael R. Page, 2017)

57 *Wells Meets Deleuze: The Scientific Romances Reconsidered* (Michael Starr, 2017)

58 *Science Fiction and Futurism: Their Terms and Ideas* (Ace G. Pilkington, 2017)

59 *Science Fiction in Classic Rock: Musical Explorations of Space, Technology and the Imagination, 1967–1982* (Robert McParland, 2017)

60 *Patricia A. McKillip and the Art of Fantasy World-Building* (Audrey Isabel Taylor, 2017)

61 *The Fabulous Journeys of Alice and Pinocchio: Exploring Their Parallel Worlds* (Laura Tosi with Peter Hunt, 2018)

62 *A* Dune *Companion: Characters, Places and Terms in Frank Herbert's Original Six Novels* (Donald E. Palumbo, 2018)

63 *Fantasy Literature and Christianity: A Study of the Mistborn, Coldfire, Fionavar Tapestry and Chronicles of Thomas Covenant Series* (Weronika Łaszkiewicz, 2018)

64 *The British Comic Invasion: Alan Moore, Warren Ellis, Grant Morrison and the Evolution of the American Style* (Jochen Ecke, 2019)

65 *The Archive Incarnate: The Embodiment and Transmission of Knowledge in Science Fiction* (Joseph Hurtgen, 2018)

66 *Women's Space: Essays on Female Characters in the 21st Century Science Fiction Western* (ed. Melanie A. Marotta, 2019)

67 *"Hailing frequencies open": Communication in* Star Trek: The Next Generation (Thomas D. Parham III, 2019)

68 *The Global Vampire: Essays on the Undead in Popular Culture Around the World* (ed. Cait Coker, 2019)

69 *Philip K. Dick: Essays of the Here and Now* (ed. David Sandner, 2019)

70 *Michael Bishop and the Persistence of Wonder: A Critical Study of the Writings* (Joe Sanders, 2020)

71 *Caitlín R. Kiernan: A Critical Study of Her Dark Fiction* (James Goho, 2020)

72 *In* Frankenstein's *Wake: Mary Shelley, Morality and Science Fiction* (Alison Bedford, 2020)

73 *The Fortean Influence on Science Fiction: Charles Fort and the Evolution of the Genre* (Tanner F. Boyle, 2020)

74 *Arab and Muslim Science Fiction* (Hosan Elzembely and Emad El-Din Aysha, 2020)

Caitlín R. Kiernan
A Critical Study of Her Dark Fiction

JAMES GOHO

CRITICAL EXPLORATIONS IN
SCIENCE FICTION AND FANTASY, 71

Series Editors Donald E. Palumbo *and* C.W. Sullivan III

McFarland & Company, Inc., Publishers
Jefferson, North Carolina

This book has undergone peer review.

Library of Congress Cataloguing-in-Publication Data

Names: Goho, James, 1946– author.
Title: Caitlín R. Kiernan : a critical study of her dark fiction / James Goho.
Description: Jefferson, North Carolina : McFarland & Company, Inc., Publishers, 2020 | Series: Critical explorations in science fiction and fantasy ; 71 | Includes bibliographical references and index.
Identifiers: LCCN 2020032648 | ISBN 9781476680897 (paperback : acid free paper) ∞
ISBN 9781476640730 (ebook)
Subjects: LCSH: Kiernan, Caitlín R.—Criticism and interpretation. | Light and darkness in literature.
Classification: LCC PS3561.I358 Z67 2020 | DDC 813/.54—dc23
LC record available at https://lccn.loc.gov/2020032648

British Library cataloguing data are available

**ISBN (print) 978-1-4766-8089-7
ISBN (ebook) 978-1-4766-4073-0**

© 2020 James Goho. All rights reserved

No part of this book may be reproduced or transmitted in any form or by any means, electronic or mechanical, including photocopying or recording, or by any information storage and retrieval system, without permission in writing from the publisher.

Front cover image © 2020 Tithi Luadthong/Shutterstock

Printed in the United States of America

*McFarland & Company, Inc., Publishers
Box 611, Jefferson, North Carolina 28640
www.mcfarlandpub.com*

For Pam

"Who ever lov'd, that lov'd not at first sight?"
—Christopher Marlowe, "Hero and Leander," l. 176

Table of Contents

Acknowledgments	ix
Preface	1
A Brief Biography of Caitlín R. Kiernan	3
Introduction	9
One. The Call of the *Sí*: Irish Supernatural Literature and Folklore in the Fiction of Caitlín R. Kiernan	19
Two. Kiernan Echoes the Literary Decadence	32
Three. The Figure of the Gothic Body	46
Four. The Folklore of Awe and Terror	61
Five. "Warnings to the Curious": Kiernan's Science and Mystery Stories	76
Six. Haunted Perceptions: Fear and Trembling in Kiernan's Fiction	91
Seven. Spectral Confessions: *The Red Tree* and *The Drowning Girl: A Memoir*	105
Eight. Dark Futures: Surveying Kiernan's Science Fiction	117
Nine. Retruthing Steampunk: Kiernan Rewrites American West Steampunk	134
Conclusion: Caitlín R. Kiernan's Modern Dark Fiction	150
Chapter Notes	159
Bibliography	171
Index	189

Acknowledgments

Several of the chapters in this book are revised versions of essays published in journals. Chapter One originally appeared in a different form as "The Call of the *Sí*: Irish Supernatural Literature and Folklore in the Fiction of Caitlín R. Kiernan" in *The Green Book*, 9 (2017), Swan River Press, Dublin, Éire. Chapter Two is a significantly revised version of "'The best Vitality/Cannot excel Decay': Echoes of Literary Decadence in the Fiction of Caitlín R. Kiernan," which appeared in *Wormwood*, 30 (2018), Tartarus Press, Leyburn, UK. Chapter Three is a revised version of "The Figure of the Gothic Body in the Fiction of Caitlín R. Kiernan," which first appeared in *Studies in the Fantastic*, 5 (Winter 2017/Spring 2018) from the University of Tampa Press. Chapter Four is an extensively revised version of "Caitlín R. Kiernan and the Folklore of Awe and Terror," which was published in *Weird Fiction Review*, 5 (2014), from Centipede Press. Chapter Five is a much-revised version of "Science and Mystery in the Works of Caitlín R. Kiernan" from *Weird Fiction Review*, 7 (2016). Chapter Six is a revised version of "Haunted Perceptions: Fear and Trembling in the Works of Caitlín R. Kiernan" from *Weird Fiction Review*, 6 (2015). Chapter Nine: "Retruthing Steampunk: Caitlín R. Kiernan Rewrites American West Steampunk" appeared in *Extrapolation* 59.2 (2018). It is reprinted here with the kind permission of Liverpool University Press, the publisher of the original article.

Many people contributed to this book. First, I am grateful to S.T. Joshi. He has encouraged me for some time to undertake and complete this book. He is an enduring source of wisdom on literature. I cannot say thanks enough for all of his suggestions, help, encouragement and advice over the years. Three of the chapters in this book are revised from articles published in *Weird Fiction Review*, edited by Mr. Joshi. Thanks also go to Jared Waters, of the wonderful Centipede Press, for publishing those three essays. I also want to thank Dr. David Reamer, editor, *Studies in the Fantastic*, and the unnamed reviewer for their suggestions and editorial directions that vastly improved my essay published in that journal. The editors, including Dr. Andrew M. Butler of Canterbury Christ Church University, and the anonymous reviewers at

Extrapolation were also generous in their help and suggestions to develop my article. I give a special thanks to Dr. Gerry Canavan of Marquette University for his advice and suggestions. And I want to mention the late Dr. Michael M. Levy of the University of Wisconsin–Stout, a scholar of science fiction, a fine and caring person, and a former managing editor at *Extrapolation*. Dr. Levy was generous with his helpful and encouraging communications with me during my article's review. I thank Brian Showers at Swan River Press in Dublin for publishing my piece in *The Green Book*. As well, I thank the unidentified reviewer and editor for their editorial improvements. Mark Valentine was kind enough to print my article on the Decadence and Kiernan in *Wormwood*, which is published by Tartarus Press of Carlton, Leyburn, North Yorkshire. The Winnipeg Millennium Library was instrumental in obtaining copies of difficult to access references through interlibrary loans. Rose Flickner at the University of Rochester Rush Rhees Library tracked down a number of especially critical articles for this book. For many years Shaun Goho and Jill Pascoe have listened to me talk about all things gothic and afforded much advice on my research directions. Their comments and suggestions improved this book. My good friend, Dave Williamson, the Canadian author, and I talked about the gothic and Kiernan at many of our routine Book Chat Brunches. Dave knows more about writing and authors than anyone else. I wish to thank the editors at McFarland for their care and consideration during the preparation of the book. As well, I thank the McFarland readers of the original manuscript for their thoughtful comments and suggestions to improve the book. It is a much better book due to all of their help. Any errors or flaws in the book are mine alone. Of course, the real source of any inspiration there might be in this book is due to Caitlín R. Kiernan; she is the creative source. And deepest thanks to Pam, who is always wonderful, for her countless hours reading and editing the manuscript.

Preface

This book explores the weird, gothic and science fiction of Caitlín R. Kiernan. She is widely acknowledged as a leading author in her field. Neil Gaiman, Peter Straub, Ramsey Campbell, Gary K. Wolfe, S.T. Joshi, and others have praised her fiction. She has won many awards: International Horror Guild Awards, James Tiptree, Jr. Award, Bram Stoker Awards and others. Her literary gothic is beginning to be recognized within the academic environment. Yet there is no extended literary exploration of her body of work. This book works to overcome that deficiency.

It is the first book-length, critical-theoretical engagement with Kiernan's writing and will be of interest to students, academics, independent scholars and readers of gothic, supernatural and weird literature, and science fiction. The intention is to create a meaningful literary map of the themes and motifs in her fiction. The book studies Kiernan's fiction through a variety of contemporary literary lenses, such as postcolonial, queer and ecological criticism. The book will benefit readers by providing an overall introduction to her fiction, a source book on what has influenced her work, critical assessments of many of her specific works and an explanation of traditional and modern gothic and uncanny themes in her work. Although the book is academic in nature, it has been written to be accessible to the general reader who is interested in dark, gothic and uncanny literature, and those who may be especially interested in Caitlín R Kiernan.

The book includes a brief biography of Kiernan, which overviews her scientific publications. Kiernan is a paleontologist with a long list of field research and scientific publication accomplishments. The book also includes an introduction, nine chapters, and a conclusion. The chapters are organized thematically and each explores a representative sampling of her fiction in relation to current literary theory. Seven of the chapters are revised (sometimes extensively) versions of articles published in academic and serious non-academic publications in the USA, the UK and Ireland. Most of these publications are printed in small numbers and are not easily accessible. The book provides an extensive primary and secondary bibliography.

Preface

This book is the result of several years of reading and study. In its preparation, I have read nearly all of Kiernan's fiction and a selection of her scientific articles. As well, my research included a study of reviews of her work, an examination of other scholarly discussions on her work and a more general study of the literary gothic and horror field and the field of science fiction. The recognition of and interest in Kiernan's literature is growing. This book is meant to address that interest and provide an overall review of her place in modern literature in relation to the long tradition of the gothic, fantasy and science fiction.

A Brief Biography of Caitlín R. Kiernan

Caitlín Rebekah Kiernan was born as Kenneth R. Wright on May 26, 1964, in Dublin, Ireland.[1] She moved to the United States as a child with her mother (Susan Ramey Cleveland). They settled in Leeds, Alabama, which is about 20 miles from Birmingham. Kiernan says she spent most of her childhood and a considerable amount of her twenties in Leeds (Kiernan, "Leeds, One Year Later"). Early in life, she became interested in paleontology and writing. As a teenager (still identifying as Kenneth R. Wright) she lived in Trussville, a suburb of Birmingham. While in high school there, she volunteered at the now-closed Red Mountain Museum. For several summer months she participated in archaeological and paleontological digs. The museum was located next to a road cut that exposed 190 million years of geological strata. The site was a rich source of fossils for paleontologists, including Cretaceous mosasaurs, which became a continuing area of study and research for Kiernan (see McDowell, "Caitlín R. Kiernan").

Kiernan graduated from Hewitt-Trussville High School in 1983. Subsequently, she studied geology and vertebrate paleontology at the University of Alabama at Birmingham and then at the University of Colorado at Boulder. She returned to Alabama from Colorado in the late 1980s to work at the Red Mountain Museum, holding both museum and teaching positions. After her university studies and back in Birmingham, Kiernan transitioned between 1989 and 1992.

Kiernan is a paleontologist with a long list of field research and scientific publication accomplishments. As early as 1983 she found a notable pterosaur fossil, a 3-centimeter femur of a fledgling. Only a few specimens have been found in Alabama (Westfall, "Pterosaurs"). In 1985 she (as K.R. Wright) published "A New Specimen of *Globidens alabamaensis* from Alabama" in the *Journal of the Alabama Academy of Sciences*. In 1988 she was the sole author of three scientific publications. In the same, year she collaborated with Samuel Wayne Shannon in describing *Selmasaurus russelli*, the only Plioplatecarpine

Mosasaur (Squamata, Mosasauridae) species so far identified in Alabama in the *Journal of Vertebrate Paleontology* (Bethany Latham, "Mosasaurs"). Also in 1988, along with D. Varner, she published "Fleshing-Out the Mosasaurs (Squamata: Mosasauridae)" in the *Journal of Paleontology*.

In 1992, now identifying as Kiernan, she designated *Clidastes propython* Cope, 1869 as the type species of the North American Upper Cretaceous mosasaur genus type species *Clidastes* Cope, 1868 in *Bulletin of Zoological Nomenclature* (Kiernan, "*Clidastes* Cope"). In 2002 she was the sole researcher and author of a survey of mosasaur material from the Eutaw Formation (Santonian) and Selma Group (Late Santonian–Late Maastrichtian) of western and central Alabama. Her research found significant stratigraphic segregation among taxa. Three distinct biozones were identified based on the survey (Kiernan, "Stratigraphic Distribution"). Following that, she and fellow paleontologist David R. Schwimmer conducted research on dromaeosaurs, familiarly known as raptors, which they published in *The Mosasaur* in 2004. Kiernan continues interest and involvement in paleontology to this day. Throughout 2019 Kiernan regularly worked on preserving fossil specimens at the McWane Science Center in Birmingham and at times has returned to collecting in the field. In addition, she is preparing papers on her current science research, for example, on an Eocene glyptosaur.

Kiernan's interest in writing also started early with two publications (as Kenneth R. Wright) in the University of Alabama at Birmingham's *The Freshman Sampler* in 1985: "The Burning" and "Another Christmas Carol" (Kiernan, *Beneath an Oil-Dark Sea* 579). Identifying as Caitlín R. Kiernan, she wrote her first novel, *The Five of Cups*, in late 1992 and early 1993, although it was not published until years later. She was soon to focus more on her writing career. In 1994 she moved to Athens, Georgia. Her first fiction sale was "Between the Flatirons and the Deep Green Sea" which was published in *High Fantastic: Colorado Fantasy, Dark Fantasy, and Science Fiction*, edited by Steve Rasnic Tem in 1995. "Persephone" (1995), in *Aberrations*, was her first published short story. While in Athens, Georgia, in 1996, Kiernan joined *Voodoo City Disco*, a goth band. Shortly afterwards, she became the group's new frontwoman. The band changed its name to Death's Little Sister (a reference to Neil Gaiman's character Delirium). In February of 1997, she left the band to focus on her emerging writing career. Her novel *Silk* had recently sold. She returned to Birmingham in 1997 and stayed until 2002.

From 1996 to 2001, after Neil Gaiman and the editors of DC/Vertigo Comics approached her, Kiernan scripted *The Dreaming* for the DC/Vertigo comic book series. *Dreaming* was an anthology comic book spun off from Gaiman's *Sandman*. It featured existing supporting characters from Gaiman's title and new ones created by Kiernan. The series concluded in 2001.

Kiernan's first published novel, *Silk*, was issued in 1998. It won the International Horror Guild Award for Best First Novel. The novel centers on the long-lasting effects of childhood trauma on its central character, Spyder Baxter, and the way Baxter's personal supernatural mythology awakens or draws forth her memories to attack friends. It sustains a perilous balance between psychological horror and the intrusion of the supernatural.

Threshold: A Novel of Deep Time (2001) features Chance Matthews, the great granddaughter of Henry S. Matthews, who was the protagonist in Kiernan's "In the Water Works (Birmingham, Alabama 1888)" (2000), which is one of her best short stories. The novel blends Kiernan's knowledge of paleontology, H.P. Lovecraft's sense that time is a terrible thing and her spotlight on characters who are outside or banished from normal society. *Threshold* won the International Horror Guild Association Award for best novel. Another main character in the book is Deacon Silvey, a sort of empath, who sometimes works for the police, but does not like it. He deals with his "powers" by drinking. Another key character is Dancy Flammarion, a strange albino young woman who battles legions of the dark world released from their underworld abode during the novel. These characters also appear in other Kiernan works. Silvey and Matthews, now married, appear in the novel *Low Red Moon* (2003), where Narcissa Snow's mental traumas seem to be transformed into external nightmares. *The Five of Cups* was finally published in 2003 by Subterranean Press. The novel traces the life of the vampire Jacob Maury Banlin from the death of his family during the Irish famine to his appalling voyage on a coffin ship to the New World, where he finally builds a fortified mansion in Atlanta, Georgia. There he confronts Virginia Percel (Gin), a rogue vampire he created that turns out to be more dangerous than he is. In 2002 Kiernan moved to Atlanta and lived there until 2008, when she moved to Providence, Rhode Island.

On April 15, 2004, Kiernan launched her online LiveJournal.[2] She has made thousands of entries since that time period, and she continues today. The entries chronicle her writing, her life, her feelings and her thoughts on many topics. In some entries Kiernan is revealing about herself. Many writers keep private journals, but Kiernan's is public. It is a way of maintaining a connection with her readers. And it provides readers with a perspective on the life of a writer, with all of its trials and challenges. Her Patreon and *Sirenia Digest* are essential economic supporters, as are the many readers who purchase her books.

After the publication of *The Five of Cups*, Kiernan's next novel was *Murder of Angels* (2004). It is a sequel to *Silk*, set ten years later in San Francisco. It explores in greater depth that harrowing web of madness and terror. The *Daughter of Hounds* (2007) features Silvey again and his adolescent daughter Emmie in an epic struggle with a murderous female character named Soldier. The background to this novel includes Kiernan's Children of the Cuckoo, which seem to be based on H.P. Lovecraft's ghouls and on the Irish *Sí*. Also in 2007 Kiernan wrote *Beowulf*, a novelization of the film. In 2009, now living in Providence, Kiernan published *The Red Tree*, one of her finest novels. It is set in rural Rhode Island and journals the gradual breakdown of Sarah Crowe by the spectral landscape surrounding and under the Wight cottage, where she seems an inmate. This was followed by *The Drowning Girl: A Memoir* in 2012, which is set in Providence, rural Rhode Island and Connecticut. Also one of her finest novels, it won the James Tiptree, Jr. Award and the Bram Stoker Award for Best Novel. It was nominated for the Nebula, British Fantasy, Mythopoeic, Locus and Shirley Jackson awards as well.

In 2012, Kiernan returned to comics, and produced a five-issue mini-series, *Alabaster: Wolves* (featuring her character Dancy Flammarion from *Threshold* and other works) for Dark Horse Comics. It was issued as a hardback in 2013 and won a Bram Stoker Award for graphic novel. It was followed by *Alabaster: Boxcar Tales* (November 2012–December 2013), which was released in hardback as *Alabaster: Grimmer Tales* (2014). *Alabaster: The Good, the Bad, and the Bird* was a five-issue mini-series in 2015 and was issued in hardback by Dark Horse Press in 2016.

Writing under the pen name Kathleen Tierney, Kiernan published *Blood Oranges* in 2013, *Red Delicious* in 2014 and *Cherry Bomb* in 2015. These dark, urban fantasy, parodic novels track the adventures of Siobhan Quinn, the part-vampire, part-werewolf heroine. But Quinn is not a lovely fantasy or paranormal creation. She has a nasty sense of humor and is good with her fists or any other weapon that is handy, and she revels in the dirt and grit and blood of the mean streets. Kiernan's recent novels include *Agents of Dreamland* (2017), which mixes literary genres and showcases Kiernan's narrative versatility in writing scenes set in varying times and at different spaces that fit together, as if a complex puzzle. In 2018 Tor published *Black Helicopters*, which is an expanded and revised version of her 2013 novella.

In addition to her many novels and chapbooks, Kiernan has written over 250 short stories. Several of her individual short stories have been lauded with awards. "Onion" (2001) won the International Horror Guild Award, Best Short Story. "La Peau Verte" (2005) won the International Horror Guild Award for Best Mid-Length Fiction. Her science fiction story "The Road of Needles" (2013) won the Locus Award for Best Short Story. And in 2014, she won the World Fantasy Award—Short Fiction for "The Prayer of Ninety Cats."

Beginning in November 2005, many of Kiernan's short stories were first published through *Sirenia Digest*, her monthly subscription-only e-zine. It is a unique way to connect with her readers, to maintain discipline in writing and to sustain a continuing source of income from her writings. Gauntlet Press published her first short story collection, *Tales of Pain and Wonder*, in

2000.³ The second edition was published by Meisha Merlin in 2002, the third edition by Subterranean Press in 2008, followed by a subsequent printing in 2016 by PS Publishing. She has published more than 15 short story collections (the Bibliography lists these), including *The Ape's Wife and Other Stories* in 2013, which won the World Fantasy Award for Best Collection. She collected her best short fiction in *Two Worlds and In Between: The Best of Caitlín R. Kiernan*, Volume 1 (2011), which contains stories written from 1993 to 2004. *Beneath an Oil-Dark Sea: The Best of Caitlín R. Kiernan*, Volume 2 (2015) collected selected stories from 2004 to 2012. In this second volume she has categorized the stories by location of writing. The 2004–2008 stories were written in Atlanta, while the 2008–2014 stories were written in Providence. This second volume also contains an extensive bibliography of all of her works from 1985 to 2015. Her most recent short story collections are: *Dear Sweet Filthy World* (2017), *Houses Under the Sea: Mythos Tales* (2018), *The Dinosaur Tourist* (2018) and *The Very Best of Caitlín R. Kiernan* (2019). Kiernan's work has been translated into many languages including German, Italian, French, Spanish, Portuguese, Russian and others.

Kiernan's work is increasingly recognized in the academic world. Recent academic articles by Sean Moreland, Gina Wisker, Kathryn Crowther, and Timothy Jarvis attest to this interest. Moreover, her work is discussed in recent Ph.D. dissertations, for example, those by Jamie Weida, Agnieszka Magdalena Kotwasińska and Alessandro Sheedy.

Kiernan's substantial body of acclaimed work is recognized in the *Caitlín R. Kiernan Papers 1970–2018* housed at the John Hay Library at Brown University in Providence, Rhode Island. The collection contains Kiernan's handwritten childhood journal, drafts of comics, edited manuscripts of her fiction, correspondence with fiction editors and with paleontologists, manuscripts and journals of paleontological work, and related artwork and objects. It represents both early and current works. Brown University has produced a guide to the collection (John Hay Library).

Kiernan's fiction is widely lauded. Dana Jennings in the *New York Times* writes that Kiernan is "one of our essential writers of dark fiction" (C4). Sean Moreland says Kiernan is "widely recognized as among the most important living practitioners of the weird tradition" ("Introduction" xxiii). Jeff Vander-Meer writes that she is "one of the most original and audacious weird writers of her generation" (Kiernan, "Interview: Caitlín R. Kiernan on Weird Fiction"). S.T. Joshi says Kiernan writes with a "prose style of wondrous luminosity, an atmosphere of languorous melancholy, and an inexplicable mixture of aching beauty and clutching terror" ("Sculptures in Prose" 5).

Her most recent books continue to be praised. In *Locus Magazine*, Paul Di Filippo says Kiernan "writes always with tactility, clarity, inventiveness and surprise, conjuring up weirdness out of the mundane, and lifting the veil of the exotic to reveal a common heritage of humanity" about *Dear Sweet Filthy World* (2017). Barry Lee Dejasu in a review in the *New York Journal of Books* remarks that "*Agents of Dreamland* (2017) is an exquisitely haunting read, full of mesmerizing prose, unsettling images, and profoundly disturbing implications." And Nisi Shawl in a brief review in the *Seattle Review of Books* calls *The Very Best of Caitlín R Kiernan* (2019) "a magnificent selection of Kiernan's eerily beautiful oeuvre." Danielle Trussoni says *The Very Best of Caitlín R. Kiernan* is "pure genius," in the *New York Times Book Review* (March 31, 2019).

In June 2018 Kiernan and her partner, Kathryn A. Pollnac, moved from Providence, Rhode Island, to Birmingham, Alabama.

Introduction

Caitlín R. Kiernan is an award-winning author with many dark fiction and science fiction publications. Beginning her writing in the early 1990s, Kiernan has now established herself at the forefront of the modern gothic, weird and dark fantasy genres and in the science fiction field. Early in life, she became interested in paleontology and writing and she remains engaged in the scientific discipline today. But Kiernan's calling is literature.

The main purpose of this book is to provide an in-depth literary review of Kiernan's fiction. The book is organized thematically and surveys a cross-section of her fiction. My analytic strategy emerges from Leslie Fiedler's approach to literary understanding. Greg Dimitriadis contends that Fielder's method of literary criticism continues to be viable and necessary today. The text itself and its literary style make a foundation, including the aesthetic quality of an author's prose, imagery, characterization, plotting, diction and narrative techniques. But texts do not stand alone; they are produced and exist in a sociological, psychological, environmental, and political nexus. This means, I think, that discussions of literature are an endeavor to learn from it, while being engaged in the world. Reading is an attempt to know and understand an author's craft and vision. Commenting on what one reads is an attempt to tell the truth about that vision as one sees it. And the truth of what one writes is mirrored by one's commitment to understanding the texts one reads. In the chapters that follow I comment on close readings of selected examples of Kiernan's fiction. In doing so, I often discuss her work in relation to contemporary literary theories. I do this because what those theories suggest is already present in Kiernan's stories and novels. That "meaning" is manifest in Kiernan's stories. It is not hidden in the depths of her stories. The theoretical lenses allow me to focus on particular aspects of Kiernan's work that seem especially important to her, informative to readers and critically important in our current world. Kiernan's fiction may be challenging to read at times as she probes the gothic and psychological disturbances of characters and describes a chaotic world, but what she writes about is clearly revealed. Hence, for me, theory shows what is present in Kiernan's texts. Within this broad strategy

I discuss a purposive sample of Kiernan's work to gain an understanding of the structure, meaning and import of her fiction. Some stories and novels are discussed in more than one chapter.

This book is not a summative or exegetical troop through all of her works. Rather, narratives are selected that provide a suggestive node of understanding influences on her work, the themes that occur in her fiction and the meaning of her work in relation to current societal issues and literary and cultural theories. The intention is to create a meaningful literary map of the themes of her fiction. Kiernan writes within the long tradition of dark fiction starting with the original Gothic literature.

What Is the "Gothic"?

David Punter acknowledges "the notion of what constitutes Gothic writing is a contested site" (1). Although nearly everyone would characterize the "classic" period (from 1764 to 1824 encompassing the works of Horace Walpole, Monk Lewis, Ann Radcliffe and Charles Maturin) with the term "Gothic," there is controversy on what it otherwise constitutes and what should be so labeled. Some, including S.T. Joshi (*Unutterable Horror*), for example, argue the term "Gothic" should be reserved for works of the original, classic period. Maurice Levy decries the expansion of the use of "Gothic," implying that it has become a junk concept with so many uses that it is nearly meaningless. Neil Cornwell says the Classical Gothic normally involves "dynastic disorders, set at some temporal and spatial distance and in a castle or manorial locale; defense, or usurpation, of an inheritance will; threatened (and not infrequently inflicted) violence upon hapless (usually female) victims amid a supernatural ambience" (66). Cornwell contends that some classic elements need to be present for the term "Gothic" to be justifiable.

Punter argues that after the classic period, nearing the end of the nineteenth century, a number of texts by such writers as Bram Stoker, Robert Louis Stevenson and Oscar Wilde shaped a Gothic renaissance (2). But Fred Botting goes further and uses "gothic" to describe "writing of excess" (1) into our current time. In part the dispute may arise from the perspective on the word. Mario Praz identified the tropes of the original European Gothic: the haunted castle, the underground labyrinth, the double, a taste for ruins, an innocent falsely accused and punished, and a repulsive authority figure (15). But these are the gothic trappings. Praz contends the original Gothic arose as a critique against religious, social and political power structures. The prisons and hideous tortures of the Inquisition were real; the ravine between the rich and poor was unbridgeable. The European Gothic expressed rebellion against the obscenities of perverse power. It illuminated the decadent social edifice for what it really was: violent in enforcing a rigid social order and full of depravity against the poor, women and outsiders.

Complicating the matter is the American gothic, which varies from the European in its topography, with the wilderness and frontier turned into gothic spaces, and its gothic figures, with Indigenous Americans transformed into gothic monsters. In addition, slavery is part of the darkness at the heart of the American gothic. Charles Brockden Brown consciously developed the American gothic against the European in his "Note to the Public" prefacing *Edgar Huntly* (1799).

In both traditions, the gothic, in my view, liberates, in altered and threatening form, what is secreted and unspoken within a society. Charles L. Crow insists the gothic is "the imaginative expression of the hidden fears and forbidden desires" (1) of people who have been suppressed or oppressed. He argues the American gothic is not defined by narrow props, but is a "tradition of oppositional literature" (2). Teresa A. Goddu says the gothic speaks to a culture's contradiction and imagines an engaged but distorted view of that reality. For Goddu the gothic gives expression to the underclass by releasing taboos and by speaking out on societal ills, dislocations and disparities. Focusing on fantastic literature, Rosemary Jackson suggests it "traces the unsaid and unseen of culture: that which has been silenced, made invisible, covered over" (4). Similarly, Roger B. Salomon claims gothic narrative unearths contradictions between the myths of society and actualities of the lived experiences of people, especially marginalized groups. Botting contends "gothic" is a term covering a long tradition of transgressive literature from colonial times to the current day in America (189). Punter agrees that the term "gothic" still has meaning in today's literature because there are continuing connections between the motifs of the gothic and contemporary issues, for example, the gothic "speaks, incessantly, of bodily harm and the wound: the wound signifies trauma" (2), which is a contemporary crisis. This trauma is related to the anxiety over the coherence of the human subject. Our bodies are fragile. In *Powers of Horror: An Essay in Abjection* (1982), Julia Kristeva finds the boundaries between our selves and the other are not secure. She explores the anxiety about the coherence of the modern subject. Moreover, Robert Miles claims there is agreement that the gothic represents the subject discovering herself in a state of fragmentation and estrangement. Sometimes the gothic expresses the feeling of being trapped in a societally enforced role, of being dispossessed from one's true nature. This sense of the gothic finds expression in stories and novels that explore the continuum of sexualities and genders.

Hence, for this book the gothic encompasses Punter's idea that the gothic today speaks about bodily harm and trauma (that is, gothic literature's continuing confrontation of the human subject with her corporeality) along with the meaning expressed by Goddu, Jackson and Botting. They argue the gothic of today has roots in the classical Gothic motifs and continues as a transgressive literature expressing, within a supernatural or fantastic mood, the submerged experiences of individuals and marginalized communities oppressed within a dominating society. In this book I follow George E. Haggerty's advice to use the proper noun "Gothic" for the classic literary tradition, while the common noun "gothic" is used for the literary motif in its continuing manifestations. Kiernan also writes within the science fiction tradition. Of course, there is academic dispute around a definition of "science fiction."

What Is Science Fiction?

John Clute and Peter Nicholls recount numerous attempts at a definition of science fiction but conclude "there is no good reason to expect that a workable definition of sf will ever be established" (314). This is not a lament; Clute and Nicholls contend science fiction is a vibrant literature, which is still evolving. John Rieder does not define science fiction, but follows Paul Kincaid in arguing the science fiction genre consists of works that have a "family resemblance" rather than specific defining characteristics (*Colonialism and the Emergence of Science Fiction* 16).

Andrew Milner briefly reviews the long history of attempted definition by writers, fans, academics and editors with a focus on the relation between utopia and science fiction. In part, Andrew Milner questions Darko Suvin's characterization of science fiction as a "literary genre whose necessary and sufficient conditions are the presence and interaction of estrangement and cognition," realized through an imagined space differing from an author's empirical environment (Suvin 7–8). This imagined space must be scientifically conceivable. Such science fiction exhibits a novum, which is an innovation that is cognitively possible. Suvin's definition sounds prescriptive, and he has argued it excludes other literary modes, such as fantasy. However, Joanna Russ's collection of interlinked fantasy and science fiction tales, *The Adventures of Alyx* (1983), confounds this distinction. In "Afterword: Cognition as Ideology," China Miéville disputes the difference and submits that science fiction and fantasy are each a literature of "alterity," that is, their estrangements are the same. It is their role in articulating an alternative reality that is different. Miéville goes on to critique the ideological, rational progress foundation for Suvin's definition of science fiction, which implies a surrender of "cognition to authority" (240). Rieder argues that Suvin defines the genre by a theoretical or formal strategy (*Science Fiction and the Mass Cultural Genre System* 5) not by observation of the elements of science fiction. Rieder contends that an historical view allows an appreciation of the shifting nature of its practice and outcomes (*Science Fiction* 7).

Kiernan says "the distinction between SF and fantasy is mostly wishful thinking" ("*A Is for Alien* in 60 Seconds"). She often uses themes of myth, folklore and fantasy in her science fiction, for example, "Little Red Riding Hood" in "The Road of Needles" (2013)—the 2014 Locus Award winner for best short story. In addition, the Irish Samhain is reimagined on an isolated, myth-seeking and war-weary Mars in "Whilst the Night Rejoices Profound and Still," and a female water spirit features in "The Melusine (1898)."

In her overview of current trends in science fiction criticism, Veronica Hollinger also writes of the "sheer diversity" (238) of its scholarly readings. She concludes science fiction studies are flourishing, while efforts to delimit science fiction through prescriptive definitions are being continuously challenged. In *Deconstructing the Starships*, Gwyneth Jones sees science fiction as a form of thought experiment, an elaborate "what if" (4) game. In a sense, it is using the scientific method in writing fiction that is critical not the science. What is important is a scientific sensibility that pervades a work of fiction. Kiernan is a practicing paleontologist and her scientific education and practice pervades her fiction. She works within the aesthetic tradition of such science fiction writers as Ursula K. Le Guin.

In her introduction to *The Norton Book of Science Fiction* (1993), Le Guin argues that science fiction is an aesthetic pursuit. She argues there are great science fiction stories where science is either not explicit or it is imaginary and the technology impossible. Le Guin says science fiction tells stories around the "mythos of science and technology," but they also have a political or ethical content ("Introduction" 23). There are many examples of works that do not have common science fiction icons explicitly, for example, Pamela Zoline's "The Heat Death of the Universe" (1967). But it does have a strong underlying science element in its handling of entropy along with a critique of the production and consumption systems within a society. It ends with chaos in a kitchen. As well, Karen Joy Fowler's short story, "What I didn't See," was criticized for lacking genre elements, but went on to win a Nebula award. Le Guin writes about such science fiction motifs as alienation, identity and the social constructs of being human, all of which Kiernan explores in her fiction.

One of the essential functions of science fiction is to dispute our current reality and to question the current human condition. Clearly this is part of Kiernan's strategy in her works. As well, Kiernan brings a gothic sensibility to her science fiction, which aligns with Brian W. Aldiss's proposed definition: "Science Fiction is the search for a definition of mankind and his status in the universe which will stand in our advanced but confused state of knowledge (science) and is characteristically cast in the Gothic or post–Gothic mode" (25). This was true at the birth of science fiction when Mary Shelley remade the Gothic novel into *Frankenstein* (1818), according to Ellen Moers. Aldiss agrees with this, as do Le Guin ("Introduction" 32) and Leslie Fielder. Fiedler writes that Shelley "invented the first myth of the age of Technology" and realigned the gothic from the past toward the "Utopian Future" ("Introduction" 12). Kiernan's dark science fiction questions our current societal structures and conditions by extrapolating surface and latent trends into the future within her gothic sensibility.

Kiernan's Fiction

In her fiction, Kiernan writes about the relationship between writing and trauma, the negative effects of the tyranny of the normal, especially on marginalized individuals and groups, and the links between memory and haunting. She writes of inherited spectrality, the gothic body, folklore and myth, and the violence of our time within a queer and transgender sensitivity. Her science fiction illustrates such themes as the falsehoods of the steampunk subgenre, the relation between science fiction and empire, and how dystopian science fiction reveals today's dangerous economic, social, ecological and political tendencies. Kiernan's fiction brings to life our fears about the other, death, the supernatural, the grotesque and the dark, inherited legacy of our past.

The first two chapters of this book explore selected influences on Kiernan's fiction. Chapter One surveys Kiernan's fiction that is influenced by Irish supernatural literature and folklore. A number of her works arise from her Irish heritage, including references to such authors as Joseph Sheridan Le Fanu and Bram Stoker. Kiernan's "Irish" fiction also illuminates the unique colonial experience of Ireland. Postcolonial theory opens ways of understanding some of the fiction of Le Fanu and Stoker, as well as Kiernan. For example, in the vampire novel *The Five of Cups* (2003), the main character is Irish and part of the novel is set during the Irish Famine. After fleeing from Ireland on a coffin ship, that character, as a vampire, seems to recreate the Irish colonial experience in America.

The following chapter suggests that many of Kiernan's stories revitalize *fin-de-siècle* Decadent motifs and echo the Decadent literary style. It traces the influence of Decadent writers and artists on Kiernan's work, while also reflecting on the extent to which Decadent literature is still possible in our age, especially in America. Kiernan's neo–Decadent fiction portrays the beauty of decay, the allure of perversity and dangerous erotica. But she does more in her Decadent works. She references and expands in more explicit ways the direct and latent LGBTTQ+ content of much of that literature.

Chapter Three explores how Kiernan deploys the figure of the gothic body to express the oppression of submerged individuals and groups. Kiernan's "gothic figure" is a body that varies from socially accepted constructs or expectations of bodily appearance, form, sexuality or gender and is usually experienced as physically unusual or grotesque, often through unwanted display or spectacle. The chapter reads a selected sample of Kiernan's fiction through several theoretical lenses, including Julia Kristeva's work on abjection and melancholia, Judith Butler's theory of subjection, Garland-Thomson's disability theory, and Elaine Scarry's work on the body in pain. These lenses reveal how Kiernan's fiction pushes upon readers the reality of physical and psychological trauma on our biological self with all of its fragility, disease and hurt. That trauma results from the tyranny of socially constructed and enforced norms and standards that differentially affect marginalized individuals and communities. The impact of personal trauma appears throughout Kiernan's fiction.

In Chapter Four, "The Folklore of Awe and Terror," I review a sample of Kiernan's fiction through the lenses of folklore and fairy tales. Kiernan infuses her dark fiction with myth to create new gothic folktales that tell about the current human condition. Many take place in landscapes that seem haunted. This links folklore to the concept of the ecoGothic, which suggests that gothic and weird fiction landscapes often depict damaged and degraded environments. Kiernan's knowledge as a scientist emerges in these stories through her connection of gothic terror with our current ecological crises. She achieves this by reimagining our environments, be they woods, lakes or the earth, as enchanted or dangerous once again. In doing so, Kiernan explores contemporary cultural and climate anxieties, especially as experienced by individuals who differ from and are marginalized by mainstream society.

Kiernan is a paleontologist, and her scientific sensibility enriches much of her work. Chapter Five studies a sample of Kiernan's work as discovery weird fiction, that is, stories wherein the protagonist experiences the uncanny through her search for knowledge, her scientific work or chancing upon an inexplicable object. In these stories, Kiernan's characters are mostly female, as is true in most of her fiction. Their explorations, investigations or discoveries resist rational interpretation. The intrusion of the irrational into the everyday is a defining characteristic of supernatural literature, yet Kiernan deepens its meaning and fright through her scientific knowledge. She is a member of the scientific community, with its evidence-based research, testable hypotheses, observations, field or laboratory testing and experimentation, simplification and abstraction, and self-correcting mechanisms. Science is a human endeavor and, akin to all human activities (including literary theory and social criticism), it is mediated by culture and values, but not everything is true. Some advocates of "science studies" (now renamed to "science and technology studies") suggest that science is completely culturally determined: that science is a subjective, socially bounded enterprise. This chapter critically converses with that field of study. Alan Sokal and Jean Bricmont critique science studies for its epistemological confusion and mis-characterization of scientific methods. Moreover, recently Bruno Latour (one of the founders of science studies) questioned some of the premises of this social criticism field. The chapter also discusses Kiernan's stories in light of the philosophy of science work of Thomas S. Kuhn, Paul Feyerabend and Paul M. Churchland.

On the other hand, some of Kiernan's stories depict the supernatural seemingly seeking out encounters with ordinary people. In the stories discussed in Chapter Six, Kiernan depicts characters experiencing a familiar world turning strange and unnerving, as something intrudes in unexplainable, impossible ways. Their experience conflicts with accepted perceptions of the world, and it is terrifying. Some stories explore what happens to people after an encounter, for example, in "Onion" (2001). While in "Standing Water" (2002), an uncanny experience or a revealed crack in the world is ignored. The characters' perceptions belie their rational beliefs. In these stories, Kiernan's characters feel afraid or exhilarated by their perception of an altered reality because it conflicts with their normative web of belief. Pierre Duhem argued that the history of science demonstrates our continuing failure to unearth the depths of nature. We live in an inter-subjectively confirmed reality that has shifted through time. What we perceive, in part, depends on our conceptual frame of reference. But there are problems with perception. Abnormal perception—that is, perceptions outside of accepted views of reality—are classified as diseased, deformed or delirious. Yet for Kiernan's characters they experience a reality, generally a terrible reality, where no explanation makes sense.

Chapter Seven argues that Kiernan draws on confessional and postmodern literary techniques to illustrate how writing one's life story works to reveal the ghosts that shape one's destiny. *The Red Tree* and *The Drowning Girl: A Memoir* confront the problem of knowing the real past and understanding the effect of that past on one's experiences in an unruly present. In doing so one confronts the trauma of one's personal history—trauma expressed in the form of hauntings in Kiernan's novels. Julian Wolfreys contends that all stories are ghost stories, that is, all stories tell of encounters with the unknown. These two novels tell of Kiernan's central characters' encounters with the unknown of the past and their attempts to salvage or recreate their life through writing. The protagonist in each of these novels reveals (and sometimes conceals) webs of personal emotional, physical and social trauma that ensnare her. Such attempts at writing about one's personal traumas (that is, to listen to one's specters) might lead to liberation but not always, which is what Julia Kristeva contends.

In addition to her dark fantasy and weird fictions, Kiernan has written a number of science fiction stories. In Chapter Eight, I explore her science fiction through four lenses. First, some of Kiernan's science fiction critiques colonization, especially the colonization of the American West. Specifically, her stories work against the American frontier myth and the glorification of space colonization in science fiction, which Carl Abbott suggests are one and the same. Other Kiernan stories may be characterized as dystopian, revealing dangerous tendencies in the present and past. In these she pictures an imaginary, future world in which current economic, social and political trends are conceptualized and characterized. Kiernan's science fiction is also about the vulnerability of the body and the mutability of identity. These stories also reflect political, that is power, responses to differences between people, be it gender, origin, or sexual orientation. Fourthly, a few of her science fiction stories are anti-heroic quests, which recharacterize the traditional male hero story into a tale of female struggle in alien environments. These stories illustrate the false mythology of such traditional quest stories.

A form of science fiction or alternate history fiction called steampunk is the subject of increasing scholarly scrutiny. Some scholars argue steampunk provides a progressive analysis of past, present and future social conditions. But it is also nostalgic for empire, ignores the historic reality of the Victorian era and fetishizes technology. The ninth chapter analyzes five short stories wherein Kiernan creates a steampunk world centered in the fictional city of Cherry Creek (Denver), Colorado, in the 1890s and early 1900s. In these stories Kiernan works against the typical way four signature steampunk themes (status of women, industrialization, technology and colonization) are portrayed in steampunk, especially American West Steampunk.

The conclusion defines Kiernan's distinctive literary achievement in the modern form of dark fiction and science fiction literature. Kiernan's writing encompasses many genres. She prefers not to be categorized as a writer of a particular genre, especially "horror" ("Interview: Caitlín R. Kiernan on Weird Fiction"). Of course, negative associations are often attached to genre fiction, because some critics view such works as inferior to mainstream fiction. John Rieder argues this is an artifact of the way that literary positions and values line up in the contemporary cultural economy of genre and mainstream literature (*Science Fiction* 23). Kiernan writes literary stories within the modern gothic, weird, dark fiction and science fiction genre traditions. She is a literary writer in the sense that she seems to respond to an inner muse, not market conditions. She has a gift of language. Her fictions are constructs of mood and emotion, where the power of language dominates. And this gift is combined with a rich imagination grounded in science and enriched by myth and folklore, but expressed in the reality of today. Yet there is an ambiguity and allusiveness in her work, as if there are things that are impossible to tell. It is a warning not to get lost but to recognize the interplay of reality, the supernatural and construct. Moreover, her fiction seems to manifest contemporary issues and anxieties, such as violence and trauma, climate destruction, and the oppression of marginalized peoples.

One

The Call of the Sí

Irish Supernatural Literature and Folklore in the Fiction of Caitlín R. Kiernan

"It's Dracula's nightout."—James Joyce, *Finnegans Wake*, 145

Caitlín R. Kiernan was born in Ireland, but she has resided in the United States for nearly all of her life. Yet her work seems haunted by her Irish heritage. This chapter centers on the influence of Irish supernatural literature and folklore on her fiction. A number of her works allude to Irish supernatural writers (such as Joseph Sheridan Le Fanu and Bram Stoker), have Irish characters, are set in Ireland or explore Irish folklore. Kiernan quotes William Butler Yeats and imitates his poetry in her stories. The *sídhe*, or *sí* (people of the faerie mounds), trouble some of her work. Kiernan's "Irish" fiction also illuminates the unique colonial experience of Ireland. Postcolonial theory opens ways of understanding some of the fiction of Le Fanu and Stoker, as well as Kiernan.

In *Inventing Ireland*, Declan Kiberd says that the Irish were the first modern people to decolonize and that they represent both the victims of imperialism and its internalization. He argues that Ireland's centuries of colonization by British imperialism[1] is unique, along with its long history of uprisings and anti-colonial efforts and its unfinished work at decolonization, that is, the continuing inclusion of Northern Ireland in the United Kingdom. Kiberd says he will not "recolonize" (*Inventing Ireland* 5) Irish cultural history by forcing it under the banner of any particular model of postcolonial literary theory. But it is helpful to consider aspects of Irish writers, including Kiernan, through the lens of postcolonial studies. Generally, postcolonial theory studies express and expose how political, knowledge and economic centers of powers work to impose their ideologies on and dominate subordinated communities and marginalized cultures (Benita Parry). This domination destroys indigenous cultures and traumatizes the surviving peoples subjected to colonization. Moreover, this trauma manifests in a variety of ways. David

Punter says the gothic speaks to trauma and that it is a mode of memory and history to express that trauma (3). Kiernan's form of the gothic explored in this chapter expresses Irish trauma resulting from centuries of colonization. Parry argues that postcolonial theory represents a confrontation with oppression and marginalization.

My intent in this chapter is to stay true to the Irish cultural history that Kiernan reflects but also to show how her fictions reflects on the colonial history of Ireland. Kiberd (*Inventing Ireland*) suggests that absorbing, reusing and rewriting Irish folk tales and literature are ways of working to expose and overwrite the colonial experience from memory. Aoife Dempsey identifies a gothic propensity in Irish and Anglo-Irish writing, which she contends arises from the colonial experience in Ireland. She argues the colonizer and the colonized used gothic motifs, such as spectral encounters and monsters, to express the impact of colonization. The indigenous Irish could camouflage their critiques of imperialism and tell their own stories through gothic images. On the other hand, the colonizers in their narratives depicted the colonized as an uncivilized cultural other, or as monsters, or as the primitive savages of another race.

Throughout her writing career Kiernan has drawn from Ireland. A recent novel, *Black Helicopters* (2018), begins in Bewley's Café on Grafton Street in Dublin, with Ptolema sipping black coffee under Harry Clarke's stained-glass windows. The ancient Irish festival Samhain is reimagined as the "Phantom Night" on the planet Mars in Kiernan's "Whilst the Night Rejoices Profound and Still" (2012). Similar to what happens on Samhain, the Phantom Night wind brings the cries of the dead, because the Martian *sidh*—mounds of the dead—open to the otherworld on that night. A creature from that otherworld, a *cú sídhe*, a supernatural black dog, appears in "Apokatastasis" (2002). This ghost story is set in a modern comfortable apartment haunted by that dark dog, which may be a harbinger of buried guilt or fear embedded in an old painting. In "Murder Ballad No. 7" (2012)[2] a *sí*, who is fresh as a summer afternoon, is happy to be a changeling in our human modern time that is so devoid of wonder that she would never be caught out. She lures a young pixy-led man to his doom. And the 1996 story "Stoker's Mistress" tells of a *leannán sí*, or vampire, that haunted Bram Stoker throughout his life and inspired him to write *Dracula* (1897). This latter story is explored in detail in this chapter.

Kiernan's stories often meld the factual with the fictive. In her stories discussed in this chapter, she does this to embed her stories in the reality of the Irish colonial experience and to celebrate the Irish story telling tradition. The Irish faerie world may be presented as fantastic in some children's books, but the *sídhe* do not bring wonder; they bring misery as did the colonization of Ireland. Some Irish faerie tales may be thought of as hidden critiques of British imperialism.

This aspect of Irish folklore, a vision of the faerie world without its glamour, provides the impetus for Kiernan's story "A Child's Guide to the Hollow Hills" (2006). In Kiernan's tale a faerie girl, who is chasing a lizard, looks under a stone and falls into the lair of the Queen of Decay, into the timeless rotting stink of loss and suffering. This setting might reflect the influence of Yeats, whose poem "Quatrains and Aphorisms" (1889) includes the line: "The Child who chases lizards in the grass" (*Collected Works* 528). Another possible inspiration may be Joseph Sheridan Le Fanu's "The Child That Went with the Fairies" (1870). Le Fanu's story is akin to common Irish folk narratives, where children are taken by the faeries. In Le Fanu's story, two women in a glittering coach abduct little Bill, also called Leum, from his impoverished family. In *Folklore and the Fantastic in Nineteenth-Century British Fiction* Jean Marc Harris contends that Le Fanu linked fairy tales and imperialistic imagery in this story. More than that, Harris says the story articulates forms of imperial oppression, such as slavery (133–34). In Le Fanu's story, Bill, or his phantom, briefly returns to the cottage, wearing rags, barefoot, pale and gaunt, as if drained of his life essence—symbolic of the facts of being colonized.

In Kiernan's story the Queen of Decay with her rusty needle teeth and leathery wings is akin to a bat or vampire. Robert Tracey argues the *sí* are in fact akin to vampires in that they live off the vitality of their captives. Kiernan evokes the suffering, loneliness and terror of a child lured into the otherworld of the *unseelí*, the fairies' imaginative realm of terror. Similar to "The Child That Went with the Faeries," Kiernan's tale reads like a bedtime story, though one that is many shades darker, explicitly telling of the faerie child's torture and rape by an evil Queen who consumes her. Le Fanu's story takes place in the human world and is not explicit, while Kiernan graphically shows the experience of a child in the world of *sí*, which is a metaphor for a colonized country.[3]

Another Irish tale about the suffering of children is the source for Kiernan's "The Last Child of Lir" (1997). It invokes the Irish myth of *Oidheadh chloinne Lir*, or "The Fate of Children of Lir," also known as "The Four White Swans" (P.W. Joyce, 1–36). Briefly, Aoife, a wife of Lir, bewitches her four step-children, turning them into swans. Kiernan sets her story in a cold and forbidding New York City, where the three main characters are young, homeless people. They are the modern world's children, forsaken as were the children of Lir. The characters are Glitch, who has recently lost his job at a pizza parlor; Jamie, a young woman fired from her retail job after being accused of stealing $20; and Ladybird, a man with HIV who dies mid-story, buried in a doorway by his companions. Kiernan deftly builds a world of hopelessness. Their squat is in an abandoned warehouse basement, and they regularly scrounge for meals: a stale cherry Danish, a couple of hard rolls, and a Coke bottle full of water. In one scene, Jamie hugs a copy of *The House at Pooh*

Corner, a talisman from a happier childhood. These characters are the marginalized people of modern America. In this story, Kiernan provides a voice for those silenced and exiled by dominate economic and ideological powers.

As in other Kiernan fictions such as the novel *Silk* (1998), young people are abandoned and they form alternative family units to guard each other against the powers of the night. In "The Last Child of Lir," on an upper floor of the warehouse, Glitch finds a treasure of wonders in wooden crates, which he opens as a child would his Christmas gifts. One particular crate contains a tall glass display case exhibiting enormous wings on an iron bar. He falls asleep and dreams of flying free with Jamie and Ladybird; he dreams of the children of Lir and their stepmother Aoife. After awakening Glitch spots the shattered display case; the wings are gone. An intrusive drift of snow draws his attention to a newly broken window, as if an opening to an otherworld, to the fantastic, for the last child of Lir—or Ladybird. Here Kiernan imaginatively links the swan transformation from the Irish myth to the transformation of Ladybird in Glitch's dream. But below in the basement, the real world of squalor, exclusion, hunger, cold and death awaits.

Le Fanu's "Green Tea" (1869) may provide the inspiration for Kiernan's "A Key to the Castleblakeney Key" (2011). Castleblakeney (*Gallagh* or *Gallach* in Irish) is a village in County Galway. The story reads as the documentation of research on an odd relic found in Ireland—a bronze key clutched in a clawed, mummified hand. That relic, or rather the large rat it conjures, stalks Mrs. Jacobs in much the same way as a demonic monkey stalked the Rev. Mr. Jennings in Le Fanu's story. Kiernan's story starts with a quote from the fictional *Archaeological Marvels of the Irish Midlands* by Hortense Elaine Evangelistica:

> and is undoubtedly one of the more curious and, indeed, grisly side notes to the discovery of the "Gallagh Man" bog mummy. The hand clutching the key is severed just behind the wrist, bisecting the radius and ulna bones (short sections of which protrude from the desiccated flesh) ["A Key to" 225].

There is a real Gallagh Man, a bog body, found in 1821 in County Galway. But in Kiernan's story the relic may be a hoax akin to the Piltdown Man; or it might be impossibly ancient, possessing an evil force that affects whoever touches it. Originally housed in the National Museum of Ireland, the relic was stolen and lost while on long-term loan to Brown University in Providence, Rhode Island. Before its disappearance, the main character, Mrs. Margaret H. Jacobs photographed the relic. Now it haunts her. She sends letter after letter to the museum curator, Dr. Lambshead, describing her increasingly elaborate and realistic nightmares, arising from, she claims, the grotesque claw. A rat-like thing begins to taunt her, calling her by name and leading her through a hideous underground. Her increasingly disturbed missives depict how dreadful an encounter with the uncanny can be. Kiernan's tale, like Le Fanu's, ends with an inevitable suicide. Both Le Fanu's monkey and Kiernan's clawed hand/rat are inexplicable entities that intrude viciously and persistently into the lives of the main characters.

This figure of the monkey in "Green Tea" seems to be another of Le Fanu's signifier's of imperialistic colonization that are refashioned into gothic stories expressing the tension of the Anglo-Irish inhabitants of Ireland, as Harris and Ridenhour find in his tales. On the other hand, W.J. McCormack cautions about reading political context into Le Fanu's stories and novels. However, Aoife Dempsey argues that le Fanu's gothic works can be re-read as postcolonial texts. She contends that as an Anglo-Irish writer, Le Fanu was both colonizer and the colonized. His tales illustrate the tension between the imperial center of power and the colonial outpost of Ireland. "Green Tea" suggests a moment of colonial encounter within the consciousness of Jennings, the English clergyman, where the repressed facts of colonization (memories of violence and guilt combined) return in the form of the monkey to haunt him. Le Fanu's gothic text recreates a colonial encounter as a physical and psychological encounter with something that is a gothic other. In Kiernan's "A Key to the Castleblakeney Key," the rediscovered grotesque claw triggers the return of traumatized memory of the violence of the colonization of Ireland in the form of a rat that recalls Le Fanu's monkey. Her gothic story may be read as a recovered story of colonization where the experience returns as other and spectral, frightening figures that represent colonial repression and attempted erasure as Michael F. O'Riley argues. As well, Kiernan's story can be appreciated as an example of gothic or weird literature, which is a powerful and ambiguity-filled form of artistic expression.

Kiernan's "The King of Birds" (1998) reflects directly the continuing colonization of Ireland. The story tells of three IRA operatives, Fergus, Gerry and Bernadette, after an attempted hit that went wrong. The trio witness an unholy dark thing, that appears as a thousand dark birds, rising from a dead-end alley in Belfast. This image is a metaphor for the "troubles" in Northern Ireland, or the force of continuing colonization in the northern counties of Ireland. Abandoning their task, Fergus, Gerry and Bernadette race to a safe house in Crossmaglen, County Armagh. As the night goes on, Fergus and Gerry grow increasingly afraid, while Bernadette stays stern as stone. Fergus counts his prayer beads and tells a story of a man who made a deal to come back from the dead during the famine. Bernadette identifies the story as from a Yeats poem, "The King of the Birds," which is in actuality a lyric of Kiernan's own invention:

> Hark, whispered the pale woman beneath the hill,
> Her eyes and mane and lips hoar-white,

> Only a crow, said she, can bring the soul back across
> To make the wrong things right [*From Weird and Distant Shores* 154]
> [...]
> And *sometimes* a crow will bring the soul back across
> To put the wrong things right [*From Weird and Distant Shores* 159]

At the end of the story the three hear the crunch of tires and wrathful voices—sounds of death approaching—or the sound of the continuing violence arising from the colonization of Ireland in the north of the country.

Kiernan's novel *The Five of Cups* (2003) is replete with violence and death. In part, it is a rewriting of part of the colonial experience in Ireland. The novel traces the life of the vampire Jacob Maury Banlin, from the death of his family during the Irish famine to his horrific voyage to the New World, where he builds a fortified house called *Tír na nÓg* in Atlanta, Georgia. The climatic scenes are set in *Tír na nÓg*. Gin gains entrance to the fortress and battles Banlin, who has already mutilated his housekeeper and butler. The novel ends in a great conflagration, with only Gin escaping. This may reflect the ending of Elizabeth Bowen's *The Last September* (1929) with the burning of the County Cork mansion, Danielstown, during the Irish War of Independence, symbolizing the end of the leisurely, ruling lifestyle of the Anglo-Irish country elite. Kiernan may also have in mind the torching of many Anglo-Irish big houses between 1920 and 1923; John Dorney recorded 275 torchings.

Tír na nÓg refers to the otherworld or country of the young in Irish mythology. The house is essentially an Irish "big house" in America, that is, it is an emblem of the English colonial rule in Ireland for hundreds of years. As a human Banlin was a farmer and laborer, as vampire he turns into an aristocrat. At *Tír na nÓg* he confines his wife, Evangeline Duval; a butler of sorts, Ethan Dansby; and a housekeeper, Blanche Sutton, each of whom he governs with a ferocious temper. Evangeline is effectively a prisoner, often locked into her bedroom, as Maud Ruthyn was locked into a bedroom in Silas Ruthyn's claustrophobic Bartram-Haugh in Le Fanu's *Uncle Silas* (1864). Banlin's iron-fisted rule mirrors that of the English in Ireland. And Kiernan's story recreates the female confinement of the Victorian period. But like Maud, Evangeline eventually escapes from the house, but Evangeline embraces the rising sun and turns to ash, drifting away to darkness, expressing the existential void at her life's core and the outcome of many rebellions in Ireland in colonial times.

The novel invokes Bram Stoker's *Dracula*, but from a thematic perspective perhaps owes more to Le Fanu's *Carmilla* (1871). However, Kiernan's novel is more violent and more sexually graphic than either. She displays forthrightly the underlying violence and terror latent in Stoker's and Le Fanu's fiction, that is, the violence and terror at the heart of colonization.

The other central character in Kiernan's novel is Virginia Percel—called

Gin—an American teenager, a street kid, and sometime hooker, with no family, turned into a vampire by Banlin after he brutally rapes her. Gin is the young, indigenous "savage," in counterpoint to the aged, aristocratic Banlin, who is, after all, now a colonist overlord in America. Gin lives in a hovel and on the streets, in contrast to Banlin's fortified mansion, which reflects the distance between colonizer and the colonized.

In Le Fanu's novella, Laura's father is English and they live as aristocratic overlords in Styria, which is really just a cover name for Ireland. Smart and Hutcheson point out that it was common for English publishers of Irish gothic writers to insist that locales not be Ireland. Smart and Hutcheson argue that like Styria, Transylvania is also Ireland. James Fairhall and Vincent J. Cheng document the depiction of the Irish people as "savages" by the English colonizing power. Cheng reprints cartoons from magazines such as *Punch* and *Harper's Weekly* to illustrate how the turn-of-the-century British press pictured the Irish as savage and ape-like. Kiberd in *Inventing Ireland* points out that distorted English picture of Ireland has a long history. Edmund Spenser in 1596 characterized the Irish as a savage people. Stephen D. Arata says that the British pictured the Irish as brutish and the subjugation of Ireland was particularly brutal. David Spurr documents how part of the colonial discourse is to identify and label colonized countries as savage (5). This occurred in America, where the indigenous peoples were also labeled as savages and identified as akin to the devil. Kiernan's setting in America mixes Ireland with America, which has its own history of violent colonization and destruction of indigenous cultures and peoples.

Banlin in Kiernan's novel is akin to Laura's father in *Carmella*. Banlin flees Ireland for America, but America becomes another Ireland. He erects his great house to separate himself from the indigenous population, whom he views as beasts. Gin is akin to Carmilla in Le Fanu novella. Carmilla as a Styrian (read Irish) represents the native power and also is portrayed as a predatory *sí* lusting after Laura's life force. In his 2009 introduction to *Carmilla*, Jamieson Ridenhour suggests Carmilla is Ireland personified in the novella. And Ridenhour also suggests she signifies a fear that the colonized may reverse the empire's oppression. Arata calls this "reverse colonialization," which is the imperial anxiety over the dangers from colonies that threaten its control and power. I explore reverse colonization in Kiernan's science fiction in Chapter Eight. In *The Five of Cups* Gin is the American (or Irish), in her own land (as Carmilla had been in hers) working to overthrow Banlin, the colonizer.

Kiernan provides a startling retelling of the impact of *An Drochshaol*, the Great Hunger or Irish Famine of 1845–51[4] through the eyes of Banlin. He finds his Eileen, of the hazel-green eyes, on a cot hugging the dead body of their son, Donncha, his face bloated and black with Typhus. He lies in his dead mother's arms—the cot a mass of lice. As Banlin buries them, the *bean-sídhe* howls in the winds. The *bean-sídhe*—banshee—is said to be the woman of the otherworld, or woman of tumulus or mound—a woman of the dead. Banlin seems to be in the otherworld as he wanders the island from Dublin to Donegal, where he finds men, women and children, who seem more dead than alive as they beg for food or huddle within their sod houses praying for salvation. The *bean-sídhe* pursues Banlin across the island, wailing with death. Ireland is a graveyard as only death can find anything to feed on.

The Irish Famine caused mass migration of the Irish to America and Canada. Kiernan includes this in *The Five of Cups* and links it to *Dracula*. She also provides a genuine historic connection in her novel. Banlin ships to Quebec on a barque called *Sarah and Elizabeth*. Together with Máire Dolan, the vampire who bestowed undeath on him, they feast on the ship's passengers, with its hold of dying Irish fleeing death in their homeland but finding something worse on a storm-tossed sea. This scene bears a resemblance to Dracula's iconic passage to England, where the crew one by one die and the *Demeter* turns into a ghost ship. Interestingly, *Papers Relevant to Emigration to the British Provinces in North America* (1847) records a real barque travelling to Quebec named the *Elizabeth and Sarah*. Numerous cases of death occurred on board the barque during the passage from Killala to Canada (31, 34). The *Elizabeth and Sarah* landed at Grosse Isle, Quebec, where there is now an Irish Memorial National Historic site (27). Again, Kiernan seems to have drawn upon real life.

Two of Kiernan's stories spring directly from the pages of *Dracula*. "Stoker's Mistress" (1996) is structured as a treatment for a play in honor of Stoker's lifelong work with the actor Sir Henry Irving.[5] The story has a prelude, five acts and a finale. Kiernan weaves strands from Stoker's life, Irish folklore, *Dracula* and "Dracula's Guest" (1914) into her narrative. There are three main characters in the story: Count Dracula, Molly Breen (a *leannán sí*) and Bram Stoker.

Dracula and Molly are center stage in the prelude set in the Whitby graveyard in 1841, plotting their ensnarement of Stoker. In Kiernan's story Dracula says, "My revenge is just begun! I spread it over centuries, and time is on my side" (*From Weird* 61), which is a direct quote from Stoker's *Dracula* (267). Molly first haunts Stoker when he is a sickly child in Dublin in 1854. She is a *sí* at his window, a pale face framed by wild black hair. Of course she is Ireland, the "Dark Rosaleen" (1847) of the poem by James Clarence Mangan. Rosaleen is an anglicized Róisín, an Irish female name. Mangan's patriotic poem, based on the Irish *Róisín Dubh*, is camouflaged as a love poem, as a form of subversion against the colonizing English during a time when any form of nationalistic expression was banned in Ireland.

Kiernan reveals this connection when Molly appears as a drift of "dusty, pressed rose breath" (*From Weird* 64) surrounding Stoker. *Róisín* is rose in Irish. Stoker feels a sharp prick at his neck and Molly's eyes appear as dark holes, which bless him a sight of darkness, of an ultimate nothingness, perhaps of Dracula himself. This scene resembles Laura's childhood "dream" of Carmilla. That apparition has a "pretty face," Laura feels "two needles," and Carmilla's eyes fix on her (Le Fanu *Carmilla* 4).

In Kiernan's story the *sí* guides Stoker into the Irish past, where he beholds victims of the famine and cholera epidemic strewn like dying ravens on the streets and roads of Ireland. Stoker was born in London in 1847, the worst year of the Irish Famine. Kiberd in *Irish Classics* tells how Stoker's mother told him about the cholera epidemic in Sligo during the 1830s. She wrote an account of the epidemic in the 1870s for him. The Famine highlighted the rule and savagery of the British landowners, who exported food during that time (Kiberd, *Irish Classics* 381). In Keirnan's story the *sí* brings the horror alive to the character Stoker. She makes explicit the suffering of the Irish during the colonial period. The real Stoker may have used the vampire image, among other things, as a symbol for the British landlords of large estates in Ireland (Kiberd says eight million acres, *Irish Classics* 381), who lived off the labor of the Irish.

Kiernan also connects this story to Irish folklore. In *Fairy and Folk Tales of the Irish Peasantry* (1888), Yeats notes that some families are attended at death by ravens. He also suggests in "Irish Fairies, Ghosts, Witches"(1889) in *Writings on Irish Folklore, Legend and Myth* (1993) that the *leannán sí* are vampiric, living off those they haunt.[6] But in this story Molly seems to invigorate Stoker. In Chelsea during the winter of 1881, Molly again inspires Stoker as he lounges with a volume of Le Fanu and drifts dreamily asleep. In his introduction to Le Fanu's *In a Glass Darkly*, Robert Tracey observes that Yeats suggested that the touch of the *sí* makes one fall into half-dream (xxviii). Stoker wakes in a "fog of flowers pressed between yellowed scrapbook pages" (*From Weird* 67); out the window he spies naked footprints in the snow.

Stoker's journey to Nuremberg with Irving in 1885 is dramatized in the story as well. Part of this section of Kiernan's story merges scenes from "Dracula's Guest" and *Dracula*, along with *Carmilla*. As Stoker rides out of the city in a carriage, he sinks into a gloomy obsession over his recent visit to a dank museum. At a crossroads Stoker halts the carriage and asks about a lonely pathway, not unlike the path Harker takes in "Dracula's Guest." The driver says it goes nowhere, but finally admits that it leads to an unholy village. There is a broken cross at the intersection impaled by an iron spike, again reminiscent of the cross in the mausoleum in "Dracula's Guest." Jacob, the driver, explains it marks a suicide. In *Carmilla* it is suggested that a villainous suicide may become a vampire. The cross may also reflect the stone cross in *Carmilla* that startles the horses of Carmilla's carriage and deposits her into the care of Laura's father. Startled by a plaintive cry, Stoker and the driver flee through the dark forest, pursued by wolves, as Harker's carriage had been on his journey to Dracula's castle in *Dracula*. A giant wolf, appearing as a blast of darkness, slams into the side of the coach; Stoker and the driver are spilled out onto the road. The *sí* appears and commands the wolves to retreat, thus protecting Stoker in the same way Dracula (in wolf form) protected Harker from Countess Dolingen in "Dracula's Guest."

Another scene recreates a dinner in the Lyceum Theatre's Beefsteak Room. There Stoker dines with guests, but Kiernan also adds a strange woman whose hair is black like a night sky with no stars. That *leannán sí*, that is Ireland, continues to haunt Kiernan's fictional Stoker.

A more explicit scene in Kiernan's story has Stoker dreaming. He is led by the black-haired girl (again the image of Ireland) through a battlefield drenched with blood and studded with the impaled. The *sí* takes his penis with animal teeth, while blood rains incessantly across the field of the dead and dying, as hordes of ravens and wolves watch with hunger. This scene makes explicit the latent violent sexuality of *Dracula*. And it exhibits plainly the facts of the violent colonization of Ireland.

The final act in "Stoker's Mistress" is set in Cruden Bay in August 1911, where Stoker worked on *Dracula* and he and his family holidayed. Stoker is walking the shoreline and finds a young woman with hair the dark shade of night reading *The Lair of the White Worm* (1911). Of course it is the *sí* or Ireland again. She kisses him, kisses him goodbye. He catches again the "musty nostalgia of her breath" (*From Weird* 80), which in Kiernan's story is the pervasive memory of Ireland.[7] In this story, Kiernan links her fictional characterization of Stoker to *Dracula*, to Stoker's real life, to fictional Irish folklore through the intersession of a figure from Irish folklore, and to the colonial experience in Ireland. Appearance and reality intermingle in this story, which itself masquerades as a play. Stoker lived in London most of his adult life, yet Ireland haunted him. That haunting is manifested in Kiernan's story through the image of an Irish *sí*.

An additional story that finds inspiration in the novel, *Dracula*, is "Emptiness Spoke Eloquent" (1997). The title is a phrase from Chapter XXVII of *Dracula*, speaking of the sleep of the three female vampires that Van Helsing is about to butcher. Kiernan's story is an alternate supernatural ending for Mina Harker, one that extends her life for decades. Jonathan Harker's note at the end of *Dracula* strives to portray a return to innocence and hope, a reestablishment of true Victorian values, and the return to the natural colonial order, with the reverse colonization from Transylvania vanquished. But how could Mina overcome her blood kinship with the vampire, her ardent relationship with Lucy and her urge to become a journalist?

Jonathan Harker dies in the Great War, while Mina's son Quincey[8] is taken by the influenza pandemic after the war. His death releases Mina from her sexual chains. For she is not haunted by Jonathan or Quincey, but by Lucy. In *Dracula*, Lucy is initially portrayed as a victim of Dracula, but she turns into a vampire *femme fatale*. In Kiernan's story this happens to Mina, who had sucked at Dracula's breast. Here Mina hearkens to the siren chant of the three vampire sisters.

The story starts in 1969, with Mina as an old woman. She is in a New York City hospital, where she reminisces on her life. Even the television footage from the Vietnam War does not muffle Lucy scratching at the window. This is a direct incursion of the reality of the continuing struggle against colonialism into the story.[9]

In Kiernan's story Mina is not a reliable witness, as the story illustrates the sideways and selective properties of memory. She is always keeping something away, hiding something, perhaps even from herself. In 1904, the survivors survey the desolate waste surrounding Dracula's castle, while Lucy mocks Mina, whispering that Dracula is gone. In November 1919 Mina is at the windswept graveyard in Whitby and then in her hotel room where she dreams of Lucy. Are those Lucy's hands like cool silk on her shoulders? Lucy whispers, "*we loved you, Mina*" (*Two Worlds* 23, emphasis in original). In 1922 Mina is with the elderly and dying Van Helsing. She sees herself in a mirror, still young, but her hollow, dead eyes betray her. She has become a *sí* and represents Ireland, perhaps especially the Irish diaspora.[10]

Then it is 1930 (the scenes of the story are dated) and she is in Paris at Shakespeare & Company to hear Colette read from her new novel, perhaps *La Seconde* (1929). James Joyce also attends the reading. Mina is now a writer of supernatural fiction and she now goes by Mina Murray, her birth name. She has a one-night stand with a Lucy look-a-like and then kills her, or the Lucy Westenra look-a-like committed suicide. After World War II, she goes back to a ruined London. At the remains of Carfax Abbey, she kills a boy, and wonders if perhaps she has left a trail of dead children across the decades. She is the bringer of a reverse colonization back to English shores. Mina loves her meds now, but outside on the streets of New York she can hear the fall of wolf paws and Lucy's incessant fingernails at the window, like mating calls. Mina is in a strange middle ground between two worlds, she is young and old, vampire and human, Victorian and modern. And she represents the colonizer and the colonized now as the English woman takes on the characteristics of an Irish *sí*.

Kiernan's story is more than a tribute to Bram Stoker. She rewrites themes explicit and latent in *Dracula* and gives them a currency and relevance in today's world. In Kiernan's story, Mina Murray/Harker is no longer a dutiful, proper Victorian wife but a strong twentieth-century woman who endures all of the horrors of the century. She is not the embodiment of hope expressed at the end of *Dracula*, but the embodiment of existential emptiness living in a century of war and holocaust. In *Dracula*, Mina's role is of an innocent, but as Kiberd argues in *Irish Classics* the specter of the New Woman haunts Stoker's novel. In Kiernan's story Mina asserts her independence and lesbian sexuality.

From a structural perspective *Dracula* is a novel of appearance contrasted with reality. Dracula is a Count; he is an aristocrat in the class hierarchy era of Victorian England. At night he is a vampire stealing life from the blood of others. The novel itself is a construct of realistic but fictional artifacts such as diary entries, letters, notes, telegrams and newspaper reports. This narrative style itself enhances the appearance of reality of the novel. Kiernan inverts this. Her story is a fictional journey through time set in the reality of war and death,[11] which contrasts real horror with the false horror of vampire narratives. In Chapter VIII of *Dracula*, Mina notes the emergence of the Victorian New Woman in her diary. The New Woman of the late Victorian time was a threat to the male-dominated culture. The common image was of mother, wife, and sister as Kelly Hurley notes, characterized or idealized by childlike innocence. The *fin de siècle* was a time of the morphing of gender roles and perhaps a revulsion of many men, but not all, against such a shift. At that time, Bram Stoker portrays the vampire women in *Dracula* as sexual aggressors, perhaps she-devils or monster women. Kiernan brings that fear of self-assertive women and sexuality to life in her story. Lucy and the three vampire sisters all are killed in *Dracula*, because they express the latent theme of lesbian sexual desire. The men protect Mina because she was the image of the proper Victorian woman. In Kiernan's story, Mina reasserts her non-married name, transforms into Ireland and reunites with Lucy (who becomes an image of the colonized through Dracula) and the three sisters from Transylvania (read Ireland) in a lesbian colonial revolt against the rule of England.

In Summation

Caitlín R. Kiernan is a prolific writer. In this chapter I have explored a small sample of her fiction that shows evidence of being influenced by Irish folklore and literature and the impact of colonization on the country. Of course the centuries long English rule in Ireland affected much Irish writing. In the late eighteenth and early nineteenth centuries W.B. Yeats and others worked to recover Irish history and literature and to extinguish the impact of England over all aspects of the country, including language. This is yet a work in progress from economic, political, geographic and cultural perspectives. James Joyce rued writing in "the language of the conqueror" (*The Critical Writings* 212), but one of his forms of revolt was to command the English language.

Much of Kiernan's weird, gothic fiction explores the outsider worlds of the marginalized and oppressed. In her Irish fictions, Kiernan foregrounds the impact of imperialism on the colonized in Ireland. She links her stories with Irish gothic fictions that expressed (often in hidden ways) the colonial experience and in some cases makes the experience more overt. Kiernan mines that rich treasury of gothic writing to express an aesthetic of loss, an aesthetic of menace through the harrowing experiences of characters encountering the inexplicable, but which reflect the facts of colonization of Ireland. Her characters' supernatural specters reflect the trauma of colonization. But she enriches this with the ambiguity inherent in gothic and weird literature. She expresses this as an experience of an ultimate darkness, as Glitch in "The Last Child of Lir" suffers in a warehouse basement with a "dark so deep and solid" and a "musty smell of a place closed away for a long time" (*Candles for Elizabeth* 21), as if locked away in a colonial prison.

Two

Kiernan Echoes the Literary Decadence

"The best Vitality/Cannot excel Decay."—Emily Dickinson, Poem 403

Chapter One explores how Kiernan's Irish heritage surfaces in many of her works and how those works reflect upon the colonial history of her birth country. This chapter describes how her dark fiction echoes the Decadent writers and artists of the *fin de siècle*. Many of her works replay Decadent motifs, allude to authors of the Decadence and echo the Decadent literary style. Kiernan's neo–Decadent fiction portrays the beauty of decay, the allure of perversity and dangerous erotica. But she does more in her decadent works. She references and expands in more explicit ways the direct and latent LGBTTQ+ content of much of that literature. Kiernan's decadent stories and novels also show the extent to which Decadent literature is still alive today, especially in America.

The Decadence can be traced back to Edgar Allan Poe, but blossomed in the work of Charles Baudelaire and flourished in French and British artists during the *fin-de-siècle*. At first "Decadence" was a derogatory term. But Baudelaire in "Further Notes on Edgar Poe" (included in *Paris Spleen*) appropriated that negative phrase of his critics as an expression of liberation for his art. He celebrated the term in defining his work as the ultimate progression of artistic expression from birth to maturity and on to decay.

David Weir argues current literary critics contest the precise meaning of "literary Decadence." Yet, even if "Decadence" is an elusive or purposely indeterminate term, some clear motifs and themes characterize it. These include a sense of decay, a challenge to realistic prose, hedonism, perversity, madness, "*l'art pour l'art*" and the superiority of artifice over nature. As well, misogyny haunts some Decadent works. Not all Decadent artists championed all of these themes. The Decadence literary style favored language and phrasing over plot and action. Decadence writers produced novels and stories that exposed and gloried in the underside, the hidden aspects of nineteenth-century life. Their works extolled aestheticism and individualism, often in an elusive style. But the Decadents felt a deep pessimism. This arose from their sense of decay, either real or perceived, within their culture and nation. Nevertheless, the Decadents always valued works of art. The Decadents also challenged the sexual and gender norms of the *fin de siècle*.

Kiernan's neo–Decadent fiction reworks many of the themes and motifs of the original Decadence. But her fiction is of today and can be appreciated for its aesthetic elegance as well as through contemporary literary analysis, which helps to reveal the social criticism layered throughout her work. Queer theory emerged in the late 1980s and early 1990s as a means of addressing issues of gender, sexuality and subjectivity in politics, history and literary criticism. The term "Queer" was used consciously to challenge and overcome its offensive meaning similar to what Baudelaire did with the word, "Decadence." Using "Queer" in a positive and affirming way critiques a society where only specific people, beliefs and sexualities are valued. In *Epistemology of the Closet*, Eve Kosofsky Sedgwick argues that sexual definitions and challenges to such definitions are at the heart of literature and that any discussion of literature is incomplete without an exploration of its meaning for and across the spectrum of sexualities. Queer theory is a continuously evolving perspective,[1] but for the purpose of this chapter, which focuses on the relation between some of Kiernan's fiction and that of the Decadents, Queer theory will help to explore the ways LGBTTQ+ issues on gender, sexuality and subjectivity are manifested in her texts. Her narratives tell the stories of sub-cultures that challenge the hierarchy of today and the marginalization of those marked as different, especially those so marked due to their sexual and gender orientation.

Kiernan's fiction is in the tradition of the original Gothic and the revived late nineteenth-century gothic, which coincide with the Decadence. George E. Haggerty in *Queer Gothic* argues that the gothic was a testing ground for illicit genders and sexualities, because the genre's traditional motifs provided an existing framework and readership for exploring proscribed themes and issues. Similarly, Paulina Palmer (*The Queer Uncanny*) says that gothic fiction is rich with motifs, such as secrets, monsters, doubles and spectrality, and unnatural behaviors, that establish a frame for the exploration of taboo subjects. Kelly Hurley sees the gothic as a speculative art form that provides a framework to imagine new human form realities. These motifs offer a way for readers to appreciate how authors have explored gender and queer issues in their fiction. Although there may be more freedom in some aspects of some societies now for those outside traditionally "normative" gender and sexual roles, Palmer, along with Lauren Berlant and Michael Warner, point out that they still endure ostracism, hate, abuse and banishment in many, if not most, public contexts.

People as Works of Art

Kiernan's fantasy "*La Peau Verte*" (2005) creates an atmosphere of languor inspired by the *fin de siècle* Decadence. Hannah paints, but her artistic career is troubled so she takes jobs as a model. For a masquerade party, called *La Fête de la Fée Verte,* make-up artists leisurely transform her into a naked green fairy in a room where the air "smells and tastes like dust and old furniture, like the paint on her skin, more faintly of the summer rain falling on the roof of the building" (*Two Worlds* 343) in St. Marks Place (a trendy neighborhood in New York City). While she drinks, Hannah marvels at her new self in a mirror. She becomes a work of art. A young person (called a boy, but of ambiguous gender) with poppy red nails, rouged lips and sharp teeth enters the room. That person ushers Hannah down a short hallway to a green door, which opens into a hallucinatory room vaster than any rational space.

The story tells of a performance and a coming out. Hannah's story of coming out as she performs as the green fairy is an expression and a retelling of uncounted stories of coming out, of revealing one's true LGBTTQ+ self to friends, parents, the world. In Kiernan's story Hannah celebrates her performance because she reveals her true self. Awaiting her in the green room, the other guests will assess her performative role (that is, how everyone else responds to one who comes out). Judith Butler in *Gender Trouble* suggests, among other things, that gender is performance where the performance allows for or in fact exhibits one's real self (xv–xxvi). Hannah's performance of gender itself creates her gender, as the "green fairy," which will be revealed to the people in the green room.

The story mentions Oscar Wilde, Paul-Marie Verlaine, Arthur Rimbaud and quotes a poem from Marie Corelli's *Wormwood: A Drama of Paris* (1890). Albert Maignan's painting "The Green Muse" (1895) makes a cameo appearance. The numbered sections of the story belie any plot order because Hannah, the green fairy, flits here and there in time and space, as Kiernan distorts Hannah's perceptions and memories, mirroring the effects of absinthe. Kiernan's story changes the whole body into art, while Jean Lorrain's "*L'Homme aux têtes de cire*" (1893), ("The Man who Made Wax Heads") emphasizes body parts. But the glorification of art as art is the same.

Kiernan's view of humans as art takes a darker turn in the science fiction story "A Season of Broken Dolls" (2007). A journalist, who is always stoned, struggles over the beauty or the monstrousness of humans altered into art. In that near future, artists strive for an ultimate anti-naturalism where they become pure art, perhaps with no trace of humanity. Covering the stitchwork scene, Schuler frequents *Corpus Ex Machina,* a bar displaying art installations for the uber-wealthy. The living flesh walls creep her out, but the drinks help her focus on the assignment. So she stares at one piece suspended from the ceiling: a living chandelier composed of flayed muscles and rearranged bones linked by circuitry with perhaps the dim consciousness of the female artist. The story's first-person narrative is composed of the journalist's nearly incoherent sequence of notebook entries, chronicling her increasing intoxication and despair. This masterwork of living art seems formed of anguish and artifice. Kiernan dubs this story her "portrait of the artist as a young atrocity" (*A Is for Alien* 147). It pictures a future where a ruling ideology of the powerful rich results in the grotesque mis-shaping of one's body and identity in order to satisfy its preferred artistic forms. I discuss the post-humanist implications of this story in Chapter Three.

Dangerous Erotica

Apparently, Kiernan wrote "*La Peau Verte*" while drinking *Mari Mayans* absinthe. And the fragmented and dreamy narrative style of the story suggests a mind becoming intoxicated and enamored with the wondrousness of that other world. The language and narrative structure of the story subverts realism. In a sense, Kiernan reproduces intoxication and so-called deviance at the textual level. Rachilde[2] in *Monsieur Vénus* does not disrupt narrative structure, rather she cross-dresses her text. Janet Beizer identifies how Rachilde disorders culturally sanctioned gender and sexual role by providing her transvestite characters (Raoule and Jacques) with opposite and changing gender signs in her book.

Intoxication and textual ambiguity ignite hedonic excess in Kiernan's "The Sphinx's Kiss" (2007). The title comes from Franz von Stuck's painting "The Kiss of the Sphinx" (1895), which depicts the sphinx as a buxom, voracious female with her lion's claws wrapped around a naked man. She drains the life from him with a kiss. Kiernan also alludes to the sumptuously erotic content of Wilde's "The Sphinx" (1894). Her story is an elaborate fantasy, reveling in dangerous erotica and the allure of perverse, violent pleasures. High on x (the drug, Ecstasy), ketamine and gin, the narrator's perspective blurs during an all-night masquerade sex party. He and his boyfriend, who dresses as Marie Antoinette, exchange fellatio throughout the night. Old men masked like birds prowl the party room. The party culminates with a performance[3] of a scene from Wilde's *Salomé* (1893). But the lines are changed and the beheading is real. The androgynous actor playing Salomé shows teeth like a wild beast while she kisses Jokanaan's (well, the unfortunate actor's) bleeding head, reimagining Stuck's art. Many of Kiernan's female characters bear these sharp teeth. Such teeth allude to Edgar Allan Poe's "Berenice" (1835), wherein Egaeus rips teeth from his beloved Berenice's dead body. These mouths of Kiernan's heroines suggest a dangerous erotic zone, akin to the terror of female genitalia dreamed of in the eighth chapter of Joris-Karl Huysmans's "breviary of the Decadence" *À rebours* (1884). Kiernan's picturing of many of her heroines with sharp teeth ridicules the terror of women's bodies in some Decadent works, especially *À rebours*.[4]

Elaine Showalter argues that Salomé was emblematic of the Victorian New Woman and the personification of the Decadent ideology. That's because the Decadent was the masculine counterpart to the New Woman. Together they blurred the distinction between the sexes and genders. Oscar Wilde's trial for homosexuality in 1895 created a pall on the Decadents in England.[5] Moreover, Showalter claims that *Salomé* became a closet drama. Kiernan takes that play out of the closet and foregrounds the New Woman with an aggressive sexual appetite along with directly showing the play's gay sex content within her story.

As "The Sphinx's Kiss" demonstrates, explicit sex is commonplace in Kiernan's work, be it lesbian, gay, inter-species or occasionally heterosexual. "Derma Sutra (1891)" (2008) describes in gynecological detail the ravishing of one woman by another woman. In "Breakfast in the House of the Rising Sun (Murder Ballad No. 1)" (1997), Rabbit works in a gay sex house. Kiernan describes in detail the degradation that he endures at times. But there are also moments of love. And to illustrate the violence directed toward gay men, Rabbit's one true male lover, Arlo, ends up mistakenly killing him in an American orgy of gunfire. The fantasy "Skin Game" (2007) tells of the brutal love of a werewolf, at his time of month, for a man. One long paragraph forms Kiernan's story "Lullaby of Partition and Reunion" (2008), where the female narrator yearns to fuse fully with her female lover. Together they reminisce on a sculpture exhibition of lesbians graphically merging during sex, of making two into one. But they question the sanity of the sculptor who glued her body to her female lover. The narrator justifies the rawness of the exhibit: "Anyway, that's the proper function of art isn't it? […] To unsettle us?" (*Confessions* 184–5), which was virtually a pledge for the Decadents. Nonetheless Kiernan does have a humorous side, as did the Decadents, for example, Théophile Gautier in "*Le pied de la momie*" (1840) ("The Mummy's Foot"). In Kiernan's "The Collector of Bones" (2008) an elderly woman fetches a young boy up to her antique apartment for sex. Afterwards she ushers him into her extensive ossuary, where he poses for a photograph. She eyes him as another trophy for her bizarre museum of decaying bones.

Decadent Art and Artists

Art and artists appear in many of Kiernan's works. Performance art is featured in "Untitled Grotesque" (2007): a live sex act between two young people with unusual sex organs. Gathered close around the basement stage, an audience appreciates the show. The members of this first audience have modified their bodily form in a diversity of ways. They are also on display, but they do not know it. That is because a hidden set of spectators spy on them. The members of this second audience consists of seven men, seven women and seven more, "who keep matters of gender fluid" (*Confessions* 73). This is a story about sexual and gender performance, and surveillance. Kiernan's story suggests that performance spaces are everywhere, and that a performance shapes how we see ourselves and make ourselves and how others see us. This is what Judith Butler argues in *Gender Trouble*. The story also questions about control over how we are viewed in a society, which is increasingly surfeit with surveillance. That is, today an individual may not know when she is being viewed, hence she is always performing. In the story, Kiernan establishes three spaces: the stage, the audience space surrounding the stage, and the upper story, hidden room with its bank of screens. The performers are aware that they are viewed by the audience and they talk about it on the stage; they are not ashamed of their bodily form but use it to earn a living, as was the tradition of circus performers. Rosemarie Garland-Thomson shows that people with unusual bodily form have a long history of being put on display ("The Politics of Staring"). The first audience views the performers as artists and they identify with them, because they share non-normative bodies, which they have modified themselves. They see the performance as liberating and validating their bodily modifications. The hidden audience represents society's universal gaze on those with non-normative human bodies. They view the show on the stage and in the surrounding space as a spectacle of unusual bodies for their amusement. The spectacle of the unusual bodies confirms their image of the ideal body. They also represent where privacy vanishes in our society. In the modern world the marginalized are always under surveillance.

An artist is the central character in "Random Thoughts before a Fatal Crash" (2011). Part of the influence on Kiernan's story may be found in Robert W. Chambers's weird and Decadent collection, *The King in Yellow* (1895). Several of the stories in the book, for example "The Street of The Four Winds," tell of artists experiencing a strange Paris, where Chambers studied art.

In Paris, Albert Perrault combats inner and outer demons with drink, drugs, and trysts with a pretty boy who calls himself Gautier, perhaps after Théophile Gautier. Perrault represents a Decadent artist. He shuns society, wanders "*Le Cimetière du Montparnasse*" (where Baudelaire is buried), stalks la Rue Saint-Denis for rough trade sex and hangs out with Dorothée, an older woman with false teeth. He shows her canvases he cannot complete. Named after Charles Perrault, Albert Perrault paints grisly, sexual works of wolves and little girls that mock the moralizing behind "*Le Petit Chaperon rouge.*"

Perrault or his art appear in several other Kiernan stories and novels. This story is composed nearly entirely of a dated sequence of Perrault's journal entries (from 15/7/98 to 5/8/98). But the story ends with a 2006 art review of Perrault's final painting by Gautier Baillargeon (who may or may not be Perrault's pretty boy whom Perrault may have only dreamed he killed). Kiernan portrays Perrault as an outlaw artist with gay street virility (expressed in his notebook words), who produces violent and powerful art. Yet she ends the story with a limp, verbose and confusing review of Perrault's art. She contrasts the creative power of artists to the impotence of artistic criticism that was directed against such Decadents as Oscar Wilde.

The Beauty and Despair of Decay

Many of Kiernan's works reveal the beauty and despair of decay. Her decay is modern: an urban archaeology of the wreckage of the industrial age. In the "Afterword" to *Wrong Things* (2001), a co-collection with Poppy Z. Brite, she writes of her fascination with abandoned warehouses, dilapidated steel mills, derelict shipyards and corroding scrapyards. She believes in Emily Dickinson's lines that "The best Vitality/Cannot excel Decay" (Poem 403, 186). In her novel *Murder of Angels* (2004) Kiernan describes an urban scene of squalor: "cement walls and abandoned brick ruins, rusted, disused train tracks sprouting sickly weeds between their ties and trash littering the streets" (242). Her characters often haunt these lost places. They are the outsiders of today: street kids, hookers, freaks, junkies, goths, transgenders, runaways and squatters, similar to Charles Baudelaire's ragpickers, beggars, gamblers and poor old men and women of "*Tableaux Parisiens*" in the second edition of *Les fleurs du mal* (1861) and in *Le spleen de Paris* (1869). Of course, the Decadents extolled outcasts and deviants to counter the bourgeois lifestyle they abhorred. Kiernan gives a voice to those marginalized by their social status, their sexual/gender orientation, or their despair.

Kiernan's "Glass Coffin" (1999) tells of a group of young misfits, including one with HIV, another who killed her stepfather for raping her and yet another whose face is horribly scarred. All fled their natural families to become an artificial family trying to survive in an abandoned shipyard in New Jersey. This failure of family permeates Kiernan's fiction. It represents the failure of modern society. In "Glass Coffin," Salmagundi[6] Desvernine, who is one of the last of a rich American capitalist family that built the shipyard, cuts her thumb on rusted steel and slowly dies from an infection. She inherits her disease from that "Gilded-Age [1870–1900] spirit grounded in soot and lifeless, oil starved machineries" (Kiernan, *Tales of Pain and Wonder* [2016] 365). Her friends cannot save her. But her lover, Jimmy DeSade, returns and welds a steel and glass coffin to immortalize her as the "Scrapyard Cinderella" or "Sleeping Beauty of Weehawkin" in the tabloids. Written in a gritty, yet lyrical style, "Glass Coffin" refashions the Snow White fairy tale into a modern fable of group trauma in the industrial wastelands of America.

"Glass Coffin" is one of a linked set of short stories wherein Kiernan traces the decay of the wealthy Desvernine Family. Even in America a sort of declining aristocracy can be found. It is 1941 in "Estate" (1997) and Silas Desvernine has retreated to his isolated castle on Pollepel Island in the midst of the Hudson River in New York State. A typical American capitalist, Silas made a fortune building ironclad steamers for the Great War. He is part of an aristocracy based on earned wealth, a phenomenon Jean des Esseintes in *À rebours* loathed. Silas obsesses over his museum of oddities, grotesqueries and mythical artefacts collected from around the world, as did Des Esseintes in his retreat at Fontenay-aux-Roses. Salmagundi and Salammbô, Silas's great-granddaughters, are the last of the line. In "Salammbô" (1999), which is set during the Vietnam War, they grow up on the island in the servants' cottage under the shadow of the high and empty castle. Salammbô's name came from Gustave Flaubert's novel, which rests on a nightstand in the cottage. Snakes are her fetish, which she houses in a ruined greenhouse on the island. At fourteen she escapes the island and flees to California. She is a lesbian and becomes a herpetologist. In "Salammbô Redux (2007)" (2008) she returns to the northeast of America. In her Watch Hill, Rhode Island (a village where wealthy Americans summer) cottage, Salammbô complains every wall seems to contain a deadly mirror now that she is fifty-three. Conversations between Salammbô and Sebastian comprise the bulk of the story. A young man, Sebastian, claims to be writing a book about her. He exhibits the fluidity of gender. He is beautiful, dresses in drag and appears to shape-shift his gender in the story. Salammbô can hear him frown, but nothing happens in the story.

Salammbô's sister lives a decadent lifestyle as a performance artist in "Salmagundi (New York City 1981)" (1998). Salmagundi distances herself from a repugnant reality through her stylistic life and art, as did the *fin de siècle* Decadents. The narrator of the story, Elgin, hopes to interview Salmagundi. He tracks her to SubAllegory, an art house and bar. On stage she emerges from a mass of bones and gelatinous membrane, covered in maggots to the sound of screeching iron and chainsaws. Her performance may be a continuing act to reimagine herself, to recreate herself in a world that has marginalized her and her art. It is a performance to unsettle her audience. And it is a scene to unsettle readers of the story. From a performative point of view (that is, how it affects a reader) the performance disorients the reading of the story. Perhaps it is meant to suggest the emergence of the libido in all of its anguish and desire, or perhaps the emergence of a new artistic self-identity that is counter to mainstream art. After the performance Elgin gets to see

Salmagundi. A print of an Aubrey Beardsley work hangs on her dressing room wall. Jimmy DeSade ushers Elgin out. One suspects that Elgin is part of the surveillance network of modern society.

DeSade stars in other Kiernan stories, but especially poignant is "Between the Gargoyle Trees." Ten years after Salmagundi's death DeSade finally locates a lost art film in which she starred. The film was banned because it was degenerate and harmful. Virtually all copies had been destroyed, as Salmagundi herself had urged. High on whisky and cocaine, DeSade watches the film alone in a condemned, decaying movie theater that reeks of semen, piss and cigarettes. He longs to see her, his wasted, terrible beauty on that artificial screen of life. In one scene, a living tangle of wire and scrap crawls across nails and glass to attack the naked Salmagundi. Tough guy DeSade closes his eyes at Salmagundi "writhing like a poisoned dog as the nails and glass bite at her body" (*Tales of Pain* 362). The scene depicts the wreckage of American industry killing the artist.

Another decaying aristocratic family appears in *"Les Fleurs Empoisonnées: or, Dans le Jardin des Fleurs Toxiques"* (2002). Miss Aramat Drawdes, another last of her family, is the great-great-great granddaughter of an American Civil War Confederate munitions merchant. A lesbian, Miss Drawdes populates her antique Savannah, Georgia, mansion with a coterie of Southern belle acolytes, who "paint their lips like open wounds, their eyes like bruises" (*Two Worlds* 242). This lesbian sisterhood acts like grave robbers and cannibals. The basement becomes a sick playground for profane autopsies of the dead. This story of corruption and madness, coupled with forbidden appetites, depicts the American southern plantation elite in total decline, playing at being ghouls. Written with a flamboyant, fantastic flair that is part comedy, part satire and part grotesquery, the story is an example of the decadent Southern Gothic style. Yet the story also reflects the fact that lesbians, perhaps especially in the American South, need safe houses where they are protected. Kiernan deploys gothic elements to showcase the solidarity of those outside sexual norms.

The Decadent Style

Similar to authors of the Decadence, Kiernan's style emphasizes language and mood while it downplays realistic narrative. Often storylines are non-linear and told by unreliable narrators, where the relation to reality is consciously indeterminate. Of course, her work arises from a maze of political, social, sexual and cultural issues, as did the original literary Decadence. But fundamentally the texts are creative works. Some of her stories, for example, "Madonna Littoralis" (2005), are vignettes or prose poems, as they exhibit Kiernan's lush language, yet have little plot or action in their narrative flows. "Madonna Littoralis," a fusion of eroticism and fantasy, may be a story of a "*felo-de-se*" (a suicide) or a lesbian erotic encounter with a sea creature. That thing of the seashore has eyes that are dark and bottomless; they are the eyes of the sea. The tale flows in luxuriously rhythmic language that sounds like the spray of waves on a shore.

Another disorderly story appears in Kiernan's *The Yellow Book* (2012). "Ex Libris" (2012) is headed by a quote on immortal books from Wilde's *The Picture of Dorian Gray* (1890), perhaps alluding to the yellow book (likely *À rebours*) sent to Dorian by Lord Henry. Kiernan's story tells how strange, ancient books spread a deadly infection to an unfortunate buyer. The unnamed narrator, who is an artist working endlessly on her masterpiece, but doing lots of commissions, says the story will seem like disconnected episodes and come out in bits and pieces. And that is exactly how it reads.

Dreams enrich much of Kiernan's fiction. In this Kiernan follows the Irish-American Fitz-James O'Brien who often used dreams as a central narrative technique, for example, in "The King of Nodland and His Dwarf" (1852) and the fantasy "A Voyage in My Bed" (1852). Kiernan's "Pickman's Other Model (1929)" (2008), which riffs off H.P. Lovecraft's "Pickman's Model" (1927), tells of a search for the background of a mysterious woman, Vera Endecott. She has eyes a "stony, sea-tumbled shade of grey" (*Beneath an Oil-Dark Sea* 213) and looks like Theda Bara, an American silent film and stage actress who starred in the 1918 silent film *Salomé*. Mr. Blackman narrates his attempt to find the truth about Vera, but his bizarre investigation leaves him, and a reader, more confused than enlightened. Kiernan's story mixes real and dream sequences, often challenging to separate. The dream distortion effects recall those of Ambrose Bierce in his puzzling and nightmarish "The Death of Halpin Frayser" (1891). In Kiernan's fiction, dreams may express the mental disturbances of characters, work as distortion effects, represent the intrusion of something supernatural or remake a grim reality. Films play a similar role. Kiernan creates a cinematic experience in "The Prayer of Ninety Cats" (2010). It is a multi-layered work. Written partly in second person, as if addressing the reviewer of the film, the story incorporates snippets from a screenplay about the bloody Countess Erzsébet Báthory, the reviewer's reactions to the film in a seedy theater and an obsessive commentary on the history and aesthetics of filmmaking. Through fast cuts and flash-forwards and back, the story seems like a movie. It immerses a reader in artifice.

"The Prayer of Ninety Cats" shuns traditional plot sequencing of beginning, crisis and resolution. Indeed, Kiernan says she is not interested in plot. But this is much less revolutionary now than during the *fin de siècle*. She does salt her writing with scientific terminology, as if following the lead of Gautier who urged the use of "technical vocabularies" in his preface to the third edition (1868) of *Les fleurs du mal*. The short story "Salammbô" uses the Latin names of snakes. In "Tears Seven Times Salt" (1996) Kiernan refers to fish characteristics such as their "hyomandibular, interopercum, supraoccipital crest" (Two Worlds 69). In the dark science fiction story "In View of Nothing" (2007) the female narrator briefly escapes from her cyborg-like, female interrogator out onto a fire escape. Sprawling around her is a decaying city or perhaps not. It resists description with its magnificence, terror and loathsomeness. Kiernan describes the narrator seeing strange spiraling structures "which *might* be the skyscrapers of an unnamed or unnamable city, they are as intricate as the calcareous or chitinous skeletons of deep-sea-creatures" (*Beneath an Oil-Dark Sea* 141). The city may be organic, but the rattle of vast machines fills it. It seems *le cauchemar* of artifice and nature as one.

The Decadence in America

In *Wormwood 17*, rj krijnen-kemp traces the uneven descent of American Decadent literature from Poe to Clark Ashton Smith and beyond. Kiernan stirs the embers of that tradition. Some of Kiernan's work finds its source in Poe's psychological fiction. She channels Lovecraft's cosmic indifference, florid language and existential despair. Chapter Three examines how some of Kiernan's fiction reflects Lovecraft's notion that supernatural literature arises from and appeals to our primal biological imprints.

Kiernan's protagonists are generally women, while Lovecraft's are nearly always men. Lovecraft's baroque "The Hound" (1924) features an unnamed narrator and his cohort St. John, who adhere to the "philosophy of the Decadents" (*Dagon and other Macabre Stories*, 171). The story references Baudelaire and Huysmans. The heroes strive to overcome their ennui through grave robbing. In an underground hideout the two savor their strange trophies, which are similar to Prince Zaleski's ancient curios kept in his "darksome sanctuary" (*Prince Zaleski and Cummings King Monk* [1977] 41) room at the top of a tower in a ruined palace. In M.P. Shiel's stories, Zaleski's room wafts with hashish and opium, while the stench of the grave fills the air in Lovecraft's story. Unlike Lovecraft, Smith channels Shiel, and Gautier's "*Le Club des Hachichins*" (1846) for his poem "The Hashish Eater; or, The Apocalypse of Evil" (1971) where a dreamer experiences new worlds through drugs. As well, in *The City of the Singing Flame* (1931) Smith's luxuriant prose illustrates drugs and drink expanding one's consciousness. In some of her works of dark fantasy, Kiernan's prose style recalls the rich sweep of Smith's language. Yet much of her work roams the dark streets and ruins of modern cities and not a fully imaginative world, as Smith created. Her work also has an edge of realism (expressed often though gothicized images) with its exploration of different forms of sexual activity and gender identity that assault many societal norms.

krijnen-kemp concludes Decadence morphed into Modernism and that traces may still be found in American literature, for example, in the continued questioning of the American frontier myth and manifest destiny. Kiernan addresses this in five of her stories set in the late nineteenth- and early twentieth-centuries in America during the *fin de siècle*. Chapter Nine of this book explores in detail how her alternate history stories do not glorify the expansion of empire across North America, but question the dominant colonial, gender and industrial power relations in the old American West. The stories also work to undermine the false history of the science fiction subgenre, steampunk. Each of the stories is dated, as if the stories chronicle the history of Cherry Creek (a fictional Denver), Colorado. Only one will be discussed briefly here. "Derma Sutra (1891)" reads like a Decadent work with its voluptuous language and sexual explicitness. Two female characters lead the story, but the nameless woman with the Kiernan sharp teeth sexually dominates the other, Stephanie Brockett. They represent both sides of the Victorian view of women: ethereal creatures on the one hand, while their bodies were seen as dangerous due to their sexual power—either saintly or demonic. Arousing from a drug coma, Brockett finds her body completely tattooed with profane writings (hence the title "Derma Sutra" may mean a skin text, or a set of aphorisms sewed into or tattooed on skin). Then it gets worse (or better), as the nameless woman sexually assaults Brockett repeatedly. Nevertheless Brockett welcomes the physiological agony and euphoria of change from angelic. That is because she has been released through lesbian love from the chains of the Victorian sexual prescriptions and has become a New Woman.

Kiernan's fiction echoes many Decadent motifs. And her stories combat realism and emphasize language, prose rhythm and elegant description. But the full *fin de siècle* experience of the Decadent Era is impossible to duplicate. The originators of the Decadence lived in a unique time period and their work was innovative, shocking and pulsed with a strange, weary power. Yet Decadent artists sensed their work would fade. Walter Laquer writes that pessimism underlies the Decadence. In Poe's "The Masque of the Red Death" (1842) Prospero creates an abbey of art in the countryside as a haven for aristocrats away from the ravages of the plague in Florence. But during a masquerade ball nature invades the abbey and spreads a disease killing all. Time and nature will win out in the end, as the Decadent artists knew, indifferent to them and their works of art. Even Des Esseintes returns to society. Baudelaire's "*La chambre double*" (1862) evokes the tyranny of time with that knock on the door that recalls the poet from his vision of a wondrous room back into its shabby reality. Kiernan captures this sense of despair in "Salammbô" where she describes Salmagundi and her sister sitting on the crypts of their ancestors as the Hudson River flows by deep and cold and indifferent as time flowing away. Baudelaire voiced the existential limits of artistic expression in "*Une charogne*" ("A Carrion"). This mock love poem questions the hope of immortality through art in its ending phrase: "*Qui j'ai gardé la forme et l'essence divine/Des mes amours décomposés!*" ("I've kept the sacred essence, saved/the form of my rotten loves!") (Richard Howard's translation, 212, 36). Many Decadents shared the pessimistic philosophical views of Arthur Schopenhauer and despaired for the enduring value of their art. Yet the Decadents strived for artistic expression. Bierce shared this pessimism, forged by his American Civil War experience and especially evident in his newspaper columns, but he held fast to his *l'art pour l'art* sensibility and distaste of realism. Kiernan voices her pessimism in "Houses Under the Sea" (2007) where the narrator describes the story as a fable of "eleven thousand words cast like a handful of sand across the face of the ocean" (*Two Worlds* 567).

In Summation

In his preface to *Les fleurs du mal*, Gautier suggested the artists of the Decadence arose at a particular point of history in response to a dissolute society. It was a literature of the struggle of the individual artist against a tyrannical and dominating economic, social, and sexual order, including a literary hierarchy that extolled unity, realism, objectivity and formalism. Part of the meaning of the Decadence was to challenge all of the prescriptions of a powerful society in decline. This was true in the *fin de siècle*. It was true in the *fin de millénaire* and continues now in early twenty-first-century America. Huysmans in *Là-Bas* (1891) observed the "tail ends of centuries all resemble each other" (*The Damned* 219). Paradoxically America now seems the center of both power and dissolution. The original Decadents devoted themselves to an adulation of art, hedonism and decay as weapons against a dominant set of corrupt moral and cultural norms. Kiernan's fiction draws from that spirit to write against the American grain of realism, consumerism, celebrity pop culture, and the continuing marginalization of those outside societal sexual and gender canons (that is, the LGBTTQ+ community). Because it was a pioneering and liberating movement Decadent art often shocked the established artistic hierarchy with its expressions of sickness and hedonic excess in a subjective, ornate vernacular. Kiernan writes in another time with some similarities but vast differences. Kiernan reframes Decadent anti-heroes from an ill culture's outcasts, dandies and New Women to an ill culture's young street people, assertive women and defiant gays, lesbians and the transgendered. Her fiction often expresses this through fragmented postmodern narratives that are built from elements of the fantastic and the gothic, challenging straightforward realism and subversive to power and oppression. In her stories Kiernan valorizes the LGBTTQ+ community, while she exposes the subjugation and surveillance they live under.

Three

The Figure of the Gothic Body

> "And twice a thousand more
> Starved upon the shore
> And withered to a bag of bones!"
> —W.B. Yeats, "Demon and Beast,"
> *Collected Works*, vol. 1, p. 187

The first two chapters examine how Irish supernatural fiction and folklore and the writers and artists of the Decadence influenced Kiernan's fiction. The fiction of H.P. Lovecraft is another especially strong influence on Kiernan. Indeed, in 2018 Centipede Press published Kiernan's *Houses Under the Sea* which collects her Lovecraftian stories. Although the tales are inspired by Lovecraft, it would be more accurate to say that they reflect on, reinterpret and write beyond the work of Lovecraft. Among Lovecraft's stories, it is those that emphasize the trauma, decay and the ultimate strangeness of our bodies that appear to have particularly affected Kiernan.

In *Supernatural Horror in Literature* (1927), Lovecraft suggested that supernatural literature arises from and appeals to our "inmost biological heritage"[1] (26). Based on this idea, Jack Morgan argues physiological fear is at the root of much gothic, dark fantasy and horror writing, film and art. Morgan sees gothic literature confronting readers with our primary biological reality. Gothic literature resurrects "flesh's primal mystery and power" (Morgan 108) to haunt our rationalized world. This biological horror arises from the dread of contagion, suffering and death. Such fear materializes in William Maxwell's short story "The Actual Thing" (1938), where death asserts its sovereignty via a foul odor in an attic, originating from a dead bird. That bird is "the dry horrible thing" (Maxwell 17) Mr. Topper aches to throw far, far away. Touching it turns his hands black. Such a foul thing represents "the abject" in Julia Kristeva's conception. The abject is the stuff of disgust, while "abjection" is the horror we feel when confronted by the abject—something nauseatingly other, unclean and loathsome. The concept of abjection helps us understand the ongoing power of horror in literature. According to Kristeva, when we confront the abject we both fear it and identify with it. We are repelled. But it attracts us and we may become fascinated victims (9).[2] This sense of human body trauma pervades Kristeva's *Powers of Horror: An Essay on Abjection* (1980).

Bodily trauma also pervades Kiernan's fiction, for example, in "Salammbô Redux (2007)" (2008). Salammbô Desvernine finds a body on a beach. A brown-skinned girl kneels there, seemingly praying with a rosary clutched in her hand, but her throat has been cut ear to ear and her eyes eaten away. For some time Salammbô stays with the girl, close to death, next to that abject thing. Kristeva contends a "corpse, seen without God and outside of science, is the utmost of abjection" (13). It signifies the breakdown of the difference between subject and object that is at the core of self-identity. Abjection means we are in continual danger of losing any distinction between self and something other. The initial experience of abjection happens when a proto-I begins to create a separate identity. Kristeva says it is terrifying; it initiates a primeval repression and lingers as a body memory. Something alien or threatening to one's separate identity activates that primal memory. And a corpse evokes that primal emotion of fear because it reminds us of that danger and of our essential materiality.

A similar scene with a dead body occurs in Kiernan's "The Mermaid of the Concrete Ocean" (2009). On the beach off Atlantic City a painter finds the cadaver of a young woman. Nothing remains from the ribcage down. He bears her away from the threatening sea and sits on the beach, keeping a vigil by the woman's body. She haunts him evermore and inspires his obsessive painting of mermaids throughout his life. In Kiernan's *Murder of Angels* (2004) a Berkeley graduate student drags another body away from San Francisco Bay. While he stares at the girl's battered body, her slate-gray and blue skin and her kelp-like hair, it appears to him that awe and terror merged into one. The abject body causes the graduate student to experience beauty and loathing simultaneously.

These bodies and others in Kiernan's stories represent what Steven Bruhm calls the "gothic body." Bruhm argues gothic literature presents readers with the reality of the body's repressed vulnerability, forcing us to see our inexorable corporeality. Bruhm defines the gothic body as a human body "which is put on excessive display" and has a "violent, vulnerable immediacy" (xvii). Nowell Marshall argues Bruhm's definition is too narrow because it focuses on the body in pain and as a gothic spectacle. Marshall broadens the definition of gothic bodies to include those bodies that are seen as ruined or monstrous, have suffered physical or psychological trauma and those bodies that disorder the normal view of family and sexuality (129).

Marshall focuses on melancholic, mad and masochistic bodies, which arise from narrowly defined gender roles. He contends that gothic literature depicts characters who are not able to embody socially expected gender norms.

Those characters feel normal gender as something lost to themselves, regardless of their sexual orientation. This perceived loss results in either self-directed or other-directed violence. In part, bodies become gothic because they reject orthodox human taxonomy or subvert standard ideas of what constitutes a normal or socially acceptable body, according to Xavier Aldana Reyes (5).

As noted in the Introduction, I use the term "gothic" to encompass David Punter's idea that the gothic today speaks to bodily harm and trauma. In addition, my use of "gothic" also speaks about the underclass, articulating societal disparities and dislocations, while revealing what is hidden away, found in subcultures and covered up in society, as Teresa A. Goddu, Roger B. Salomon and others have defined the word. As well, I follow the advice of George E. Haggerty to use the proper noun "Gothic" for the classic literary tradition, while the common noun "gothic" will be used for the literary motif in its continuing manifestations (205).

This chapter examines how Kiernan deploys the figure of the gothic body to express the oppression of submerged individuals and groups. Founded on but expanded from Stephen Bruhm's notion of a gothic body, Kiernan's gothic figure is a body that varies from socially accepted constructs or expectations of bodily appearance, form, sexuality or gender and is usually experienced as physically unusual or grotesque, often through unwanted display or spectacle. Kiernan's stories create a space for the different, the marginal and the odd. In the stories explored in this chapter, Kiernan writes about bodies in pain, extraordinary bodies, queer bodies, melancholic bodies and anthro-technological bodies. Her characters are women, the physically challenged or different, transgendered people, the mentally challenged and the poor. She writes about individuals or groups who are other to the dominant image in a society, especially modern American society. Many are in danger of losing autonomy over "their most intimate property, the human body" (Scarry 136). Kiernan pushes upon readers our biological self in all of its fragility, despair and hurt as a primal source of the continuing power of gothic literature, but more importantly to illustrate the destructive force of socially constructed norms and standards that marginalize individuals. Her stories are read here through several theoretical lenses: abjection, disability theory, subjection theory, queer theory, bioethics and melancholia theory. These lenses reveal the essential emphasis of Kiernan's writing on illustrating the trauma experienced by individuals who are treated as different or inferior in a society.

Bodies in Pain

Bruhm argues the gothic manifests the fragility of the body through the display of pain. Physical pain through its terrible dominion returns us to the

Three. The Figure of the Gothic Body 49

truth of our precarious materiality. Kiernan's neo–Decadent story, "Concerning Attrition and Severance," explores the power of this pain. Using a straight razor, a tall, unnamed woman tortures a kneeling and bound woman. But the torturer is not looking for confession. She inflicts pain for the pleasure it brings her and her responsive audience. Bruhm suggests that the delights of pain inflicted on another are heighted by nearness, not eradicated (119). In the story the torturer shares a stage with the prisoner. Yet there is a distance between torturer and prisoner. Based on her phenomenological study of torture, Elaine Scarry argues that during torture the body and pain are overwhelmingly present for the prisoner while "voice, world and self" (46) are nonexistent. Yet for the torturer, voice, world and self are overwhelmingly present while pain and body are absent.

In Kiernan's story the torturer speaks and the other screams; there is no voice for her, except for feeble replies to threats. The story recreates the theater of torture in its aim to decompose the voice of the prisoner. Scarry illustrates how the ability to articulate sentences, and then words, disappears for one who is in pain. Pain disintegrates language. That is the physical fact of pain. Kiernan emphasizes this fact with the phrase "We need not note the screams" of the prisoner, which is used three times (*Confessions* 88, 89). The prisoner's screams tell of pain, but real pain is untranslatable, impossible to articulate. Pain is demanding because it unmakes one's self. Pain shrinks the world to the body and then to that part of the body that is in pain. There is no escape for that bound woman.

According to Bruhm pain obliterates the self, and that is the purpose of pain during torture. Scarry clarifies this by pointing out that a torturer uses pain to unmake objects of consciousness, which means to destroy a person's worldview and sense of their self within a set of cultural and societal beliefs. In torture the external world is progressively eliminated while the tortured body is reduced to a contracted, inarticulate state in which nothing exists for it other than its own pain.

Kiernan graphically depicts the sexual mutilations and degradations inflicted on the body of the bound woman. Those mutilations represent, through their concreteness (their visible "voice" of pain), the power of the torturer. In Kiernan's story the prisoner's body becomes the palpable sign of the torturer's power. In that theater of pain, the torturer violates and deforms the prisoner.

The torturer controls the stage (the world), and she adulates herself. She inflicts pain; therefore she exists. The prisoner is a mere object, not a self. This story's theater of pain illustrates the savagery of torture, where the "lesson is Control" (*Confessions* 91) and power over others. It is disturbing because the torturer gains the participation of the audience in her cruelty. By calling on the audience to appreciate her mutilations of the bound woman's body, the torturer works to adulate pain and claim it as her power. The subject of torture is in a room, on a stage in that room, bound tightly on that stage, bound by the mocking and commanding voice of the torturer and bound in agonizing pain. The voice of the torturer becomes the only world for the woman. She is submerged by pain. Her bloodied body is displayed for the audience, who participate in the dissolution of the woman's world through the mutilation of her body.

Another torture scene occurs in Kiernan's "A Canvass for Incoherent Arts" (2009). This vignette illustrates physical vulnerability in the body of a chained, naked woman alone in a pitch-black room. Cuffed to a chain fastened to a bolt driven into a wall, she lies on the floor. She waits to be frightened by her lover. This story recalls the original Gothic, which Camille Paglia says stylized "claustrophobic sensuality" and withdrew into a "chthonian darkness" (265). Kiernan's vignette rewrites that original Gothic trope of female confinement into a modern sex game. But it is a one-sided, brutal game, with a woman's body trapped in a dark, carceral space. The cell is small and the woman's movements are constrained by the chain and the darkness, which engulfs the room until for a brief moment a door opens and closes quickly.

Kiernan probes the psychological and physiological dimensions of one tormented, yet one so afraid she identifies with her lover (or tormentor), dramatizing the condition of being a subject, that is, in a position of extreme subordination. The chained woman is in mandatory submission, which Judith Butler (*The Psychic Life of Power: Theories in Subjection*) says is necessary for one to become a subject. The attachment to her lover does not mean that she is at fault for seemingly sustaining her own subordination. Rather, as Butler argues, subjection is brought about by the use of power (*The Psychic Life of Power* 6). And this story narrates one of the most sinister outcomes from the extreme exercise of power over someone. The chained woman is in a position of complete dependency in a small, dark cell. Her lover/tormentor controls everything: the lights in the room, the key to the door, the key to the shackles and when the chained woman may speak. She is isolated. She is cut off from anything but one "passionate attachment" (Butler, *The Psychic Life of Power* 8), admittedly a brutal attachment. This attachment through dependency leaves the woman in subordination and exploitation. There is no space for resistance. The lover/tormentor seems aware that the "desire to survive, to be, is a pervasively exploitable desire" (Butler, *The Psychic Life of Power* 7) and uses this to abuse the chained woman. And she so wants to survive she endures the sado-masochistic desires of her lover.

The torture in this story is not just psychological but also physical. From a psychological perspective, the chained woman experiences waves of panic. She has cognitive disturbances including disorientation when she is not sure where someone may be in the enclosed space of her cell. She also loses her sense of time. In addition, she has perceptual distortions. She is not sure if something more than her lover has entered the cell. In fact, it could be that her entire experience in the cell is hallucinatory. Kiernan hints at this possible interpretation by inserting quotes from *Hamlet* and from *Paradise Lost* about the dangers and terrors the mind creates in a vacuum.

The woman has often endured extended time alone in the cell (although the exact length is unclear to her). She is in solitary confinement. Enclosed in a smothering, total darkness, and in chains, she seems a sex slave. When her lover (not identified as male or female, making the other an ambiguous and more terrifying figure) enters the room, the lover's voice dominates. But the voice sounds disembodied, so it could be anyone's voice. It is a voice that commands, mocks and laughs at her. Scarry emphasizes that voice is overpoweringly present for a torturer, while a prisoner becomes lost in her body and has no voice. The power of the torturer arises from this opposition of voice and body. Kiernan's story depicts the lover's voice as the sound of power over the subordinated woman.

In her reactions to her lover/tormentor, the woman focuses on her physical agony. She is nauseous, her throat aches, sweat stings her body and her lips crack. As in "Concerning Attrition and Severance," the tormentor bears a straight razor, or perhaps a knife. The bound woman cannot see anything in the darkness, but she feels a sharp edge press against her neck. That physical touch signals her complete entrapment, obliterates her autonomy. Scarry argues that physical pain has the power to destroy all parts of the individual self and her world. For the chained woman, the world, contracted into the cell, now contracts into her body. The lover/tormentor demands complete subordination. In this "game" the chained woman cannot even scream because she has been ordered not to. For the woman there is only the carceral space in the dark, where she cowers in psychological and physiological pain, waiting in complete subjection for the next fright.

Extraordinary Bodies

Xavier Aldana Reyes argues that "deformity" is nearly a defining characteristic of gothic bodies (6). But contemporary disability theory insists on uncovering the material reality of the lived experience of individuals labeled "disabled." Kiernan's "Daughter Dear Desmodus" (2011) tells the lived experience of one different from the societally valued body image. Because Ileana was born "deformed," her horrified parents abandoned her as a child, selling her to a carnival, afraid that some devil devised her teratism. But in Kiernan's story Ileana is not presented as monstrous. Rosemarie Garland-Thomson notes that circus folks are among the "extraordinary bodies" outside the dominant culture's valued body, which she designates the "normate." The normate is a constructed identity possessed by people who do not have branded, generally physical, identifiers of disability (which is Garland-Thomson's central concern), race, class, or gender and who represent themselves as standard humans (*Extraordinary Bodies* 8). She argues that "disability" is a social construct where a dominant group achieves, maintains and enforces its image of valued physical appearances by imposing a sense of cultural or bodily inferiority on those who are different. Garland-Thomson's thesis focuses on the Western world, where she claims people with disabilities have a history of being on display, of being visually conspicuous while politically and socially erased ("The Politics of Staring" 56).[3]

An "extraordinary body," for example Ileana's, is excluded from "normal" society. Ileana is on display as a gothic body not to just shock audiences, but to reinforce a culturally enforced view of the valued "normal" body. In the ableist world Ileana's body only matters because it is a warning to others of what can happen to a standard body. But in the carnival, she is accepted among the others who are displayed for audiences. Kiernan portrays Ileana being raised by a dwarf in a battered Airstream he shares with another carnie, who shoves ice picks and nails up his nose. Ileana is the other who signifies our fear of physical deformation, but also our fascination with malformations. "Normal" people respond differently to those perceived to have an unsettlingly deviant physiological form. Ileana's parents' response was to dispose of her, which has been the fate of many deformed people. In *Freaks: Myths and Images of the Secret Self* (1978), Leslie Fielder documents how people with unusual bodies have been revered or ritualistically killed in other times and cultures. These responses have the same root, a sense of terror and wonder, a deep feeling that we are at the organic gateway of something strange, mysterious and uncanny.

Put on display, the "freak" helps demonstrate the normality of the audience. In our current time, Garland-Thomson argues people with physical disabilities are no longer considered portents but pathologies. But as Fiedler identified there is a tyranny of the normal to stigmatize those different from the "normate."[4]

In Kiernan's story, Ileana grows up to be displayed as the spectacle of the batgirl, grotesquely made up and hanging in a cage. She earns a living in the carnival, similarly to how many other "non-normate" people earn a living and are not dependent on society, which Fiedler shows in his *Tyranny of the Normal*. But late at night Ileana flips through a Parisian fashion magazine glancing at the valued bodily images of all those beautiful women. She lives in a society governed by ableist assumptions about which bodies matter.

Kiernan continues to explore "disability" in one of her anti-steampunk stories "The Steam Dancer (1896)" (2007). This is one of Kiernan's best stories. It is included in her recent collection, *The Very Best of Caitlín R. Kiernan* (2019). The story exhibits Kiernan's command of lyric prose, character development in the short story and historic setting. It is an alternative history story set in the American West and is part of Kiernan's set of five that work against the false history of the science fiction subgenre, steampunk. Kiernan's five anti-steampunk stories are explored in detail in Chapter Nine. Here I study how the story's protagonist confronts standard views of what it means to be a person with physical challenges. Missouri Banks represents those who are marginalized by their physical differences and sidelined economically because of those differences. But Kiernan's story also tells of the experience of someone with physical challenges who overcomes those challenges.

After her mother and father die, Banks ends up "one of a thousand or so dispossessed urchins" (*The Ape's Wife* 15) scrapping out a nasty, brutish and short existence on the streets and in the alleys of Cherry Creek, Colorado, in the 1890s. She finds food in trashcans, wears rags and ends up on a soiled mattress among rusting mining debris, as if just another waste cog from the industrial machine. A mechanic (who is unnamed throughout the story) finds her attacked by bloatflies and with maggots eating away a leg, an arm and an eye. He rescues her and makes her a prosthetic arm and leg and secures her an artificial eye. Missouri Banks becomes a steam-powered cyborg, another form of a gothic body. But her differences from the norm are her strengths in the story.

Banks overcomes her "disabilities" through her prosthetic limbs and earns a living as an exotic dancer. Kiernan notes the influence of C.L. Moore's "No Woman Born" (1944) through a dream of Missouri Banks, or rather, through a story she makes up for the mechanic that she calls a dream. In the dream, she says she was "burned away" but the mechanic made her "a pretty metal face and a tin heart, and [...] breast" so she could dance again (*Ape's Wife* 23). Moore's early female cyborg story tells of Deirdre, whose body was destroyed in a theater fire. Maltzer, a scientist, transplants her brain into a metal body that Deirdre controls with her thoughts. She returns to the stage and is a huge success. Susan Smith says Moore's story "imagines the potential of the female as an empowered human machine" (24). Kiernan's story reimagines female empowerment using steam-powered prostheses to overcome physical challenges.

In Kiernan's story, the need for prostheses not only foregrounds the fallibility of the human body, but also presents the variability of the body and works to disrupt the idea that bodies are the same and uniform. Kathryn Crowther argues the story works to transform physical challenges and protheses into an erotic image of the merging of the female body and beautiful technology (90). Crowther points out the story depicts the lived experience of someone with a disability. For example, when Banks's prostheses need repair, she laments that crutches limit her mobility to such an extent that she must stay within the confines of her room. Banks's "disability" is not a metaphor in Kiernan's text. Rather Kiernan emphasizes the humanity and materiality of the experience of someone with physical challenges.

As a cyborg, Banks confronts standard views of what it means to be a person with disabilities. Donna Haraway suggests that for women, a female cyborg "reveals both dominations and possibilities" in a patriarchal society (295) such as the old American West. Banks exhibits this contradiction. She is alive and artistic due to her prosthetics, but she depends on the mechanic to keep them working. More importantly, Haraway argues that cyborgs challenge normative views of man or woman, be it as human, member of a race, gender, individual identity, or an organic body. A cyborg is an anomalous body. It is visibly constructed; it is outside normal expectations. A cyborg's hybrid identity, which is other to the norms of culture, a different form of a body, disrupts the categories of human identity. The figure of the cyborg, in part, represents those marginalized within an ascendant culture. Garland-Thomson sees Haraway's notion of the cyborg expressing a prototype for making a self that overcomes the seeming incompatibility between "disability" as a physical fact and social identity, and what it means to be a full, recognized person in the human community.[5] Missouri Banks represents that achievement, and in Kiernan's story Banks is not a "supercrip" (Garland-Thomson, "The Politics of Staring" 61); that is, her dancing display is not beyond belief and does not disrupt a sense of equality between viewers and viewed. In Kiernan's story Banks represents all of those who are different, those who are marginalized by their physical differences, and those sidelined economically and socially. Banks's identity diverges from the ideal woman, but she does not see herself as grotesque; she sees herself as beautiful, feels no shame and has no self-hatred.

Queer Bodies

Kiernan has remarked that "Faces in Revolving Souls" (2005) illustrates the "prejudices, the social and medical difficulties faced by transgendered persons" ("Author Spotlight Caitlín R Kiernan").[6] In Kiernan's story, Sylvia finds herself trapped in a body that is not hers. It does not represent her true nature. She undergoes "interspecific genetic modification," or the integration of genetic material from different species, to realize her true self by becoming a parahuman (*A Is for Alien* 50). Throughout the story, Sylvia agonizes over her acceptance by parahumans, her ostracism by humans and the outcome of her genetic modification. At a conference of parahumans, Sylvia feels estranged from the parahumans. She stays clothed while the parahumans display their interspecies characteristics. She is also estranged from her mother, who calls parahumans perverts and queers.[7] In this science fiction story polymorphism (having multiple species' genetic characteristics) is considered by some a sickness, by others a crime and by yet others blasphemous. Kiernan's story underscores the multiple medical, social and political challenges faced by transgender and transsexual[8] people, especially challenges when medical treatments fail or go awry. Such a failure occurs to Sylvia's body in Kiernan's story. Sylvia becomes trapped in an alien body. Her real identity becomes unachievable.

Kiernan's story destabilizes the border between human and animal with its hybrid parahumans, paralleling transgender and transsexuals, as ambiguous beings threatening social norms. Transgendered individuals embody gender ambiguity and reconstructive surgery threatens a world of gender normality. Although there may be more freedom in some aspects of society now for those outside normative gender roles, Paulina Palmer documents how such roles still generate extreme prejudice and much hostility. Sylvia experiences what Judith Halberstam says the transsexual experiences, that is, living in a state of cross-identification with a sense of personal identity that conflicts with her body (59). Such individuals are trapped by the constructed nature of the normative concept of the gender of a human body. Judith Butler says gender is socially compelled and "masculine and feminine are not dispositions [...] but indeed accomplishments" (*The Psychic Life of Power* 135). These accomplishments may trap individuals in bodies within a socially identified gender differing from their personal sense of gender. In Kiernan's view, Sylvia represents such individuals in her struggle to achieve true identity.

At the end of the story Sylvia's attempt at constructing her true self fails. Her false body traps her; it rejects the gene treatments. She faces an even darker future. "Faces in Revolving Souls" depicts the loneliness, despair and heroism of a character who desires a different path in life. She takes a risk. But her risk will lead to ostracism from everyone and will result in more pain, suffering and loneliness. It is clear that Sylvia faces devastating illnesses "following from the rampant emergence of retroviruses in her body, cancers and autoimmune disorders" (*A Is for Alien* 57). The body's fragility always wins out. Tonia Poteat, et al. provide evidence that stigma and discrimination are fundamental causes of health disparities for transgender people. They confirm conclusively that these lead to an increased risk for depression, suicide and other ailments. This is the future that looms for Sylvia in Kiernan's story.

A similar failed attempt at body modification occurs in "Tears Seven Times Salt" (1996).[9] Jenny Haniver (the protagonist's name is also a term for the carcass of a skate or ray that has been disfigured to look like a fantastical creature, popularized in the sixteenth century) aches to escape her body. But she lacks the resources to find the medical care to help her manage her physical and mental health challenges. Her room is lined with bubbling aquariums and tables heavy with formalin-clouded jars, dissection trays and scalpels. But when Haniver tries to surgically alter her body on her own, she fails. Her body ends up wrapped in bandages. Similar to Sylvia, Haniver feels consigned to a body that is not hers: a body which society constructed for her through a long history of social conditioning. After this failure, Haniver becomes delusional. She cannot bear the reality of her alien body. So she descends below Manhattan for a journey through labyrinthine tunnels and sewers of crumbling masonry, rubble scree and fallen concrete in search of a miracle metamorphosis into a mermaid. Haniver's subterranean passage recalls Isabella's flight from Manfred through the "long labyrinth of darkness" (26) in Horace Walpole's *The Castle of Otranto* (1764), but Jenny Haniver is fleeing from her body. Her underground flight creates a harrowing descent into her subconscious to escape a painful reality.

Kiernan writes of people trapped in bodies defined by societal norms, but which do not match their feelings of what they really are. Haniver is another of Kiernan's marginalized characters. In this story, Kiernan writes about what some people do to their own bodies when they feel trapped, when they are prevented from expressing their true selves. Haniver self-cuts her body, which is trapped in a world of pain. The world views her to be mentally unstable because she will not accept her socially constructed bodily form. Her existential search for her real self closes in suicide. At the end of the story, Jenny Haniver's abhorred and self-mutilated body washes out from subterraneous sewers into the polluted harbor.[10]

Haniver represents those who self-mutilate because they hate their bodies but cannot escape from them. The story also leads readers to suspect that Haniver's father's beatings may have caused her to hate her own body. Once after a beating, he took her, with tears in his eyes, to the New York Aquarium where she marveled at the "sleekest nightmares" in the dark water (*Two Worlds* 71). She sought to join those nightmares.

Melancholic Bodies

George E. Haggerty argues that Gothic fiction can be understood in part through the figure of loss, which often engages with an unusual eroticism (3, 21–44). Loss is the key to Kiernan's "The Ammonite Violin (Murder Ballad No. 4)" (2006). The story focuses on three characters. The unnamed, rich man is a serial killer with sixteen kills and a collector of fossilized ammonites (ribbed, spiral-form shell fossils). Ellen struggles to survive as a musician and mourns for her missing (and presumed dead) sister. Ellen is melancholic.

She and her sister were united in their love of music and often performed together. Now Ellen is adrift and alone, but she ends up playing a violin for the collector. Unknown at first to Ellen, the collector had murdered her sister and supplied a luthier with bones from her body for pegs, bridge, chinrest, and tailpiece; hair for the bow; breast fat distilled into rosin; and part of a small intestine, dried into gut for the strings. Not only is the violin a gothic body, but also it is the abject. But that body was artistically formed and this story suggests that through that art, as Kristeva argues, it is transformed into a form of liberation from abjection.

While playing the violin the melancholic Ellen hears her sister's voice within the music. That music helps Ellen overcome her melancholia. The music acts to sublimate her loss, as Kristeva suggests in *Black Sun: Depression and Melancholia* (1989). For Ellen, the "harmonics and drones and double stops" work to alleviate her loss (*The Ammonite Violin & Others* 100). Linked to Haggerty's notion of the gothic figure of loss, Kristeva's notion of melancholia helps us understand Kiernan's story. Kristeva theorizes a form of depression or melancholia where a depressive person feels an existential loss. Stuck in a condition of suffering without being able to articulate it completely, the depressed person is trapped by a melancholic Thing. In playing the violin, Ellen confronts the loss of her sister and through "melody, rhythm" secures "an uncertain but adequate hold over the Thing" (Kristeva, *Black Sun* 14). That Thing is her murdered sister, whom Ellen gets to embrace, because her sister has now become a gothic body, the violin. And at the end she takes her beloved home. Ellen regains her figure of loss and desire. The collector is another melancholic body. Joel Norris hypothesizes that seven phases describe the awful agency of serial killers. During the story Kiernan portrays the totem phase (the sixth phase), where killers take souvenirs from their victims. Norris says the seventh phase is depression, when some serial killers commit suicide. In Kiernan's story while the music plays the collector shoots himself. His melancholia is destructive, first against women and then against himself.

Anthro-Technological Bodies

Bioethicist Fabrice Jotterand argues the "development of emerging biotechnologies is on the verge of redesigning the boundaries of human existence" (617). This future potential with biotechnology and genetic engineering raises ethical questions that Kiernan explores in several of her short stories. For example, Kiernan's neo–Decadent story "A Season of Broken Dolls" (2007) raises questions around genetic engineering and increasing the human technology and technology interface. As noted in Chapter Two, the story is presented in the form of field notes of a jaded, middle-aged journalist, Schuler, chronicling her encounter with the display of surgically and bio-technologically altered humans into art forms. They are displayed in a warehouse bar and art gallery for a future, rich avant-garde. Schuler has seen nearly every disgusting thing in a dystopian future of a sea-engulfed New York City with toppled skyscrapers and a bombed Brooklyn thanks to a corporate mini-nuke. She muses that the installations are "bad art, […] pretentious carnage and willful suffering" (*A Is for Alien* 152). All of the displays trouble her. Installation #17 especially haunts her, yet she stares at its six eyes and wonders what the correct way of referring to the thing may be: is it one or are they three? It seems to be a surgically assembled artwork of three women with their body parts rearranged with hooks, wires and flesh.

Kiernan presents readers with a challenge about these humans transformed into art. Are they still sentient? It is not clear in the story if Installation #17 has any remaining human consciousness. The journalist doubts it. She is dismayed at the exhibits of humans crafted into art. And she is more dismayed that she must report on it for mass consumption, as if the technologically changed humans have been commoditized for the tabloids. But another character in the story, Sabit, who is younger than Schuler, relishes the exhibits and sees them expressing a savage modern art, appropriate for that future age of misery. It is not clear in the story what the specific legal status may be of the humans who undergo such changes. But the human art installations are allowed because of fears over lawsuits claiming censorship and violations of the freedom of expression and First Amendment rights. It is also not clear in the story who profits from the displays. There is medical attention (through painkillers and antibiotics) provided to the now anthro-art devices. But this pain and infection implies maleficence by the facilitators of the creation of the human art installations. A lingering question is: Do the art installations surpass the ethical limits of body modification?

On the other hand, the new human art pieces may be a transhumanistic release of the creative force of the human mind to express itself in another form in order to become something more fulfilling. Pro-technology non-profit Humanity+ notes that transhumanism seeks to advance "human potential by overcoming aging, cognitive shortcomings, involuntary suffering, and our confinement to planet Earth" ("Transhumanist Declaration"). The argument is that all deployments of technological and other human modifications should be pursued aggressively. Humanity+ contends that such changes will improve memory and mental functioning, extend the life span of humans, expand reproductive choices, advance space colonization and lead to advanced cryonics procedures. Such technological advancements will also provide opportunities for even more creative expression by humans.

Gwyneth Jones ("The Icons of Science Fiction") suggests that part of the purpose of science fiction is to raise questions about the impact of technology on the nature of humanity. These questions include: What is the status of a genetically engineered biological human being? In Kiernan's story "Faces in Revolving Souls" Sylvia fails in her attempt to genetically alter her body. But others succeed in becoming parahumans by integrating their original genetic material with that from a different species. And often these parahumans become shunned and degraded by many humans. They find comfort and acceptance from their own kind. Jones also wonders how we would define someone born human who chooses to alter some or all of her body parts for hardware, or to metamorphose into a non-human body? In Kiernan's story "Riding the White Bull" (2004) after Sarah becomes part technology she is classified as a cyborg and loses her human lover Deet Paine, because she is no longer a human. In "Blind Fish" (2012) Aden is a human/marine hybrid, who keeps her human lover, but she always dreams of being in the sea. She is valued for her ability to travel underwater without a breathing apparatus and her kinship with marine beings. Kiernan offers no easy resolutions; she tells stories of humans undergoing technological and biological modifications and how these affect their relationships with others in society.

Jones also asks: What is the status of an artificial being, who achieves some form of consciousness? In Kiernan's "Ode to Katan Amano" (2005) a synthetic human, of sorts, breaks into an art exhibit to grope a statue, but she does not do it. She feels guilt at using the beautiful statue as merely an object of her passion. This robot has her own problems with her human owner who asks her to remove her face while they make love. It is the ultimate degradation. Should such sentient robots be abused for the pleasure of their owners? In Kiernan's story the synthetic human hesitates at the violation of a piece of art and in a manner exceeds the morality of her owner. The story depicts the results of a society of objectification. The robot in the story has self-awareness but is still treated as merely an object by her owner. The story hints at the fragility of self-awareness, or rather, the non-exclusivity of self-awareness to humans.

Several of Kiernan's stories present possible futures where biotechnology is unleashed, so to speak. She offers no answers but the point is to encourage readers to think about the consequences of our advancing technology on our concepts of what it is to be human and what it means to be self-aware. Do the art installations in "A Season of Broken Dolls" represent a new height of personal enrichment through an expression of personal and individual freedom by leaving one's humanity entirely for an otherness expressed through art? Perhaps, but it seems these new things may have lost critical human capacities, for example cognitive functioning. If so, would the loss of cognition be unethical, or would it be the free choice of the individual? Trans-humanists argue that all mechanical and biological enhancements should be allowed and perhaps mandated. Others argue such a stance overthrows the fundamental principles of bioethics, namely respect for autonomy (expanded at times to include respect for human dignity, integrity and vulnerability), non-maleficence, beneficence and justice (Beauchamp and Childress). Kiernan contributes to this debate on the potential future of anthro-technological devices, that is, technologically augmented individuals, by illustrating a possible future of biotechnological change into art installations. In that future, some individuals strive to overcome living and dying by merging with bio-technology. But the protagonist in "A Season of Broken Dolls" sees some anthro-technological devices as monstrous bodies (now with no autonomy) put on display, as if freaks for onlookers to feel good about their normalcy.

In Summation

This chapter explored a sample of Caitlín R. Kiernan's fiction that deploys the figure of the gothic body to illustrate the traumatic experiences of marginalized individuals and communities. Such individuals are marked as different or other to a culture through their gender, bodily form, mental health, or social class status. Her gothic bodies are bodies in pain, extraordinary bodies, queer bodies, melancholic bodies and anthro-technological bodies. Interpreted through several theoretical lenses including Julia Kristeva's work on abjection and melancholia, Judith Butler's theory of subjection, Garland-Thomson's disability theory and Elaine Scarry's work on the body in pain, Kiernan's fiction pushes upon readers the reality of corporeal terror and psychological trauma. That trauma results from the tyranny of socially constructed and enforced norms and standards that differentially affect marginalized individuals and communities, who are treated as different or inferior in a society. This bodily trauma represents a primal source of the continuing power of gothic literature, which Kiernan deploys to illustrate the destructive force of societal ideologies and practices that force individuals into subjection, stigmatize those with physical differences, enforce gender and other socially constructed roles and marginalize those with mental health challenges.

Four

The Folklore of Awe and Terror

"I love folklore and all festering superstitions."—E.M. Forster, *Howards End*, 74

In Chapter One, I survey the influence of Irish folklore on Kiernan's fiction. Here I broaden and deepen that exploration across the folklore and myths of other places and times. Supernatural fiction often springs from the world of folklore. The American Folklore Society shies away from a single definition but says that folklore reflects and shapes a people's belief system. Folklore is found in many forms, including traditional art, knowledge and practice that flow through a culture.

Folklore comes from the oral tradition of stories told around camp fires, outposts and hearths late at night in the shuddering cold as the shadows from the wood crept too close and the animal howls grew too loud. The oral tradition helped people find their place in an unruly world of strange phenomena. But folklore is more than old stories, it is a "rich and meaningful source for the study of cognition and values," according to Alan Dundes (xi–xii). Oral knowledge and stories tell of the way the world is and how we should act in that world. Such stories articulate how to live within a natural world as part of it. Folklore helps make sense of the world. And such stories reflect our desires, our aches and our fears. Dundes argues that folklore is not a relic of the past. He shows it is an artistic process that is still meaningful today. For him, folklore is not to be assigned to primitivized others either historically, culturally or socially. It is part of everyone's knowledge and behavior, as Simon J. Bronner points out (1). In part, folklore allows a release from reality, although it is not disconnected from reality (Bronner 3). Many tell of experiences in particular places or landscapes that seem haunted. This links folklore to the concept of the ecoGothic, which maintains that gothic, uncanny and weird fiction landscapes often depict damaged and degraded environments.

Akin to folklore, fairy tales link to the gothic. Christina Bacchilega says that fairy tales are directly related to folklore, indeed, she says they are literary appropriations of older folktales (3). Maria Tatar contends that fairy tales are similar to folktales, but they vary because folktales tend to be more realistic. She says fairy tales are "narratives set in a fictional world where preternatural events and supernatural interventions are taken wholly for granted" (*The Hard Facts* 33). In "Reading the Grimms' Children's Stories" Tatar says that fairy tales are still alive today. They help us navigate through experiences to make sense of them. She goes on to say that fairy tales help us manage personal and social anxieties that run deep. A specific example of this is Victoria Tedescui finding that nineteenth-century fairy tales expressed anxieties about ecological devastation. This ecological anxiety is more pronounced in today's world. Tedescui goes on to argue that fairy tales are always alive in our collective mind. That is why so many writers have and continue to recycle or revise folklore and fairy tales to address current experiences. As an example, Jack Zipes notes thirty-eight different version of "Little Red Riding Hood" from 1667 through 1990. There are even more. Kiernan rewrites that fairy tale.

Karen Armstrong says that myths, broadly understood, are about the unknown, which is what Kiernan explores in her fiction. It is a dark writing—a folklore of awe and terror. Kiernan is a folklorist of our fears. She is also a scientist and that knowledge emerges in these stories through her connection of gothic terror with ecology. Kiernan achieves this by reimagining our environments, be they woods, lakes or the earth, as enchanted or dangerous once again. The forests are not lumber stands, lakes are not just sources for municipal water supply or dumping toxic chemicals, and the earth is not merely to be quarried. In her work, nature is not just a source of commodities. It seems sentient and often malevolent, as in myth and in folklore. In her novel, *The Red Tree* (2009), the red oak tree is triumphant with its ancient, awful majesty. In that novel Sarah Crowe glances out a window and sees farm land that has grown into bush and a mass of trees crowding around Ramswool Pond. The pond is a quarry reclaimed by nature.[1] Even the cellar of the Wight farmhouse in *The Red Tree* returns to nature. Landscapes become gothic haunts.

Many of Kiernan's landscapes become feral again, which suggests the return of a gothic nature, or perhaps, records the impact of ecological damage within a dark fiction context. Tom J. Hillard writes that the field of ecocriticism now recognizes that gothic writing addresses such matters as environmental degradation, climate change and the violence that humans inflict on its own and others creatures' habitats. In brief, ecocriticism is a method of critical study that arises from an awareness of environmental crisis and danger and explores how that crisis is portrayed. Cheryll Glotfelty says ecocriticism studies the relationship between literature and the physical environment. It takes an earth-centered approach to studying literature (xviii). Sara L. Crosby argues that given the range and degree of global environmental destruction, it seems that terror is an environmental norm now (514). Some of Kiernan's stories transform the pastoral into the apocalyptic. Or more broadly, in some of Kiernan's stories settings, places and landscapes reflect changes happening due to the impact of human activity. Some of her stories could be characterized, in part, as ecoGothic in that they display gothic bodies in gothicized environments.

Kiernan portrays this through mythic, folklore or fairy creatures that journey into the everyday world or through the desire of her human characters to become impossible beings. Such human characters ache to be abhuman, as defined by Kelly Hurley.[2] For Hurley morphic variability typifies the abhuman, which signifies something that is becoming other to itself or losing its own nature (7). Hurley contends the modern gothic reveals and ignites cultural anxieties and conflicts through the figure of the abhuman. In Kiernan's fiction explored in this chapter, such a figure surfaces environmental anxiety. Some of Kiernan's characters express their cultural or environmental trauma through the urge to embrace the abhuman. That is, they want to cross a threshold and become an impossible being. It may be a reaction to the changes in the natural world, that is, the transformation into the abhuman is an attempt to adapt oneself to an environment made dangerous by human activity. In doing so, Kiernan expresses contemporary cultural and climate anxieties, especially as experienced by individuals who differ from and are marginalized by mainstream society.

The Ecological Gothic

Kiernan presents *The Red Tree*[3] as Sarah Crowe's found journal, fronted by a scholarly preface. In that preface, the ancient oak looms as a site of homage, portrayed as surrounded by *Red Rose Tea* figurines, as if mocking folklorists. Kiernan depicts the landscape surrounding and beneath Crowe's rented farm house as a gothic space. Brad Tabas argues that gothic or weird fiction emphasizes deformed places, surroundings and environments.

In the cellar of the farm house, Sarah Crowe finds a manuscript written by Dr. Charles L. Harvey about the history of the Wight farmhouse and its environs. Crowe compares her rescuing of the manuscript to Hecate rescuing Persephone, as if she wrenched it away from hell. But in the myth Persephone must go back to Hades, and her attendant during her season in hell is Hecate.[4] Is this a foretelling of Crowe's fate? People who have inhabited the Wight house find ways of dying, seemingly under the sway of that ancient, everlasting red tree, including Dr. Harvey, who hanged himself from the tree. Dr. Harvey was a folklore professor. Another folklorist in the novel, Joseph

Olney, who researched the history of the red oak, kills himself. This landscape seems to exact revenge on the humans, especially those who work to domesticate it.

The cellar is another gothic space. It is an enormous, shape-shifting space, especially once Crowe crosses the "rough-hewn stone threshold" carved with symbols, as if hexes against evil, similar to those "on barns in Pennsylvania Dutch Country" (*The Red Tree* 72). This is an intrusion of reality because there are such barns. Don Yoder and Thomas E. Graves display and comment on such hex signs as folk art that may have started as protective emblems. Crossing that threshold, Crowe moves into another zone of space and time. It becomes gigantic, perhaps a cavern, or maybe a vault, something underground that is vast and unending and dangerous. Kiernan conjures up a strange claustrophobic but immense underground space drenched in a chthonian darkness. This may be an image of Crowe's disintegrating mind as she slips nearer and nearer to madness, as if the red tree spreads an infection of psychosis.

Such an infection may explain a central scene in the novel where Sarah Crowe and Constance Hopkins (a character who rents the attic of the house) walk to the red tree. But they become lost in the woods mere yards from the house. They cannot find the tree; they retrace their steps and try again. But they seem never to get closer to the tree. They sense danger, as if time and space are warped. They turn back toward the house, but they are unable to reach it. Then they hear something large splashing in the nearby stream. The panic of the woods has them. Hopkins freaks first and runs, and Crowe follows. They end up facing the front of the house, which seems crazy to them. In her journal, Crowe writes that their experience was impervious to rationalization; to "any explanation that does not assume or require a violation of the laws of physics or recourse to the supernatural" (*The Red Tree* 166), as if defining the gothic and weird fiction tradition.

Tabas says weird fiction empathizes distortions in the environment and thereby disrupts our normal sense of being home in the world. This is what the characters in *The Red Tree* experience. They become increasingly estranged from the natural space they inhabit. This mirrors our current circumstance where there no longer seems an interconnection of humans with other natural things, because human activity has caused significant environmental change. Now nature appears as strange and other, or hostile to humans. We now live in the Anthropocene Epoch. Simon L. Lewis and Mark A. Maslin find that human activity is now global and is the chief cause of most contemporary environmental change. They argue that the effects of human activity will likely be found in the geological stratigraphic record for millions of years into the future, which means there is a new epoch (171). Planetary disruptions in climate, landform and weather result from our machinations, which harm nature and us.

Four. The Folklore of Awe and Terror

The Red Tree, in part, is an example of what Hillard (28) and others[5] call "ecoGothic," that is, it exhibits ecocriticism in a gothic manner. Shoshannah Ganz says the ecoGothic is about the earth as ravaged by climate change (67). Kiernan's novel re-enchants nature as a raging force, recovering from damage. A deep terror underlies the novel, as if there is something in the landscape that spreads a deadly fungus. A fungus that human activity may have started. The novel paints a disturbing folklore of the wood, a wood that is taking back its rightful place full of awe and terror. Hillard sees such gothic or neo-gothic[6] fiction as revealing anxieties about the destruction of the natural world and our place in nature (11). Such ecologically focused gothic literature expresses an intensifying dread over human-caused environmental change. Gothic fiction is a literature of fear, and the ecoGothic expresses our fear of the effects of climate change and terror at our role in causing that environment change.

This fear also dominates Kiernan's story "In the Water Works (Birmingham, Alabama 1888)" (2000). Building on the traditional dangers of mining, she fashions a startling image of terror found in a mine shaft. In mines, especially mines prior to the introduction of large-scale mining machines and remote operations, miners worked in conditions of constant uncertainty and exposure to death. Gabriela Dumbrava suggests that miners' ancient folklore voices the fact of working close to death. She says mines were viewed as a magical and haunted space with both evil and good spirits, because a mine itself may give riches or death. Dumbrava describes how Roman miners saw mines as an evil realm, where demonic creatures became dangerous, if stirred from their hidden places. One of these creatures is known as the *Vâlva Baii* in Romanian folklore. This happens in Kiernan's story. But in her story the things found in a shaft of a tunnel being drilled through Red Mountain suggest a deep disturbance in nature.

Henry S. Matthews is a schoolteacher, a fossil hunter and an outsider. He is from the north and works with his mind, not his body, as do the workers on the tunnel being cored through Red Mountain to bring water to Birmingham. Yet he is up there with them, although he is hunting for fossils in the spoil piles, while the workers labor in the dark tunnel. One day the foreman, Warren Wallace, shows him a strange dark thing coiling and uncoiling in a nitro bottle. Matthews has never seen anything like it. He doesn't know what it is; he has no taxonomy for the thing.

Wallace leads him through the tunnel drift to a wall fissure. Kiernan evokes the claustrophobic feeling of an old mine drift with its scarred rock faces, low ceiling, slippery bed and weeping walls. At the fissure Wallace removes the metal barrier. The stench is overpowering. Wallace urges Matthews to peer down into the hole. At first, he sees only black water. When his eyes adjust, Matthews makes out a swarm of black coiling things, and then a large dark tendril rushes up the pit. Wallace yanks Matthews out of the fissure and slams the corrugated tin back in place. They shudder at the repeating "meatmallet thud" (*Tales of Pain* 274) of the thing against the tin.

Afterwards they share a whiskey in the foreman's shed. Wallace shows him another sort of fossil: a piece of hematite, scored, as if by the coiling things. This seems a metaphor for the ecological damage that results from mining, for example, spoil piles and tailings. Spoil piles consist of all the excavated materials abandoned during construction of mines and tunnels. Tailings are the waste products of mining. Where mining uses toxic chemicals to extract the desired material product, for example gold, from ore, these remain in the tailing ponds and dams that surround a mine site. These toxins leach into ground water and destroy habitat. An example of this destruction is the Giant Gold Mine (a mine and environs that I have personally visited), which was an underground gold mine on the northern arm of Great Slave Lake near Yellowknife in the Northwest Territories of Canada. H.E. Jamieson itemizes how this long-lived mine (active for fifty years, between 1948 and 1999) created wide-spread environmental destruction. Arsenic was used in the mining and processing refractory operations. The use of arsenic resulted in a complex and continuing legacy of devastating contamination.

Kiernan's story is an effective tale from an aesthetic point of view with its realistic descriptions of the tunnel counterpointed by the horror in the shaft. Kiernan finely draws both characters. Matthews is young and a rationalist rattled by his experience, while Wallace is a tough foreman, who has seen it all underground, but there is a crack in his hard rock visage caused by those things found in the mineshaft. The story is also an effective gothic ecological story in its depiction of the gothic terror arising from a spoiled earth. And she does this by linking the story to mining folk legend. In the story, Matthews does not want to remember that darker shape rushing up the shaft towards him. This darker shape is similar to a description of the *Vâlva Baii*.[7] Dumbrava says these supernatural creatures are described in different ways; one is as black and hidden, another is as a shadow that lurks in the depths of mines. They seem akin to what Matthews saw in the depths of Red Mountain. In Kiernan's story the *Vâlva Baii* are reimagined as those strange, dark coiling entities deep in that shaft. That darkness is a metaphor for ecological disaster. "In the Water Works (Birmingham, Alabama 1888)" ends with Matthews hiding all the evidence, as if ecological damage can be ignored.

But that impossible thing in the nitro bottle comes to light again one hundred years later in Kiernan's novel *Threshold* (2001). Chance Matthews, great-granddaughter of Henry S. Matthews, is studying to become a paleontologist, just like her grandmother. With the help of Dancy Flammarion, a strange, albino young woman, Chance finds an old crate containing the impossible thing, the oddly scored hematite, other unknown fossils and her grandmother's journal. This discovery pulls Chance and her friends into a rendezvous with the return of those impossible beings.

Threshold is subtitled "A Novel of Deep Time." It is the phrase used to express the immense age of the earth confirmed through geological research starting with the work of James Hutton and Charles Lyell. Prior to their work, biblical creation time was the accepted standard. The shift in the time horizon was from thousands to billions of years. A measurement that remains difficult to comprehend fully. *Threshold* is set within a context of such time. In its depths, Red Mountain hides something terrible and primeval. But Chance and her friends release again the *Vâlva Baii* (the dark spirits of mines). It seem that drilling into the earth has released an environmental disaster that is gothicized into the shape of violent subterranean hordes. Yes, part of the gothic genre deals with the supernatural. But, as Tabas says, the genre also explores changes and deformations in natural landscapes. *Threshold* is also discussed in Chapter Five.

Estranged from Nature

"I am lost" (*Confessions* 21), says the young wolf/woman in "The Wolf Who Cried Girl" (2007), as if speaking for many of Kiernan's characters. She is lost between two worlds, estranged from her life as a wolf in the forest with its feral smells and her bloody feedings, and not at home in the city of constant noise and perfume. Or is it the other way? Is Anastasia a human, delusional, as she says? Does she long to be a wolf, to be another, and have elaborate dreams about it? In her wolf form, she says a skinwalker[8] stole her pelt, claws and teeth.

The young wolf/woman is ostracized by her pack so she wanders into the city, where she is cured of her wildness through medications and then released onto the streets of the city, which happens to many people with mental health challenges. This is a harrowing tale of growing up with madness, being abandoned and left alone on the mean streets and rooftops. A photographer rescues her and she has sex with him. She regrets it. Wrapped in a wolf pelt, akin to a skinwalker, she waits for him with a long knife, sharp as a wolf fang.

This story and others are set within a folklore of loss and despair, where the monsters seem to suffer as much as so-called normal beings. In several of her stories, Kiernan reverses (or at least creates ambiguity about) who the monster is. The wolf/woman represents an increasing split between humans and nature, although humans are animals, but we are losing our sense of belonging in nature. In the story, the wolf/woman refuses to be domesticated, exploited and abused by the photographer.

A story with a similar theme is "Unter den Augen des Mondes" (Under the Eyes of the Moon) (2008), where a female werewolf is caged and beaten by an angry man, a cowardly woman-beater. This is another story in which the roles of monster and victim are reversed. The werewolf worships the moon and all the old gods, yet she suffers behind iron bars while the man sputters insults and beats her with a broom handle during the day. At night when the moonlight pools on the basement floor, the werewolf recalls Juliet's lines from *Romeo and Juliet*. But the wolf changes the gender: "[s]he will make the face of heaven so fine/That all the world will be in love with night/And pay no worship to the garish sun" ([*Confessions* 112] and [*Romeo and Juliet* 3.2.23–25]). This is a modern folktale reframing the image of an outlaw and dangerous werewolf as a woman beaten by a drunken man. She is a woman caged within a violent and gender controlling society. And she also represents abused wild creatures, for example in entertainment zoos and circuses, within the gothic context of the story.

Consider also how the selkie suffers in Kiernan's short story "For One Who Has Lost Herself" (2006). This is a story that reflects on the hurt and agony that wild creatures face for the amusement (that is abuse) of humans. The selkie seeks her stolen skin, tricked away from her by a young man on the forlorn, red sandstone beach of Veantro Bay in the Orkney Islands. In the Irish and Scottish folk traditions, Patricia Monaghan writes, the selkie is a mythological creature, an enchanted seal and enchanted human. Monaghan says that in some traditions seal women were said to make wonderful wives, but a man had to steal their seal coats and keep them hidden or the selkie would go back to the sea (411). In this, as in other stories, Kiernan is writing from the perspective of the outsiders, so to speak, to show us their fears, their night terrors and their despairs. Here the selkie longs for her skin, her freedom, but stands sadly across the street from a fossil shop, as if she is afraid to find what she needs. On that corner she encounters "someone like her, one thing pretending to be another" (*The Ammonite Violin* 40) who goads her to search the fossil shop for her skin. This ambiguity or uncertainty about one's true identity is found throughout Kiernan's fiction.

This story reclaims an old folktale, but it is also a tale of all who are lost, who search for themselves, who seek their true self. The selkie's skin is found in a place of stolen things, a museum of robbery, of things that belong elsewhere. It is a shop that smells of dust, as of ages. The owner brings out an old chest containing a piccolo and sealskin. Seeing the sealskin transports the selkie—transports her back to her "lost sisters and brothers" (*Ammonite Violin* 50). Back to the sound of the "crash of breakers […] the raucous cries of […] gulls," where she feels again "the cold water flowing all about her," catches the "taste of a codfish on her tongue," smells the "salt and seaweed," and once again sees "darting seal shadows" (*Ammonite Violin* 50). Kiernan arrays all the senses to express this experience of the selkie in her sea.

This story tells of a search for identity in a booming, buzzing, confusing world, stylized as that busy corner the selkie haunts, while she gets up her nerve to cross the street and enter the fossil shop. That street is in contrast to her home in the sea. Growling buses patrol the street, venting diesel fumes and soot in contrast to the serenity in the sea. But she is trapped in a city, which appears to her as a canyon of concrete, steel, glass and electricity.[9] On that corner she fingers the small treasures in her pockets the way a small child protects herself with a hoard of stones, coins and shells.[10] Kiernan illustrates the loneliness and the fear of those others, because they are us. She writes this loneliness and fear as a folktale from the point of view of a sea creature caught in a modern urban environment where she is estranged from nature by the action of a human.

"Bridle" (2006) is another tale of a folk creature, a kelpie, which is said in Celtic legend to be a supernatural water horse haunting rivers and lakes, according to Katherine Briggs. The only way to control it is to keep its bridle. Traditionally the kelpie was depicted as male in human form; however, this image is not uniform. Herbert James Draper's painting *The Kelpie* (1913) depicts a lovely nude young woman on a stone, poised to slip back into the river or perhaps to lure one into that water.

Kiernan locates her story in a city, not in the wilds. That is because, as Ruth D. Weston writes, "we are aliens in the natural world" (97); we no longer see ourselves as part of nature, but use it as a source of commodities or as a place for entertainment or sport. Yet we cannot escape its mysterious power, which seems to creep into or under our cities. This story is centered on an old fountain, forgotten about in an abandoned, seemingly desolate area of a city. The narrator of the story lives near the fountain in an ancestral house, where she finds an old bridle. A young boy is found dead in the fountain, drowned, reportedly an accident, but she wonders about the weird hoofprints in the mud near the stone bridge over the pool.

Mysteriously she receives a package. In it, there is a clipping of the killing of an *each-uisge* (Scottish Gaelic for water-horse) and a print of Jan Preisler's *The Black Lake* (1904), which depicts a young boy and a white horse by a jet-black lake. The narrator writes of her dreams of riding the dark kelpie horse through modern streets, and loving the kelpie woman in the stone fountain, while the dead boy stares at her through the holes that were his eyes, because "[o]ne does not need eyes to see such things" (*Ammonite Violin* 36). But the narrator watches him die, for the kelpie entranced the boy into the unknown depths of that shallow fountain pool. She wakes in her bed covered in mud and weeds. What is real and what is dream in a folk tale? Kiernan transforms an old folktale into the reality of desolation and loneliness in a big city. But a city that seems to becoming reclaimed by nature through the intersession of folklore creatures.

In this story and others an image of a young woman in water is a powerful image of fear, attraction and loss. The narrator in "The Bridle" is startled by a young woman with long dark hair and black eyes wading through the fountain toward her. In *The Red Tree* there is a similar scene where a naked, black-haired girl moves through the waters of a quarry pond toward Sarah Crowe. It is not clear in either work if the young woman is real or a dream image. In *The Red Tree*, Crowe thinks of Thomas Millie Dow's painting, *The Kelpie*. This image is different from the dense coloration and stylization of Dante Gabriel Rossetti's paintings of beautiful, dreamy-eyed, sensual women, such as *Jane Morris* (1868), *Lady Lilith* (1868) or *Proserpine* (1874). Dow's *The Kelpie* (1895) is in black and white. It depicts a naked young woman on a stone above an oily lake; she is pulling on her long black hair as she stares darkly, threateningly, directly at the viewer. And in "As Red as Red," Ms. Howard dreams of a naked Abby Gladding, with her long dark hair, standing ankle deep in a stagnant green pool. These recurring images signal a deeply traumatic experience for the characters as they are engulfed by natural or supernatural forces.

Becoming the Abhuman

"Fish Bride (1970)" involves another mythic, impossible creature. A man sleeps with a young woman on a damp bed in a dilapidated cottage. It is November and the winter season creeps near, rattling the hut. The man is from the good part of town—the village on the hill—far from the sea. It is the abode of upstanding citizens, away from the old myths and old folktales and the poor folks.

Acolytes surround the young woman. They seem to adore her, or marvel at her strangeness. All live by the sea. He listens to their mutterings and to their whispers that slip through the slender walls of the hut. He is a voyeur into the forbidden side. For the "fish bride" (the young woman) is symbolic of all those thrown away, or abjected in Kristeva's sense, by their society. She lives by the sea among the outcasts from the town: squatters and drunks, lunatics and mystics, and the poor. The people of the town try to forget that appalling storm—the storm from the sea. Or rather to forget their ostracizing of those few left by the sea after the storm. That shantytown was once prosperous, but a wind came out of the sea, blew up out of the sea, and a tempest came and took so many away. The shanty by the sea is an abode of loss, because of an ecological disaster.

In this story Kiernan finds beauty in the appalling. See the fish bride, see her "iridescent skin," feel the "thin, translucent webbing stretching between her long fingers."[11] She has "teeth like those of a very small shark" and "peculiar welts just below the line of her chin," as if forming gills (*Beneath an Oil-Dark* 276, 278, 281). The young woman celebrates her different body form, her gothic body. She embodies the abhuman. The abhuman is a being that retains part of its human identity but is, or is becoming, an unspeakable other thing. Such a thing is loathsome because it threatens, or indeed overcomes human identity, yet is also alluring. That is what the narrator of the story feels.

After the storm, strange things emerged from the sea, things that slithered and lurched from the sea, as if the shantytown is Lovecraft's Innsmouth. They flooded streets and basements. But they were not monsters, they were the dead bodies caused by the storm now thrown back by the rising sea. This story represents the sea as a gothic force, as nature damaged, yet Kiernan also depicts the sea as a place of solace and healing.

As in many tales, the "fish bride" must go back to the sea. She walks into the sea, confirming she is an impossible creature. She embraces becoming abhuman, that is, she celebrates and exhibits her differences from the norm and swims away from that man. This young woman represents those ostracized and abandoned by contemporary society, expressed by Kiernan in the form of a modern folk tale. The happy ending in this remade tale is not marriage, but a young woman's exhibition of her differences and her gothic journey into a night ocean. This story alludes to Lovecraft, but it is much more. With a tone of elegiac wonder, Kiernan writes about the joy of becoming one's true self in spite of being in a decaying landscape.

Elise in "Paedomorphosis"[12] (1998) is a direct kin to the fish bride. After Elise and Annie make love in the Seven Deadlies band's practice room, Elise lures the naked Annie through a fissure in the room's concrete wall, down to a black, underground lake. Annie does not swim, but Elise dives into the oily water. When she comes out and starts to pull her shirt over her head, Annie sees crimson slits where Elise's armpits should be. Annie stares at the gasping slits, which are bright with blood. She vomits into the black water. Later Annie gives Elsie the cold shoulder, but Annie is haunted by her continuing dreams of wide caverns and dark pools that sprawl somewhere far beneath her. She listens to the call of the abhuman.

Rewriting Fairy Tales

The fairy tale, "Little Red Riding Hood," and its images of dangerous wolves and little girls are continuously rewritten. It is found in many modern works, for example, Margaret Atwood's[13] *The Robber Bride* (1993), Tanith Lee's *Red as Blood* (1983) and Angela Carter's *The Bloody Chamber* (1979). Caitlín R. Kiernan appears to be haunted by the fairy tale.[14]

Kiernan's "The Road of Pins" (2002) reworks "Little Red Riding Hood" or perhaps more correctly "The Story of Grandmother" (sometimes called "The Path of Needles or Pins") as known in the French oral tradition.[15] In a version of this tale the wolf asks Little Red which path she is taking to her grandmother's house, and she says the path of needles, so the wolf takes the path of pins. The wolf kills and eats the grandmother. When the child arrives, the wolf demands that she strip off all her clothes, but in the end the child tricks the wolf and escapes on her own.[16]

In Kiernan's story Alex Marlowe has writer's block and is angry. The story starts at a gallery exhibiting the dark works of Albert Perrault.[17] Alex's roommate Margot is running the show. Another character in the story, Jude Sinclair, is writing a review of the show. Jude tries to explain one of Perrault's paintings, saying it exhibits our fear of wolves—the dark images are drawn from our deepest fears, from a primal source of terror.

Later Alex goes to a showing of Ingmar Bergman films, but the second film is unknown to her. It is shot in black and white with disturbing scenes: a dead sheep, a man and dog, a wolf killing a sheep, a blind young woman at a window of a house, a young boy killed, an organized party of males off to hunt the wolf, something big moving in the shadows, a man fires a gun, there is a scream, a group of peasant women cry, a skull, then the daughter again. She is asked: what road will you take, the one of needles or the one of pins? The film stops. That is the question asked of Little Red.

Back at the apartment she shares with Margot, Alex receives a package from Jude. There is a picture of a wolf-like thing attacking a young woman surrounded by bodies. There is also a videotape, which shows the ending of that black-and-white film. While Alex watches it, Margot calls. She is crying because she has witnessed a vicious attack in which a dog killed a young child. Margot returns to the film. The blind girl says she will take the road of pins, while a dark shape bends over her.

This is a modern fairy tale centered on a disturbing image of a wolf nearly hidden in a painting, then more real in a film, and finally realized in a vicious dog-like thing that kills a little girl. The story tells of an ever increasing violence in art, film and in city streets. It is a troubling rendition of the Little Red Riding Hood tale, where the wolf is an image of enduring violence against women. Sharon Rose Wilson argues that modern fairy tales written by women often speak to characters' transformation from alienation towards greater freedom, but this is not true for Kiernan's gothic story. The film ends with the camera panning out to reveal a vast, bleak landscape. The house appears an insignificant feature in a cruel terrain of nature. There is no escape from estrangement in this gothic landscape that seems alien to human life.

Kiernan's "The Road of Needles" (2013) also uses elements from "Little Red Riding Hood." Nix Severn pilots the space-freighter *Blackbird* to Mars.

Four. The Folklore of Awe and Terror 73

But the load of terraforming engines go berserk. It seems a tale of the revenge of nature against technology. Severn struggles through the exploding terraformed isotainers, as if she is lost in endless forests. Of course, she wears a red jumpsuit with a hood, and a bzou (werewolf) hallucination hounds her, while she tries to control the terraforming machines.

Kiernan sets the story in a distant future when the Earth is fouled. Flora and fauna are extinct or nearing extinction. But the rich still rule. They pay genetic outcrossing labs to create freaks for the future zoos of disfigured humans. There are no longer any animals. But a wolf haunts Severn. During her youth, a wolf stared at Severn with the eyes of all wolves, who are extinct at the time of the story. From its cage, the wolf stared at her with amber, hateful eyes. It paced as animals do in zoos, especially big cats and bears. They are of course all crazed, squeezed behind bars and hounded by pale humans staring and mocking them. They are lost in delirium, caged, dreaming of open spaces, and crushing that ice-cream cone licking kid between their jaws. Severn sat there as a child knowing it and fearing it. It becomes a phantom. Nicolas Abraham argues that "the phantom" is an intergenerational haunting. It is the return of a family's repressed secret to subsequent generations. It is a secret buried in the tomb of the unconscious that passes from a parent's unconscious into a child's. Abraham writes, the "phantom's periodic and compulsive return [...] works [...] like a stranger within the subject's own mental topography" ("Notes on the Phantom" 289–90). In this tale, the phantom is the wolf. Nix Severin's child, Maia is disabled and is afraid of wolves, passed to her from her mother. The image of the wolf grounds the tale within the power of myth and fairy tales. It expresses the trauma of humans and animals in a time of ecological crisis. Kiernan's story is not only "Little Red Riding Hood" in space.

Adam Trexler and Adeline Johns-Putra see climate change as a force impelling authors to move beyond using the environment merely as a setting. They argue it can work to distort plots, produce unusual narratives and changes in characterization. "The Road of Needles" does this to a traditional fairy tale within a recognition of the current trajectory of environmental trends. For example, the term "bzuo" comes from "The Story of Grandmother," yet in Kiernan's story it is a hallucination, but also a phantom wolf, and a signal about the revolt of terraforming engines (that is, a gothicized nature). Kiernan takes climate change into space.

In two stories, Kiernan rewrites nature images from Scandinavian fairy tales. "Drawing from Life" (2009), originally "Untitled 34," features a skogsrå or skogsnufvar, which in Swedish folklore is a female fairie who captures young men (Theresa Bane). The frame story of the tale centers on a male character who is sentenced by a skogsrå to draw her repeatedly. The skogsrå tells the young man a fairy tale about the revenge of a skogsrå on a man who betrayed her and tried to throw her to wolves. It seems a threat to the young man to keep drawing her or else. And that is what he does. He draws her naked back of peeling birch bark, moss, and green lichen above her long tail. "Drawing from Life" is more of a vignette than a complete story, but it exhibits Kiernan's command of fantasy description. The title is likely from M.R. James's "Canon Alberic's Scrap-Book" (1895). The fear-inspiring sketch in that story was "drawn from life" (12).[18] The drawing in Kiernan's story does not inspire fear, rather it inspires awe. Tabas says that weird fiction at its best can prod readers to think about the places they inhabit. Of course, in Kiernan's story the skogsrå is nature personified. And the male character is forced to think about nature.

Another Scandinavian fairy tale creature, a huldra, finds a gentle way to expose her true self to her lesbian lover in "Fairy Tale of Wood Street" (2017). The story seems one of hope for reconciliation with nature. Awakening from a disturbing dream of a forest, the narrator finds that her girlfriend, Hana, has a tail. Throughout the day (the story takes place in one day) the narrator wonders how to speak of it to Hana. Or was the sight a hallucination, she wonders? Hana is the huldra (in Norwegian folklore, the huldra is said to be an elusive and seductive fairy-woman of the forest [Theresa Bane]). She takes the narrator to see a movie. Of course, the magical huldra ensures the film on screen tells a fairy-story of the tribulations of a huldra as the world of humans invade her forests. The narrator is again disturbed and Hana leads her home. There the narrator reveals that when she was very young she became lost in a dark forest but a kind, beautiful woman appeared and led her to safety. Afterwards the narrator would leave small gifts for her fairy lady. Hana remembers the gifts that were left for her. Kiernan writes a modern day fairy tale of magic and rediscovery, where romance triumphs over terror, fear and doubt. And where one who conserves the forest is rewarded.

After a fashion, folklore and fairy tales taught life lessons. The long oral tradition provided a story framework (or a cognitive framework) for living in a sometimes haunted or dangerous environment. That framework also shaped how people interacted with that environment. G.J. Osemeobo studied indigenous folktales in Africa and found that most old folklores influenced the conservation of the environment. But he also found that changing religious beliefs, a more market-based agricultural production, and changes in recreational activities eroded the conserving traditions on which the folklores were based. Then the role of folklore in conservation diminished considerably. Osemeobo's study is a microcosm for what has happened across the planet.

In Summation

Kiernan infuses her dark fiction with myth, folklore and fairy tales to create new gothic narratives that reflect on the current human condition.

Kiernan taps the long history of folklore from ancient to modern times. In doing so, her stories tell of our current ecological circumstances and emphasize the experiences of characters who are different and estranged from nature or society or from themselves.

Karen Armstrong contends that myth (broadly conceived to include not only ancient Greek and Roman myths but also folk narratives and oral traditions) is not about stepping away from the world. Myth enables us "to live more intensely within it" (3). Armstrong says myth is an imaginative art form that helps us make sense of the world. It arises from our experience in that world and mythic narratives help shape how we live in it. Kiernan brings the power of folklore and myth into her stories. In her imaginative art form, fiction, she portrays emotions of loss and fear within a world of loneliness and madness, often depicted at the margins of society. She mines old myths and folktales to find the truth they still tell. Jason Marc Harris found that folkloric narratives in the nineteenth century were not escapist dreams to deny Victorian anxieties. Rather, he found that such stories were aimed articulations of concerns that troubled Victorians (35). Kiernan reprises that feature of folklore and articulates contemporary issues and anxieties. But she recreates them in a modern gothic context, where we live in an increasingly uncanny and terrifying age that is called the Anthropocene.

The characters in her work discussed in this chapter experience that terror and react in varying ways. In some of her stories, folklore and fairy tale creatures are reanimated in a modern gothic context. In others, characters become the abhuman, that is, they accept their abject status in the modern age. Her stories give a voice to those outcasts, loners and the marginalized in society, who seem to be on the front lines of the madness of modern society with its continuing environmental exploitation, degradation and destruction.

Five

"Warnings to the Curious"
Kiernan's Science and Mystery Stories

> "Do I believe in ghosts? [...] I am prepared to consider evidence and accept it if it satisfies me."—M.R. James, *Collected Ghost Stories*, ix

Caitlín R. Kiernan's novels and stories are infused and enriched with scientific knowledge. Of course, she is a scientist, a paleontologist by education, research and field experience. In many of her fictions scientists and academics, along with journalists and other searchers are central characters in stories that explore the threshold between science and an unknown, which resists explanation. The intrusion of the irrational into the everyday is a defining characteristic of supernatural literature, yet Kiernan deepens its meaning and fright through her scientific knowledge. In her stories the characters are on field explorations, in a lab, performing an experiment or in an ordinary apartment where they find something outside accepted explanatory schemes. For these characters the trauma of crossing a threshold between science and the irrational is precipitated often by contact with an inexplicable object, for example, a fossil. In Kiernan's "Valentia" (2000) Dr. Morris Whitney discovers the Culloo trackway on a lonely island off the West Coast of Ireland. But this fossil remnant from the Devonian seems to reveal too much. Often the mystery of the unknown, that is, the contact with an inexplicable thing or event is terrifying and sometimes agonizingly mutational for characters. This materializes for Edith and Sammie in "The Bone's Prayer" (2009).

Occasionally a character's experience is kept secret, as if the mystery is too powerful, too deep and dark, too disruptive of normal science, or rationality to tell. For example, the protagonist, Henry S. Matthews, at the end of "In the Water Works (Birmingham, Alabama 1888)" (2000) hides away the strange coiling thing found in the tunnel through Red Mountain (this story is explored in detail in Chapter Four). The search itself may call up the supernatural, and the searchers may regret their discoveries. In "Pickman's Other

Model (1929)" (2008) Mr. Blackman fears the horrors that he has called forth from his foolish investigations of the papers and sketches of William Thurber who committed suicide. Thurber was a friend of Richard Upton Pickman from Lovecraft's story "Pickman's Model" (1927). Even insane investigations such as that in Kiernan's "Rats Live on No Evil Star" (1999) may reveal something best left unknown.

This chapter explores a sample of Kiernan's work as discovery weird fiction, that is, stories wherein the protagonist experiences the uncanny through her search for knowledge, or her scientific work, or chancing upon an inexplicable object. Kiernan's characters are mostly female, differing from M.R. James, whose stories featured a male antiquarian scholar who discovers horror through his curiosity. In Kiernan's tales, the exploration, an investigation or a discovery ends up revealing something resistant to rational interpretation. The normative explanation of the universe is disrupted. Characters find something immune to comprehension, something lurking behind the rational order of the world. Only a few, generally only one, experience the extraordinary, and who would credit their eye witnessing? How many witnesses does it take, if outside an accepted paradigm of reality? As Christopher Frayling might suggest the witnessing of an extraordinary event is discounted not because it is illusory, but because "no rational account" (32) has as yet been devised for it. In some of Kiernan's stories the characters decide to discount their own experience. The science journalist in "One Tree Hill (The World as Cataclysm)" (2012) muses on telling her editor that there is no great mystery about an oddly blasted hill. She would fabricate a piece that would debunk a rural myth, and prove the victory of science over the miraculous. She thinks better that, than believing in the impossible.

Moreover, Kiernan illuminates the content of many of these stories with her many-faceted narrative style. Her narrative alchemy creates a strange alloy of the real and unreal. There is an appearance of stark realism that is peeled away or exploded away for a glimpse of an aesthetically inspired primal mystery, expressed often though narrative ambiguity. The narrative uncertainty mirrors the uncertainty of the perceptions or events depicted in the stories. Yet, Kiernan's scientific education provides a sense of objectivity and distance within the inmost private terrors in her stories. And this distancing enhances the sense of dread. Kiernan explores the dark spaces of life, the illusions of perception, the vast spaces of awe and the hurt that everyone feels, causes and regrets within a world that is impossibly beautiful but dangerous and deadly.

Kiernan is a writer, but she is also a practicing scientist. She understands and deploys the methodologies of science. That is, she is a part of the scientific community, with its evidence-based research, testable hypotheses, observations, field or laboratory testing and experimentation, simplification and abstraction, and self-correcting mechanisms (that is, changes in intersubjectivity accepted theories and methods). This is critical in our age where climate change and other scientifically established realities are treated as if they are "fake news."

Science is a human endeavor and, akin to all human activities (including literary theory and social criticism), it is mediated by culture and values, but not everything is true. Some advocates of "science studies" (now renamed to "science and technology studies") suggest that science is completely culturally determined, that empirically collected data, mathematical testing, and logical coherence are irrelevant. That is, that science is no more than a subjective and intuitive approach to gain knowledge of the world. Alan Sokal and Jean Bricmont critique "science studies," especially its lack of epistemological rigor and its misunderstanding of elementary science and its methods (207). Science is different from the disinformation of social media, unverified conspiracy theories, and untestable literary theories. Recently Bruno Latour (who is one of the founders of "science studies") questioned some of the premises of this social criticism field. In "Why Has Critique Run Out of Steam? From Matters of Fact to Matters of Concern," Latour suggests that current academic social criticism is bordering on irrelevancy. As an example, he shows that social critical approach has led to attacks on the facts of climate change and to ignoring existing ecological crises. To overcome its futility, Latour argues that social and literary criticism needs to review and asses its own assumptions and methods. To regain credibility it must understand and use empiricism[1].

Current environmental issues highlight the importance of science, as Latour argues. Environmental change, carbon loading, land and water degradation, habitat destruction and species extinction have acute consequences for us as a species. Science remains unmatched in its methods to help us fathom the effects of these environmental changes. Science is needed to predict, moderate and adjust to future changes. Yet scientists claim no ultimate knowledge, they know that the universe is still mysterious, which Kiernan writes about. David Brewster quoted Isaac Newton saying: "I know not what I appear to the world, but to myself I seem to have been only like a boy playing on the sea-shore, and diverting myself in now and then finding a smoother pebble or a prettier shell, whilest the great ocean of truth lay all undiscovered before me" (*Memoirs of the Life and Writings of Sir Isaac Newton*, 407).

The Danger in Fossils

Our world may not be as we normally designate it. It is weirder, stranger and more hostile than we can imagine. Fossils hidden away keep turning up in Kiernan's work, for example, in the novel *Threshold* (2001), which was introduced in Chapter Four as a sequel to "In the Water Works (Birmingham,

Alabama 1888)." Chance Matthews seems cursed and stalked by death. Her parents died in a car crash when she was young. Her grandmother hanged herself, and a friend, Elise, also commits suicide. Chance's grandfather dies in the early pages of the story. There is no family to protect her, even her boyfriend Deacon Spivey cheats on her.

The novel's title is apt; it is a novel of boundaries, doorways and tunnel entrances. The dividing lines are science and superstition, self and the other, reality and dream, sanity and madness, life and death. Thresholds are breached. There seems a merging of inside and outside, of here and the beyond, of present and past, of the underground and the surface. Roger B. Salomon sees this as a fundamental theme in weird literature and what is found, or what intrudes is a "negative and deconstructive environment" (10), which is what emerges from Red Mountain.

At the start of the novel, Chance Mathews is alone, alone to confront another reality, cut off from her family and her familiar world. That old ammo crate she found with the aid of Dancy Flammarion exposes science and mystery. They find her great-grandfather's hidden artifacts, fossils and her grandmother's journal. On the flip side of a rock with several trilobites much older than expected there is a strange star-shaped impression. Chance's grandmother had also sketched the symbol in her journal, as if trying to understand it, to pin it down, to explain it. Chance takes the crate into her paleontology lab. There she tries to calibrate the angles of the heptagon, to understand it, because she has a profound regard for scientific methods and a deep faith in the regularity and predictable patterns in the world. But the discovery wrenches Chance and her friends into a rendezvous with impossible beings from deep time. In *Threshold*, Kiernan is adept at transporting a "reader from the real to the unreal," as S.T. Joshi describes her prose ("Sculptures in Prose" 5). She does this with a scientific eye for precision in observation that startles us into a belief in both Chance's ordinary world and the inexplicable world slithering out of that tunnel through Red Mountain.

Lacey Morrow finds another old box hidden in a dusty drawer in the basement of the Pratt Museum in Kiernan's "From Cabinet 34, Drawer 6" (2005). In that box, she discovers an astonishing fossil. This is a story thematically linked with *Threshold* about dangerous fossils, as if there are some things best left unexamined.

The story reads like a film treatment, possibly a spinoff from *The Creature from the Black Lagoon* (1954), which is featured throughout the piece. That film depicts the search for the whole fossil of a skeletal hand found by a previous geological expedition to the Amazon. In Kiernan's story the found forelimb fossil takes Lacey Morrow on a journey to a cold room where she is shown an impossible creature, the Gil-Man, a remnant from the military operation off Old Innsmouth Harbor in the 1920s. Throughout the tale Kiernan inserts real and fictive references. For example, the cardboard box holding the fossil is marked with the *USS Cormorant,* a real ship (the *AM-40*) in the Rhode Island area at the time of Lovecraft's "The Shadow over Innsmouth" (1936). But there are fictitious books, such as Gerald Durrell's *New American Monsters: More than Myth,* used to bolster the notion of real scaly human-like creatures in the New England seas.

The direct action happens in a matter of hours during one day; the times are neatly used as section headings. There is even a chase scene, which ends in a crash, followed by gunfire from Dr. Solomon Monalisa,[2] who rescues Morrow. Monalisa also ensures that nothing is made public about the fossil.

Cinematic flashbacks give the back-story. One of the flashbacks tells of Morrow's travel to the fictional Innsmouth where she looks across the old harbor and thinks she sees something that appears big and dark scuttling across the rocks and slipping back in the sea. The story is a bit over the top, yet also pays homage to Lovecraft's story and to old monster films, which may tell more truth than one would think.

Morrow is yet another scientist, a paleontologist. She christens her find: *Grendelonyx innsmouthensis* (Grendel's claw, originating from Innsmouth). Kiernan is meticulous in describing the bones of the forelimb fossil, as she is in her delineation of the skeleton in "Pickman's Other Model." Dr. Monalisa suggests scientists really "search for answers [...], even when they are impossible" (*Two Worlds* 309). Monalisa sees the current enterprise of science as the arbiter of truth until something better arises, speaking perhaps to the discontinuous nature of science as argued by Thomas S. Kuhn and Paul Feyerabend. Kiernan is not suggesting that science is merely culturally relativistic. Her precision in describing the fossil illustrates the care and attention to observation and analysis which are hallmarks of science.

Kuhn[3] argues that science is a discontinuous but advancing enterprise with paradigm shifts in the scientific explanations of the world. He does not contend that science is irrational. These scientific paradigms are not congruent; they are different world conceptions. A scientific statement formulated in one paradigm cannot be fully translated into a statement of another paradigm, although scientific theory correspondence rubrics[4] may help in bridging this discontinuity. The Ptolemaic view of the cosmos is not congruent with the Keplerian. And Kepler's account is not totally retained in Newton's. According to Kuhn, over the history of science, it is clear that scientific theories have shifted in explanatory structure and in their portrayal of the universe we live within. In *Against Method,* Feyerabend argues that the relationship between successive theories in science is incommensurate. Further he argues the history of science shows scientific methodology, in some aspects, itself has shifted. Of course, scientific theories still need to have some empirical basis. But the progress of science is not an entirely orderly process. Feyerabend argues that over the course of millennia the procedures of science do not always share a common structure. Methods and procedures that worked in the past may not work if imposed now or in the future. Feyerabend's point, in part, is that scientific theories should proliferate and be tested. He is not saying that everything is allowed. Our explanations for the universe need to be based on confirmed data, be testable and be logically coherent. Feyerabend does not say that science is merely culturally constructed knowledge. But he is not entirely in line with Paul M. Churchland, who seems to espouse a form of scientific realism, where proven and tested methods guide an empirical enterprise based on data standards, tested methods of analysis and verifiable observations.[5] Feyerabend is more radical in his approach to the history of science, but not in science's fundamental objective efforts to understand the world we inhabit. He does not advocate subjective and intuitive approaches to knowledge. Another point that Feyerabend makes is that there is danger in believing current science has discovered timeless truth, and the real nature and structure of the universe, because this will stifle new discovery and an improved understanding of the world. There are things yet to be known and shifts in theories, methods and scientific practice are necessary. This seems to be Dr. Monalisa's view in Kiernan's "From Cabinet 34, Drawer 6."

Kiernan combines her paleontological background and gothic sensibility in "Valentia," drawing on these elements to create a menacing story of trauma and death set on Valentia Island in remote County Kerry. The characters are scientists or students. The narrative structure of the story is akin to a short film with scenes out of time sequence in different locations with a mix of reality and dream, as if to emphasize the complexity of knowing the universe we inhabit.

The story uses the destruction of a Devonian (a geologic period of 60 million years that began 420 and ended 360 million years ago) trackway as a metaphor for the continuing power of ancient beliefs and mystery.[6] "Valentia" opens with Dr. Anne Campbell flying to Ireland after learning the body of her one-time lover, Dr. Morris Whitney, discoverer of the trackway, had been fished from the sea. She meets up with one of the students at the site.

Dr. Campbell also scans the photographs of the fossil site that Dr. Whitney shot of the undamaged site. In one photo Dr. Campbell picks out something metallic and smooth, a disc, embedded in the stone, something akin to that discovered in Kiernan's novel, *Threshold*.[7] She searches for a scientific explanation, but fails. It is an inexplicable modern object in ancient rock. No theory explains such a possibility.

The trackway appears to cause trauma. Dr. Whitney is lured somehow into the sea to die. The students seem compelled to vandalize the site and are now ill-fated because of their failure to destroy not only the fossil site, but also every photograph of the undamaged trackway. Dr. Campbell is left to tell the tale, as perhaps a warning from the dark, primordial, forbidden past. This story explores the remnants of ancient beliefs and the limitations of science to explain all of our experiences in the world.

Kiernan also explores this theme in her dark science fiction works, for example, "Blind Fish" (2012). Yet another fossil, of a sauropod vertebra, was abandoned in a cabinet drawer. But when re-discovered it propels Jeremiah to an encounter outside current science. Here the fossil is a dwarf dinosaur, which evolved on an isolated island. As with many of her stories Kiernan combines the fictive with the real. She time places the originating dinosaurs in the Mesozoic Era, and space places them on an island in the ancient Tethys Ocean between the ancient continents of Gondwana and Laurasia. Such dwarfism has occurred (see Benton, et al. 2010 and Dyke). In the story, Jeremiah is the lead paleontologist on the underwater recovery of fossils of the isolated fauna from millions of years past. The find is a boon for him in 2031, as he continues to clean, examine, catalogue and describe such dinosaur species as *Microsaurophaganax inexpectatus* (unexpected small lizard-eater), which bring him recognition and job offers. But it also brings horror, as he struggles for sanity after a harrowing encounter deep in the sea. He bemoans that the "curiosity of *all* humanity is, and forevermore will be, a curse" ("Blind Fish" 90). That curiosity led to his submergible plunging into a perfectly circular hole in the sea bottom to hit onto a patterned, metallic surface.

Science has repeatedly eroded the sense of human importance in the cosmos from Copernicus and Galileo through Isaac Newton to Charles Lyell and Charles Darwin and onto Max Planck and Richard Dawkins. Jeremiah's discovery erodes this even more. He knows the meaning of the *herpetosapient* (wise reptile) skull fragments, and the immense, constructed icosahedron, which have been banned from being published by the government. Kiernan enriches this story with many quotes concerning the mystery of the sea. For example, she quotes Annie Dillard, "if you ride these monsters deeper down, if you drop with them farther over the world's rim" ("Blind Fish" 96). This continues in Dillard's *Teaching a Stone to Talk*: "you find what our sciences cannot locate or name, the substrate, the ocean or matrix or ether which buoys the rest, which gives goodness its power for good, and evil its power for evil" (19), which sums up Kiernan's effect in this story. Jeremiah's discovery reveals an ancient mystery that illustrates the tenuousness of our understanding of even our own planet, not to speak of eroding even more the false pride in human exceptionalism in creation.

Here and in other stories, Kiernan argues against Frederic Jameson, who says science has desacralized the world. Science has removed any magical presence; there is only an "absence at the heart of the secular world" (Jameson, *Political* 134). Our explanations of the universe drain the universe of mystery. Counter to this Alan Lloyd-Smith suggests that it will be science that eventually resurrects mystery (124). In Kiernan's fiction, science is a prelude to the revealing of a liminal space where terror and grace are still found. Outside the rational chain of events, the lawless impossible yet lurks.

The Impossible Sea

Another impossible object is found on Moonstone Beach, Block Island Sound near Providence in "The Bone's Prayer" (2009). This title comes from a line in T.S. Eliot's "The Dry Salvages" (1941), where he writes about a bone on a beach (*Four Quartets* 37). Kiernan's fiction is rich with allusions and quotations from science and literature. Eliot's poem, in part, bewails the fouling of nature, as humans cannot think of the great seas not polluted with waste (*Four Quartets* 38). Kiernan's tale seems a howl of the sea from that bone on the beach. When she suffers from writer's block, Edith goes to the beach. There she discovers that strange, greenish stone, slippery and sleek, and oddly etched by unknown forces. It heralds another threshold into the supernatural. In this tale the dissolution of boundaries is expressed through the writing itself. The metamorphism sketched in the story is challenging for a reader. That is because it exhibits directly that categorical uncertainty, which is how horror fiction, at its best, expresses the instability of rationality, according to Salomon. Yet rationality through the scientific method may be our only safe hold above the abyss of darkness, which is the cosmos. But rationality is at times a tyranny of the ruling order to maintain its control and authority. Salomon argues horror narratives subvert rationalism and the call of conformism. He contends dark fictions contest realism as the only pure form of literary art (161). Rational culture (and realism in writing) rejects all that is outside, or beyond its ken. Ludwig Wittgenstein wrote: "What we cannot speak about, we must pass over in silence" (89). All that is unspeakable and subjective must be hidden away; we cannot talk about the mysterious because it is not rational. But Kevin Birmingham argues the foe of the empirical is not the illogical. Rather it is the secretive (5).

"The Bone's Prayer" is an expression of the mysterious. Edith returns with the inexplicable object to her house, where she and Sammie, her friend and sometimes lover, talk about the stone and its carvings. Sammie muses on possible Atlantis and Mu connections of the stone, yet suggests it be shown to a scientist, who may know what it means. She also proposes several possible sources, or causes of the stone, each seemingly unacceptable. Edith thinks Sammie "*sounds like a scientist*" always hunting for an acceptable explanation (*Confessions* 235, emphasis in original). One layer of this sometimes confusing tale is the conflict between a rational perspective and the awful complexity of the world that refuses to conform. These two women are at the center of the storm of reason and madness. Caused, so to speak, by that strange object, defying categorization or labeling.

More importantly, "The Bone's Prayer" is an ecological dark tale and a lament on the ongoing marine pollution that destroys aquatic habitat and life. Kiernan recounts the 1996 oil spill from the *North Cape* that savaged Trustom Pond National Wildlife Refuge in Rhode Island (see U.S. Fish and Wildlife Service[8]). This catastrophe also figures in Kiernan's "Sanderlings" (2010), which explores other strange objects found on Moonstone Beach.

In "The Bone's Prayer" the found stone sings. It seems a requiem for a great dying in the sea, perhaps the end–Permian extinction event when up to 95 percent of marine species were lost (Benton, *When Life Nearly Died*), or more likely a forecast of the future of the oceans. This tale is a dirge on the current condition of the oceans, befouled by humans. It is a message in a stone from the sea. Will anyone listen? Edith and Sammie receive the early warning signals of the dying of the sea, and the death and mutations it will bring to our planet. Shakespeare wrote "Th'imperious seas breed monsters" (*Cymbeline King of Britain* 4.2.35). But in this tale the real monsters are humans, who contaminate the oceans. Its effects are depicted through an inexplicable transformation of the characters. It seems the two are press-ganged by the sea, losing their human identities, illustrating not only the frailty of identity, but also the frailty of life on the planet. Kiernan weaves these features into an enchanting story that is mythic and cosmic, yet also realistic and personal, maybe prophetic, in structure and theme. As a scientist she knows about climate change and the impacts of increasing atmospheric carbon dioxide concentrations.[9]

In Kiernan's "Nor the Demons Down Under the Sea" (2002)[10] the two female characters experience a similar extreme disorientation, which the narrative nearly induces in a reader. The title is from Edgar Allan Poe's poem "Annabel Lee" (May 1849), which was his last poem. It is a poem of young love carried through into death, where love breaches that ultimate threshold. The rhythm of the poem echoes the sound of the sea on a coastline. It reads as if an incantation, singing the mystery of the sea, and of love and death, as does the narrative structure of Kiernan's story. Dr. Julia Winter and her lover, student Anna Foley, are hunting fossils both scientific and supernatural. The story starts with Julia driving a Chevrolet Bel Air convertible along a west coast road while Anna reads a book on Malacology, (a branch of invertebrate zoology on the Mollusca), in the back seat. Their quest for shell specimens is changed to a hunt for a haunted house that Anna suggests. There, Julia turns the car around, as she senses something dangerous, but Anna is out of the car already rushing towards the house. When Anna is at the door, Julia hurries to follow her, but on the pathway the house seems to never near. When Anna finally opens the door a darkness flows out and through her. After this event, reading the story becomes challenging.

In her "Afterword" to this story, Kiernan says, "dark fiction dealing with the inexplicable should, itself, present to the reader a certain inexplicability" (*To Charles Fort* 232). Kiernan writes us into Julia's experiences through her disorientating language. The house is alive, as it lets the sky stare at Julia through its broken windows, appearing as jaws. Julia's senses are assaulted. There is a fish stench, a squishy sound of melons splitting, and she sees a beach bloated with vomit from the sea. Then there is a hideous thing on the ceiling of the room, a deformed thing metamorphosed from many creatures. Down the hall through a door lurks a "fluttering darkness" and a door of "absolute blackness" beckons her (*To Charles Fort* 228). She is wracked with pain, and hears a mocking voice, as the house becomes a maelstrom down into the sea. It is a delirium, an expression of the unfathomable in a wondrous cacophony of phrases and images that seems to drown the reader in "the sounding sea" (Poe, *Complete Poems* 478). Near the end, Kiernan sends passages from the Mock Turtle sections of *Alice's Adventures in Wonderland*, and lines from *The Rime of the Ancient Mariner*, careening like lifebuoys through Julia's mind, as Anna calls her back from the dead. This is a demanding story that externalizes an internal anarchy, as Julia flounders in a chaos of mystery, which the language of the story brings to life. The tale concludes with Julia lying in Anna's embrace by the sea, in the same way as the narrator lies with the dead Annabel Lee by the sea in Poe's poem.

Writing Away the Impossible

A more straightforward story is "One Tree Hill (The World as Cataclysm)." Loaded with student debt from MIT and Yale and hungry for work, a science journalist is on a free-lance assignment investigating a strange event on a hill in a lonely area of New Hampshire. The story reads in part as a modern rural legend. Names are hidden as the hill is just The Hill, or One Tree Hill, and there is The Village, and distantly there is The City. The narrator is nameless. In the end, she leaves behind the mystery, those "wondrous and terrifying glimpses of the extraordinary for the mundane" of her ordinary life (*Beneath* 487). Her report will call it a sham, a rural myth, nothing more than that to help her forget, to help her regain her rational hold on reality. Early in the story, the narrator notes The Hill's exact coordinates, to prove it is real, while she senses she is beginning to slip down into the irrational. The Hill is a threshold to the mysteriousness that evades logical explanation. On that hill she hears a voice. But is it merely a voice in her head? Kiernan deftly entangles a reader in the character's dreams, thoughts, fears and hopes.

The narrator describes a sinister landscape. There is a lake whose name means to fear something. An aged, nameless cemetery decays near the lake. After eleven years a smell of soot, ash, smoke and cinders yet lingers on The Hill. She feels a prey under a "wide carnivorous sky," where a sense of dread consumes her (*Beneath* 477). She is at the apex of a landscape of suspense mysteriously infused with power. In this story the heroine is not trapped in a confined space, but under the wide sky, which seems to expose her rationality, as if mere ash drifting away from that hilltop.

The sky is so big it will swallow her identity. This scene is central to the story. It marks the disordering of her scientific mind. She nearly succumbs to the allure and terror of a supernatural force impinging upon the everyday world. Or has the devastated landscape unleashed a psychological trauma dormant within her head alluded to in the story? It is a landscape of surface and latent violence, akin to that landscape in "Valentia." The Hill is a wasteland from that lightning blast. She senses that it's a place defiled and outside her experience. It is a haunted space. The Hill manifests the "force that exists beyond the human and beyond time" (Weston 39). But the narrator struggles for an explanation. She even debates with herself about the need for an explanation. In the end the science journalist accepts the scientific construct of reality and rewrites her experience of The Hill as hallucination.

Another method for drowning the mysterious is used by Ms. Howard, a student preparing a Master's thesis in "As Red as Red," who vows she will never talk about her experience again. This is after being haunted by Abby Gladding, who may be a vampire, perhaps a werewolf or also a witch—a living fossil of horror writing.

Silence is the antidote to the experience of the inexplicable. At the end of "One Tree Hill (The World as Cataclysm)" and "As Red as Red" the impossible is dismissed by the main character. As Algernon Blackwood wrote in "The Wood of the Dead": "Reason regained its sway over a dull, limited kingdom" (458).

Researchers and the Impossible

But no such reasoning helps Mr. Blackman in Kiernan's "Pickman's Other Model (1929)" (2008). Two sketches of Vera Endecott (AKA Lillian Margaret Snow) by Richard Upton Pickman propel him into an inescapable region of mystery and danger. He discovered the sketches in the papers of his friend William Thurber, who committed suicide. The sketches reveal an odd feature of Endecott's anatomy.[11] Blackman rummages through the files of Thurber, searches police reports, newspaper and magazine clippings, and hunts down films to find out more about Endecott. He is no scientist, but his quest is similar, as he wants to verify the drawings he has found, to find out the truth. But Blackman at the end upbraids himself for pursuing "forbidden questions," which lead to "dismaying revelations" (*Confessions* 260).

Kiernan draws out an increasing sense of unease throughout the story. We seem to circle ever closer to some horrible secret that it would be best not to know. Our understanding of the world we live in may be entirely wrongheaded; the social order itself may not be what is presented to us, along with the accepted view of the natural world. Our most cherished beliefs may be nonsense. Blackman writes that he strives to keep the soundness of his rational mind during his research. But he laments he should not have undertaken his dubious attempts at scholarship. All of his records of death and misfortune, calamity and crime are hopeless attempts to understand the world of Vera Endicott. Throughout the story there is a mix of real films and fictional films to highlight the battle between reason and the unknown. Blackman views one imaginary film, titled *The Hounds Daughter* or *The Necrophile* starring Vera Endicott, and becomes haunted by a rough shadow seen in the final seconds of the film, something bestial, something dark and hazy. That shadow is a continuing image for the intrusion of the supernatural in Kiernan's stories.

Officially, the work of scientists is to increase knowledge about the world through systematic methods. That means observation, proposing and testing hypotheses, experimenting and building theories to explain events and processes in the natural world. A prime role is experimental work. Kiernan explores this activity in "In the Dreamtime of Lady Resurrection" (2007), and "Rappaccini's Dragon (Murder Ballad No. 5)" (2008). The latter is a startling reworking of Nathaniel Hawthorne's (1804–1864) "Rappaccini's Daughter" (1844). This is one of several stories Hawthorne wrote about scientists, for example, "Dr. Heidegger's Experiment" (1837) and "The Birth-mark" (1843), where Aylmer, a scientist, works to erase a birthmark on his wife's face, but ends up killing her. It is a chilling single-subject experiment. Hawthorne's "Rappaccini's Daughter" fuses a discreet eroticism with the theme of creating a new being. The new being turns out to be monstrous, although the true monster is the creator. Dr. Rappaccini experiments on his daughter, transforming her into a poisonous creature, whose touch and breath bring death.

In Kiernan's story the hero, Daniel, transforms himself into a deadly poison. Here creator and monster are one. He trains himself to be a toxicologist, and experiments on his own body. He is experimenter and experimental subject. An elderly couple had poisoned his twin after sex, so he plots revenge, relentlessly injecting all known toxins into his body. Daniel has explicit sex with that couple in the climax of the story. They die slowly, horribly beside him, as he also plunges into the abyss of death. In this story, Kiernan rewrites a common theme in weird literature where men experiment on women's bodies, for example, in Arthur Machen's "The Great God Pan" (1890) and "The Inmost Light" (1894), with deadly results. The protagonist in Fitz-James O'Brien's "The Diamond Lens" (1858) claims to be more of a poet than a scientist, yet he constructs a microscope to investigate hidden tiny worlds. He discovers an infinitesimally small woman, but his voyeuristic observations kill her.

"In the Dreamtime of Lady Resurrection" (2007) portrays an experiment in death resuscitation from the viewpoint of the experimental subject.[12] It is again a single-subject study where a single case may be decisive in explaining the phenomenon of interest. Bringing someone back from death seems to fit that protocol. The story is a first person narrative from the experimental subject's point of view. She speaks of her experience in the vivarium where she was enclosed for research. It starts with a voice whispering to her to wake up. Yet she luxuriates within an incredible immensity, as if she swims in a gigantic night ocean. The voice keeps whispering to her, but the poisoned woman seeks deeper currents, resisting the demands from the experimenter, welcoming the inchoate, irrationality of the seas of night, now that she has crossed that threshold. Again in this story, the call of the irrational seems to try to overcome the logic of science, which may be those repeated calls for the experimental subject to return from her simulated death. At the end, the narrator seems to mourn being fished back into the lab, or the world ruled by science. But she is changed in ways not foreseen by the experimenter. This story harkens back to Poe's "The Facts in the Case of M. Valdemar" (1845), but gives the experimental subject full voice throughout the story. Perhaps there are also faint echoes in this story from Gertrude Atherton's (1857–1948) stories, where she explores the mystery of death, such as "The Striding Place" (1896). That story probes the notion of the soul enduring, for a time, in the body after death. Kiernan's story may also reflect "The Caves of Death" (1886), which seems to be an account from the dead. In Kiernan's story Lady Resurrection crossed the "thresholds that separate life from death" (*Ammonite Violin* 194). From that other side, she returns a mystery to herself.

The story ends with a quote from Poe's poem, "Ulalume" (1847): "She rolls through an ether of sighs—/She revels in a region of sighs..." (417).[13] As in Kiernan's story, Poe's poem is told in a first person voice. It tells of the narrator's return to the grave of his dead lover, where she dwells with the dead. The timing of the poem is October when the dead and spirits return to wander the earth again, which Lady Resurrection echoes by returning from her death. Yet she still dwells in that region of sighs.

Not only does Kiernan explore the supernatural possibilities arising from scientific investigations, but also from an ostensibly irrational investigation as told in "Rats Live on No Evil Star," which is a palindrome from a poem of Anne Sexton. There are two characters. Olan is a paranoid with worrying eyes and seems one of the many "cursed ones," who will "die before [...] [his] time" (Sexton 19). The second is Jessie, a student living down the hall from Olan. They are friends of a sort. She brings him food and conversation. Jessie is an academic writing a thesis on Anne Sexton. Olan investigates the unknown, that is, the unknown lurking around the apartment building where he and Jessie live. He creates a taxonomy, a classification of the unknown things he sees, such as "Definitive Organic" (*Two Worlds* 117), which he sketches and calibrates, as if a field scientist. He keeps a specimen in a labeled mayonnaise jar. In three very small rooms, he has crammed books, newspapers and files. His findings are noted on nearly 1,500 index cards. Olan's wisdom is that it is impossible to get any closer to the ultimate truth no matter how one records findings or rearranges words. The "truth is like the horizon, [...] it moves if you move" (*Confessions* 123). Olan is an irregular field scientist collecting, examining, naming, tabulating, and labeling his specimens. All stored in his tiny apartment on the west side of Birmingham, an area of decay where the foundries and mills are closed.

Olan is not a scientist working within a generally accepted scientific paradigm of field of study. He researches within his own theory of the landscape on the west side of Birmingham. That theory appears to be that a set of unknown things populate that landscape and they are predatory. In the story, his research methods are a purposive parody or distortion of the field research methods of scientists. There are manuals and best practices guidelines for conducting paleontological field work, that is to excavate, document, collect, preserve, research and study, and interpret fossil and geological specimens. Among other things, this is to ensure the verification and reproducibility of research findings. Science is a collective field and is generally self-correcting because of that essential collegiality, but a collegiality that believes in and practices questioning findings and debating conclusions. Kiernan's story is a cautionary tale about today's fascination with conspiracy theories made by individuals, who claim to have undertaken research.

In Summation

Kiernan's fiction expresses the human condition in a strange world, but it is a world humans keep trying to know. Her stories are experiments in form and content to achieve an expression of the inexplicable. They are constructs of mood and emotion, where the power of language is incantatory. Yet there is an ambiguity and allusiveness in her work, as if there are things that are impossible to tell. Her stories are grounded in science, enriched by a sense of mystery, but expressed within the social reality of today. In the sample of her work explored in this chapter, Kiernan illuminates what we search to know, but find is inexplicable, often dangerous, and at times what we wish to forget. Her stories articulate Walter de la Mare's view of the essence of strange fiction, which is that "this workaday world of ours—with its bricks, its streets, its woods, its hills, its waters—may have queer and, possibly, terrifying holes in it" (21). But Kiernan takes it further with her emphasis on science in conflict with an awful mystery in her fictional worlds. Amir Alexander suggests there has been a long ongoing struggle between science and an unruly nature that hides its deepest secrets from us. Science pictures reality for us, but there is yet a shadow-land of myth, and mystery in literature that suggests something beyond, something revealed in glimpses, often missed, often dangerous, something fleeting that hints at a greater unknown.

The narrator in Kiernan's "Concerning Attrition and Severance" (2008) remarks "humanity often seeks, through nomenclature, to subjugate that which it fears"[14] (*Confessions* 81). That is, the purpose of scientific and societal discourse is to know everything, to place experiences into categories, to explain, to name things, and to keep the dark away. In her fiction it seems a hopeless quest to overthrow the darkness that yet intrudes into our mundane world. Doctor John Montague is forthright about this, as he refuses to name that which has no name in Shirley Jackson's *The Haunting of Hill House*.[15] Science does not kill awe and wonder but deepens that awe with its revelations of an ever more strange, immense and terrifying universe.

Kiernan's fiction resounds with those "chords of dark understanding" that Leonard Wolf found in Bram Stoker's *Dracula* (170). She does this with a deep understanding of science, of its power and its promise. Yet she also knows its fragility, as it is a human enterprise and not something existing outside of human capacity. Her fictions counterpoint cosmic wonder and terror with personal and emotional story lines. In her stories of science and mystery, the trauma for the characters is the failure of science to explain their experience, an experience of darkness, as they step into the unknown.

Six

Haunted Perceptions
Fear and Trembling in Kiernan's Fiction

Omnia Exeunt in Mysterium

Albert Einstein wrote that wonder occurs "when an experience comes into conflict with a world of concepts already sufficiently fixed within us" (9). He went on to say that this often leads to a change in thinking about the world and may lead to developing a new system of thinking that is in "a certain sense a continuous flight from 'wonder'" (9). So, one way to escape wonder is to transform our scientific understanding of the world. In other words, science provides the conceptual framework through which we understand our world. It defines our perception of the world. Paul K. Feyerabend once speculated that the ancients, "prepared by [their] ideology, virtually *perceived* gods, demons, wood sprites" (*Problems of Empiricism* 190–91, emphasis in original); that is, for example, the Greeks saw their gods wander their streets, roam in the woods and visit their bedrooms.[1] Along the same lines, Paul M. Churchland (*Scientific Realism and the Plasticity of Mind*) says perception is theory-laden. He means that what we perceive is filtered through a complex web of beliefs. Our knowledge of the world is a network of theories, which are tacit, familiar and completely assimilated by people. But Churchland shows this does not mean that nothing is real; rather, he argues for a hard scientific realism that evolves an ever-improving knowledge about the world. For him, our apprehension of the world is guided by accepted, testable theories of the nature of the real, which have changed over the course of human history (*Scientific Realism* 1–6).[2]

Terror, as the other side of wonder, also arises when our experiences collide with our beliefs about the world. W.R. Irwin defined fantasy literature as exhibiting an "overt violation of what is generally accepted as possibility" (ix), that is, what our belief system tells is the world of the possible. More clearly, H.P. Lovecraft argued that the point of a weird tale is to tell of something that could not possibly take place. Lovecraft wrote that weird literature inspires terror because one experiences a malign overthrow of the accepted laws of nature. Lovecraft knew that advances in science shift the nature of the possible, because our scientific perception of the nature of the universe evolves. And that this evolution affects supernatural tales:

> If any unexpected advance of physics, chemistry, or biology were to indicate the *possibility* of any phenomena related by the weird tale, that particular set of phenomena would cease to be weird [...] because it would no longer indicate a suspension or violation of the natural laws [Lovecraft, *Selected Letters* 3.434].

In her weird and dark fictions, Caitlín R. Kiernan illuminates the wonder and terror of the universe. She is a scientist (a paleontologist) and an imaginative writer. Gifted with a deep word-hoard, a power for descriptions, an insight into human psychology and a scientific sensibility, she creates stories expressing both wonder and terror. In Chapter Five I look at Kiernan's stories surveying human scientific exploration, which may reveal more than humans can truly bare, as if illustrating Lovecraft's warning in "The Call of Cthulhu" (1928) of a future science that might "open up [...] terrifying vistas of reality" (*Dunwich Horror* 125). Perhaps this is the warning implicit in Einstein's notion that wonder showed there was something hidden behind things. That hidden thing is what Captain Barton in Joseph Sheridan Le Fanu's "The Familiar" (1851) calls the system behind the world, a system which at times is incompletely revealed and is malignant. However, Barton did not search for that system, as human scientific curiosity is but one gateway into terror. Other works of Kiernan tell of the unknown reaching out on its own. Of course, this follows, because the corollary to human research into the unknown is that the unknown also probes the human experience, as if sapient, wanting to know as well.

This chapter examines a sample of Kiernan's stories where the supernatural seemingly seeks out encounters with ordinary people. She paints characters experiencing a familiar world turning strange and unnerving when something intrudes in unexplainable, impossible ways. Their experience conflicts with accepted perceptions of the world, and it is terrifying.

The Problem of Perception

Normally, perception is filtered by a reference frame consisting of a set of assumptions and beliefs about the world. Kiernan expresses this in her short story "Hydrarguros" (2010). The narrator first spies something that appears like mercury leaking from a fellow passenger's nose. But that odd, silvery, shiny stuff keeps turning up throughout the story, including at a murder scene where the quicksilver seems alive. The narrator does not know how to describe what he perceives because it is outside his current frame of reference for the world. Of course, the irrational is outside the intellectual set of criteria we use to make judgments about the world.

That irrational appears, perhaps randomly, to disrupt the everyday experience of Kiernan's characters, either brutally, as in "Tidal Forces" (2001), or quietly, as in "Tall Bodies" (2012). In *The Red Tree* (2009), an ancient red oak refuses to be just an oak, but shifts time and space as perceived by the novel's characters. Not just trees cease to be only trees, but a hallway may not be empty as in "The Long Hall on the Top Floor" (1999), or books may not be inert as in "Ex Libris" (2012). Or the laws of causality may be defied when a dreadful personal event provokes a terrible response from nature, for example, in "To This Water (Johnstown, Pennsylvania 1889)" (1996). Some stories explore what happens to people after an encounter, for instance "Onion" (2001), while in "Standing Water" (2002) an uncanny experience is ignored. In these stories the characters' perceptions belie their rational beliefs. Kiernan's characters feel afraid or exhilarated by their perception of an altered reality because it conflicts with their normative web of belief.

Are these pathologies or intrusions of the supernatural? Are they mere illusions or hallucinations or dreams? Do the characters perceive a mind-independent object? Illusions and hallucinations may be convenient explanations for perceptions that conflict with a belief system, especially when only one or a few experience them. Here I think of illusions as experiences where mind-independent things appear other than they really are (Crane 243), while deceptions are deliberately false representations of a mind-independent object. Kiernan investigates deceived perceptions in her short story "The Melusine (1898)" (2008). An ostensible melusine taunts Cala Monroe Weatherall, asking why is it that no one "trusts its own eyes and its own ears" when she perceives a wondrous thing (*Confessions* 124). But Weatherall is not taken in by the fakery, as the melusine is a steampunk illusion meant to deceive. An hallucination is subjectively impossible to differentiate from an authentic perception of a mind-independent object, but there is no mind-independent object being observed (Crane 239).

Dreams may be subjectively indistinguishable from real experiences. Yet there is no mind-independent object being perceived. Dreams have been classified as hallucinations or imaginative experiences that are similar to fantasies and daydreams. Carl Jung says dreams take humans beyond the limits of sensible or empirically-based knowledge. Often Kiernan uses dream sequences imaginatively in her fiction. Generally, the dream sequences, at least in the stories discussed here, do not suggest the characters are hallucinating or seeing illusions. They are imaginative experiences Kiernan uses in at least two ways. First, she embeds them into her stories to illustrate the motives, fears and beliefs of her characters, as they process an unsettling experience.

For example, in "Pony" (2006) the unnamed narrator's recurring dreams reflect her encounters and experiences from her waking life as she tries to reconcile an impossible happening into her web of belief. Second, dreams are used to illustrate the fragility of perception of the world and the uncertainty her characters experience. The sequences function, in part, as an anti-narrative to push the reader into experiencing the confusion of characters when the irrational intrudes on their lives, for example, with Reese Callicott in "Spindleshanks (New Orleans, 1956)" (2000).

Kiernan writes dreams into her narratives to explore inexplicable things beyond the range of human understanding. This may arise from the work of Carl Jung (1875–1961). He suggested that humans in their scientific investigations reach the edge of uncertainty. For him, dream work produces a symbolic vernacular that hints at what is beyond that edge. Roughly speaking, Jung in "Approaching the Unconscious" in his edited volume, *Man and His Symbols,* suggested that dreams are an instrument for going beyond the limits of conscious knowledge to see another reality (21–23). This is a narrative technique Lovecraft used in "The Dreams in the Witch House" (1933). Gilman's dreams turn out to be terribly true.[3] He experiences a world outside of the normative, because the stone terrace in a dream shows an otherworldly symmetry whose laws he did not know and probably could not understand. Gilman is separated from the normal human world of perception, but it is not an illusion. Kiernan's dream sequences are narrative methods to give insight into how her characters experience a supernatural reality, similar to Captain Barton in Le Fanu's "The Familiar" where he suffered through not a dream, no, it was a reality.

The Problem of Reality

No dream but an inexplicable reality frightens two women in "Tidal Forces." Kiernan begins the story with one of her lyrical descriptions: "The sun melts across her [Charlotte's] face. It catches in the strands of her brown hair, like a late summer afternoon tangling itself in dead cornstalks" (*Ape's Wife* 181). For the climatic encounter, both characters are outside their house, Emily on the porch, Charlotte in the garden close to the sea. Emily spies a strange movement or shape in the waves and calls to warn Charlotte. Then a shadow of darkness rises out of the sea, leaps over the shore rocks and sweeps through Charlotte, who falls, screaming. It leaves a hole in Charlotte's body. That wound in Charlotte's side expands quickly over eight days. It seems a "hole in the cosmos" (*Ape's Wife* 190), because it is incomprehensible. That hole shows a complete darkness—the undecipherable darkness that haunts Kiernan's work.

In a twist, this story ends happily, which is unusual for Kiernan. In the ultimate scene, Emily kneels before Charlotte and stares into the hole, now as large as a softball. Emily plunges her arm into it, an act of outrageous courage. Kiernan pens in agonizing physiological detail Emily's arm being torn apart. Yet it does not happen, because it is the only hallucination in the story. Charlotte shoves Emily away. Just before her arm is freed, Emily touches something wet, soft and abhorrent that for a moment wraps a cosmic tendril around her wrist.[4] This unwanted touching reflects a fundamental fear in weird literature. Patricia MacCormack claims the Gothic protagonist is a being within the world who fears the world will come within her (29). It is the fear of being taken over by the unknown or being consumed by the unknown. In "Tidal Forces," the unknown impregnates Charlotte; it is a cosmic violation. Charlotte speaks of the hole in her side, as if something alive, an insane, blind presence is growing inside her.

In Kiernan's stories studied in this chapter, fear originates in a source external to the subject, which is one of the major sources of fear in fantastic literature according to Rosemary Jackson. And this fear is disturbing because it suggests a takeover of one's being or consciousness and a loss of one's normal perception of the universe. It suggests an "absolute otherness" that one falls into, cannot understand and may not be able to exit (Rosemary Jackson 60).

The narrative structure of "Tidal Forces" shifts days out of standard linear time. The two characters careen bewildered and afraid through shifting storms of space/time, yet keep trying to make sense of their experience. Perhaps the non-linear telling is meant to reflect the space/time distortion effect of the impossible black hole nestled within Charlotte. Of course, it is impossible that the hole in Charlotte's side grows larger, that the spray from a shower flows into that hole, and that her skin rotates around the hole. The story is packed with questions about what the characters see and feel, questions that reel away from answers. None of Emily's scientific books provides an explanation for what she sees. Yet she works on the problem of how a shadow could knock Charlotte down, and how that widening pinprick might be explained as a simple wound. Scientists "would deny the evidence" of their eyes (*Ape's Wife* 190). What they see cannot be so—but there it grows. Perhaps it is a visible manifestation of "quantum foam" (*Ape's Wife* 194), as Kiernan interlaces science and terror in the story. John Wheeler suggested that the fundamental fabric of the universe at the quantum level was space/time foam. Roughly speaking, at that extreme minuscule scale there are tiny variations in space/time while its geometry shifts continually through complex shapes and textures, say, tiny black holes appearing and disappearing in nanoseconds with variations in the speed of light. This notion conflicts with Einstein's Special Relativity Theory, which predicts a smooth space/time with no such variations and a constant speed of light. In "Tidal Forces" Kiernan posits that something terrible lurks in the fundamental fabric of the universe; something horrific hides behind things out there in the cold void where nothing could possibly be predicted by science.

Kiernan further explores the problem of space/time and perception in "The Hole with a Girl in Its Heart" (2007), where quantum physics and wonder merge. The story suggests another possible outcome for Charlotte, if Emily had not released her from the growing dark thing in her body. The nameless girl of this story finds a lozenge in the dunes and swallows it. It may be a black hole. The story is in split screens: one in the trailer, where the young woman and her visitor talk, the other in a spacecraft around Cygnus X-1, where the visitor has been mysteriously transported, or at least so perceives. That lozenge in the young woman's body violates the laws of time and space for those who experience a terrible emptiness, all those who feel lost. Rotating inside her, that thing from some other place gifts a release for all those who touch it buried there in her chest. However, it may not be a genuine escape, because that visitor (now traveler in space) is unable to comprehend the experience. And the visitor's journey is a one-way journey; there is no return. This story contrasts realism and the fantastic. Rosemary Jackson posits that fantastic literature is the underside of realism and works in opposition to a culture's dominant discourse (25). Kiernan's text weaves together the fantastic and the scientific, suggesting a fissure in our current epistemology of the universe.

Reality, Dream or Hallucination?

What happens after such an experience? How does someone cope after she has brushed up against the irrational, that is, after the universe refuses to be as expected? In "Onion" (2001), Frank and Willa have "glimpses of impossible geographies" and impossible creatures (*Two Worlds* 219). When he was seven, Frank ventured down to the basement of his parents' apartment building and saw fields of red grass through a crack in the basement wall. It was a wonder to behold. Willa bathes in shafts of translucent beings in the small bathroom in her and Frank's apartment. She loves the experience and sees it as her true reality. She feels trapped in the world of waiting tables, eating bad food, and living in a ratty apartment. Frank seeks a cure, so to speak, while Willa wants the experiences to continue. She is not afraid, not even of the bug-like dark things skittering from her hair in the bathroom. For Willa the real terror is that she would be trapped in the everyday world. She will not attend to a silent universe. She listens for the stones to sing. Frank hopes that he was hallucinating, while Willa loves the wonder and horror she experiences and dreads her everyday life. For her the translucent beings are mind-independent.

Of course, "Onion" (which won the International Horror Guild Award for Best Short Story) is a story with layers. It reveals the agony of Frank and Willa. Are they gifted with insight into a world invisible to most, or do they have a mental illness? Perhaps it is better to be mad than have reality upended by an unknown agency, as Kelly Hurley suggests (15). The story has an undertow of menace, yet also of marvel. Frank and Willa are lost souls who somehow find each other in the ordinary world of traffic, and sirens, and jobs, and cigarettes, and lousy food. They represent the world of those with mental health challenges, who cannot access needed health or other support services. So, they form their own support groups (in Kiernan's story the talk therapy sessions led by a Mr. Zaroba) with others facing similar challenges. They try to scrape out a means of living in the ordinary world, while coping with the constant intrusions of psychoses (sometimes felt as wonder but at other times as terror).

"Onion" may have been influenced by Arthur Machen's "A Fragment of Life." Edward and Mary Darnell endure an ordinary and drab life in London until they remove to Wales where they experience ecstasy and overthrow the material world. They see the beauty and mystery veiled by common, societally prescribed perceptions of the world. Among other things, Machen's novella is a censure of Victorian social restraints, especially sexual role constraints.

Kiernan's short story contrasts the "scientific" perspective of the experience of Frank and Willa and the experience of the characters themselves. From a psychiatric view, perhaps they suffer from *folie à deux* (Lasègere-Fabret syndrome), that is, they have a shared psychosis. Yet they experience the fantastic differently and react to it with variant emotions. In addition, the story's fantastic elements reveal what society works to make invisible or absent, that is, the terror and despair of those with mental health issues who are left to manage on their own. Kiernan's texts often speak to the distress of those outside mainstream society.

In "Onion" the irrational intrudes in enclosed spaces such as a basement and a bathroom. Kiernan's story "The Long Hall on the Top Floor"[5] tells a more harrowing encounter in another enclosed space. The imaginary long hall derives from the real Harris Transfer and Warehouse Building on the Birmingham Southside. Sadie Jasper, a recurring Kiernan character, persuades another recurring character, Deacon Silvey, to accompany her to an alleged haunted floor. She wants a witness to confirm her theory of the supernatural (that there is something other than the reality commonly experienced). Wilfred Sellars argues that to have good reason for holding a theory means that there is good reason for holding that the entities postulated by the theory exist. What helps provide "good reason" is an inter-subject framework of such objects, that is, more than one (actually many) person experiences them—in a sense they become public, that is, real (Sellars 91). Another witness of the supernatural entity on the long hall will provide this inter-subjectivity for Sadie. Her sense impressions of something strange on that long hall leads her to know directly, in her mind, that the something exists as a supernatural object. After a fashion, Sadie thinks she is acting rationally. She has had a direct experience of something she believes is a mind-independent object. Therefore, she leads Deacon up to the top floor to gain a witness and confirm her theory.

Haunting Visitations

In Kiernan's story "Tall Bodies" (2012), the unnamed narrator is a loner who was dismissed from her position due to a misadventure with a student. Alone in her cottage near the sea, her human visitors are few. But other things visit her as if she is the subject of an observational field study. Strange beings, who moved slowly and gracefully, populate her views of Block Island. But she says words fail to describe them truly. Her conceptual vocabulary is inadequate to denote what she sees, that is, she cannot find a category for the tall beings within the inter-subjectively accepted view of what counts as mind-independent entities. They are incommensurate with accepted reality. But for the unnamed narrator these beings disrupt that reality. Looking out toward the Mohegan Bluffs and Corn Cove, she watches them stride so elegantly. At her window, one stared at her with eyes as dark as raven feathers and then walked away. For the unnamed narrator they are real, not hallucinations. One could interpret this story as a gentle settling into a lonely mania. But it seems more an acceptance of the intrusion of the irrational, an acceptance of the wonder. This is what occurred in Machen's *A Fragment of Life.* She will not tell others about the tall things, as if the tall, tall things are too beautiful to share with others. Or she may not tell because she may discover that they are mind-dependent. The tall bodies are inscrutable observers on Block Island from beyond the narrator's reason. They roam through her landscape and she is not afraid, just in rapture. The terror for the narrator may be the idea of returning to the normal, of not seeing them again, or being told that they are mere hallucinations.

Some people perceive a strange intrusion and do not really see what it might be, as they are set in their ordinary lives. They ignore the uncanny. Two characters in Kiernan's "Standing Water" (2002) seem to miss a glimpse of a "mightier universe" (Blackwood, "The Wood of the Dead" 458). Elvin Ross and his former girlfriend, Shanna, both work in Mr. Culliver's used bookstore. In the alley behind the bookstore, Elvin thinks a puddle is odd in the dry summer heat. It worries him even more as it seems to grow the following day, while he smokes in the dry heat. He points it out to Shanna. While they observe the pond, the surface ripples, as if it were a skin. They think it is weird. Elvin dips a broom handle into the puddle and it disappears, as through a verge into the abyss of an uncharted sea. The puddle ripples iridescently, almost with joy. Then one day the puddle is gone, and the alley is as it was. Shanna says she vaguely remembers hearing a screaming like a rabbit. They both head back into the bookstore, and their dreary jobs, and seemingly hopeless lives. From the edge of mystery, near the depths of wonder or terror, they hurry back to the dull comfort of home. This extraordinary event will drift away in their worried memories, as do the ashes from Elvin's cigarettes.

Daniel Kahneman says "associative coherence" (75) rules our interpretation of events in our perceptual world. Our existing patterns of association refuse evidence that contradicts our ingrained beliefs of a stable reality. So, everything coheres and there is no ambiguity, no disruption of our picture of a logical world. The characters in "Standing Water" ignore the wrongness of that puddle to avoid the terror of what it may hide. As Kahneman argues, we prefer safe, comfortable and familiar interpretations of perceptions, even if they disconnect us from a strange reality. That small but strange puddle in "Standing Water" may portend something deeply hidden behind things, something in nature troubling our normal perceptual world.

In "Ex Libris," the unnamed narrator tries many theories to explain what her senses cannot believe. She refuses to accept events that contradict her understanding of reality, a reality explained by science. The story's source is Lovecraft's "The Haunter of the Dark" (1936), wherein Robert Blake finds a collection of occult books in a church of the Starry Wisdom sect. In Kiernan's story, the narrator's lover, Maggie Ellen Morse, buys some books from an estate sale in Newport, Rhode Island, and deposits them in the narrator's apartment in Providence. The narrator opens the box, and odors of old leather, musty paper and an odd sourness assails her. But worse, on looking into the box, she sees an impossible profound darkness, as if the box had never harbored light or it holds the singularity of a black hole. There are miniature black holes, but that will not explain the odors, and nothing is collapsing into the box. So, she counts out eleven old, worn books, such books as *Von Unaussprechlichen Kulten* and *De Vermis Mysteriis*.[6] Over the next weeks the books increasingly distress the narrator and Maggie. The unknown here is tactile because the books feel oily and spread that oiliness to those who touch the books.

The narrator keeps trying to explain their effects. She wonders if they contain a lost knowledge and that now they are slowly un-concealing a part of the world. Perhaps it is a dangerous part that the evolution of human consciousness has adapted us to ignore for our own safety. She theorizes that the books affect space/time, that in some undiscovered manner they cause time storms. The narrator ponders this because she drove by St. John's Catholic

Church on Federal Hill in Providence, but Maggie tells her it was torn down years past in 1992.[7] This event unnerves the narrator; she seems overcome with fear and trembling.

What unnerves the narrator more is the gradual transformation of Maggie into something utterly strange. She searches for an explanation for what she senses is no hallucination. Maggie suffers an existential metamorphosis from the books. Her skin becomes oily, akin to the feel of the books and her breath smells like the "slow inevitable rot of antique, silverfish-riddled books" (*Yellow Book* 25). Then it gets worse.

The narrator conjectures that the books infected Maggie with a virus that spreads like a fungus. She needs rationalization, perhaps analogous to Hannah Arendt's comparison of evil to a fungus or an infection that has no intentions but may work according to some unknown law of nature. She must find a cause. Kahneman would suggest that is because she has limited information, she relies on one of her systems of thinking to formulate a coherent causal theory to explain her uncanny experiences (20–30). The narrator hypothesizes that her antibodies might fight off the infection, but Maggie's immune system must be faulty. The narrator elaborates a theory that the vector of the books followed the standard virus process in infecting Maggie. But Maggie's transformation violates any known biology or physics. Finally, the narrator ends her search, thinking that ignorance is a better ally. She fears she may be too close to a horrible truth. So, she must commit what she knows to oblivion, following Lovecraft's notion that some knowledge is baleful. She packs Maggie's impossibly transformed body inside a cedar box and hides it in a closet, along with the box of books locked in a safe. She knows it is not over; she will not succumb to the illusion that there are happy endings. For she has experienced the impossible and will be endlessly haunted.

Haunted Places

In "Spindleshanks (New Orleans, 1956)" Reese Callicot ignores her sense impressions in order to maintain rationality within a disruption of her known world. Escaping Cambridge, Massachusetts, for a time, she moves into a big white house on Prytania Street across from Lafayette No. 1 in New Orleans. Kiernan captures a sense of danger in the French Quarter, as if all the dead cluster on its hot, sweaty streets at night, suffocating in the scent of night jasmine. Her prose is polished, restrained, and quiet in this story, as if mirroring the ancient house on Prytania Street too near a graveyard. A lurking sense of something sinister pervades this story; there is something just there at the edge of consciousness trying to break through.

The white house is reputed to be haunted, perhaps by a young female suicide. That restless house cannot sleep. It seems alive, mumbling its thoughts and memories through its plaster walls and oak floorboards. Callicott is a writer with a block and a gin-and-tonic fetish. A recurring dream keeps taking her back to Cambridge, struggling through a snowstorm along a wrought iron fence past a small graveyard. Something dark mumbles on the other side of the fence, but she will not look. This dream illustrates the fragility of Callicott's perception of the world. And it illustrates that she will hold onto the accepted realities of the world and ignore anything that is counter to that reality. Callicott turns away from any irrational intrusion into her life.

And the strange and unnatural events in the big, white house will not shake her hold on the accepted knowledge of the world. A woman is murdered near the rented house, her throat torn out, perhaps by an animal. One evening at a party in the big dining room, an Ouija board is used to call up the dead. The planchette begins to move around the board, stopping to spell out "Spindleshanks." A shudder echoes across the dining room. Turning on the lights, a woman cries out, pointing high on a wall, where "Spindleshanks" is spelled out in dripping blood.

After the party, Reese Callicott wakes again from her recurring dream of Cambridge and that wrought iron fence over which she will not look to see what makes those soft footfalls in the snow. The house is restless again, as if troubled by unquiet memories. At the French doors opening onto the verandah, Callicott catches a quick movement of a deep gloom through the ancient magnolias and oaks. She closes the doors on that sinister world, stopping that silent call of the dark to experience what may be out there behind the accepted theory of the order of things. Churchland might suggest that Callicott's theory-laden worldview is a comfort not a blight ("A Deeper Unity" 271). That theory determines how she will perceive the world. Anything outside that perceptual screen (her dreams and the events at the white house in New Orleans) can be dismissed as aberrant. So she closes those doors of perception.

But in "Flotsam" (2009) the unnamed narrator harkens to the sea at the call of an inexplicable thing. In the first paragraph Kiernan pens one of her luminous descriptions of the ocean:

> Block Island Sound stretches out before me, restless and muttering beneath the moonlight, describing time and the night with the rhythmic language of troughs and cresting waves and breakers [*Confessions* 75].

In this vignette, a voice pulls the narrator to the sea. She aches to stop listening, to hear not, but she always goes down to the sea. And there she seemingly pulls the unknown thing up from the depths of the sea, up from the wheelhouse of the scuppered *Caoimhe Colleen*.[8] The being is a ghost, or water creature or vampire now comforted by the sea although she once haunted Stonington Cemetery, then the Seekonk River. They are lovers, but the thing from the sea feeds at the narrator's carotid artery. The story lists the many names of her incarnations, the names by which she was worshipped, including *Morrigan*,[9] as Kiernan evokes her Irish heritage.

The thing from the sea is a metaphor for the unfathomable universe and the many ways humans struggle to explain it. Rosemary Jackson suggests that fantastic literature exists as an opposing force to the accepted explanations of the world, which portray order in the universe and reinforce existing cultural hierarchies and beliefs. Fantastic, gothic or weird fiction spotlights the forces of disorder, the inexplicable and the unknown against which these explanations of order organize itself (Rosemary Jackson 20). In antiquity people worshiped and propitiated the mother goddess as a way to control and understand wonder and terror. And at one point in human history such a being would have been perceived as real, as mind-independent. In this story, the narrator wonders if the thing from the sea is only in her imagination, or a mere dream, not a mind-independent being. Kiernan uses "maybe" four times in three sentences to suggest the hesitancy at the door of wonder, which defies our scientific understanding of the world. This being walks out of the waves of the Sound unto the beach, trailing a blue bioluminescence "from dinoflagellates"[10] (*Confessions* 77). She comes with the taste of salt and estuary sediment. She is impossible, and the narrator falls under her spell. On the surface of this story there is wonder from that thing external to the subject. But at the end the narrator surrenders herself to the sea thing. She is gradually being consumed, losing herself in the arms of the unknown.

Supernatural Synchronicity

In Kiernan's stories the characters question their perception of an impossible world. Often, they ache for an explanation of their irrational experience. In Kiernan's "Tidal Forces" Emily suggests a relationship exists between Charlotte's brother shooting her with a BB gun in the past and that shadow from the sea hitting her. It may be a "meaningful coincidence […] a sort of synchronicity," referring to Jung (*Ape's Wife* 183). Any explanation provides a respite from fear. Jung's concept of synchronicity posits an alternative principle of explanation, an acausal connecting principle, in situations that seem immune to causal explanations, yet exhibit meaningful connections. We are all embedded in some form of orderly framework that may be beyond the current understanding of science (see Jung, *Synchronicity*). This is the appeal that Emily makes in "Tidal Forces"; even an irrational or occult explanation is better than deep fear. The deep fear of Oleron in Oliver Onions' "The Beckoning Fair One" (1911) came because "when all explanations had been made, there remained something that could not be explained" (34).

Similar to "Tidal Forces," Kiernan's story "To This Water (Johnstown, Pennsylvania, 1889)" fuses a personal tragedy with a dreadful natural catastrophe.[11] The story is multi-layered and yields multiple interpretations. It fictionalizes the historic 1889 gigantic storm that caused the catastrophic failure of the South Fork Dam and the subsequent flooding and near destruction of Johnstown, where 2,209 residents died. In the story a young Hungarian immigrant, Magda, is gang-raped in back of the Washington Street Saloon. Through her pain and anguish, she sees someone at the far end of the alley— her eyes plead for help. Tom Givens witnesses the rape, but turns away. Later he witnesses her suicide as she plunges into the reservoir at the top of the dam. Soon the monster storm arises to burst the dam and wreck Johnstown. Sexual violence, despair, and guilt seem to combine to call up a horrific natural event that sweeps away a town that is filled with criminal violence and anti-immigrant sentiment. Kiernan describes Magda's immigrant father in a rage for revenge, but stopped by societal powers that overlook the rape of a young immigrant girl. Kiernan also expresses the despair of Magda, who will find solace only in the cold waters of the dam's reservoir, the pockets of her skirt filled with rocks.[12] Kiernan portrays Tom Givens's guilt through a phantasmagoria distilled in his drink-addled mind. He relives the scene of her rape, sees her fall into the water, hears other men mocking him and feels her clutch at his ankle. She will "pull him down into the fish slime and silting night," which is a metaphor for his guilt (*Two Worlds* 50). Then Givens believes he sees Magda riding the gigantic waves of the flood, delivering destruction and death to the town.

"To This Water (Johnstown, Pennsylvania, 1889)" depicts an irrational connection between the rape and suicide of a young immigrant and a gigantic flood. When something seems impossible, perhaps even Jung's acausal connecting principle may allay fear. In *Synchronicity* Jung suggests that in some cases of seemingly no causal connection, there is a connection beyond the realm of mere coincidence. For him the patterns in life are not mere chance events but express a deep coherence and meaning. However, such explanations seem spurious, as Emily thinks in "Tidal Forces." "To This Water (Johnstown, Pennsylvania, 1889)" is a disquieting story of individuals and a town linked by crime and cowardice, broken by violence, suicide and guilt, and driven by despair, fear and retribution to a cosmic doom, as if by a supernatural force.

In Summation

Kiernan writes supernatural weird stories within a scientific worldview. Her stories often center on individuals experiencing a cosmic dislocation in their perception and beliefs. Indeed S.T. Joshi says the "inextricable fusion of science and artistry" and the "fusion of the cosmic and the personal" hallmark Kiernan's fiction (*Unutterable Horror* 707). In her stories, Kiernan's characters are haunted—haunted by the intrusion of the irrational, haunted by ghosts, memories, by themselves or versions of themselves. They become alienated from their normal perceptions of our world, from accepted societal modes of understanding and experience. They are separated from the world, banished from the normal or dominate system of explaining the world. And they are afraid, existentially alone and disconnected from the shared social reality. Kiernan's characters in the stories explored here do not exhibit pathology, rather something outside, some seemingly mind-independent thing affects them, forces a change in their perception of the world. Sometimes they perceive beauty, but mostly it is terrorizing.

Pierre Duhem argued that the history of science demonstrates our continuing failure to unearth the depths of nature. We live in an inter-subjectively confirmed reality that has shifted through time. What we perceive, in part, depends on our conceptual frame of reference. But there are problems with perception. Abnormal perception—that is, perceptions outside of accepted views of reality—are classified as diseased, deformed or a delirium. Yet for Kiernan's characters they experience a reality, generally a terrible reality, where no explanation makes sense. They cross the boundary of reason. Kiernan portrays how disturbing an encounter with the unknown, the supernatural, would be to someone. She imaginatively describes how such an encounter takes them away from the familiar world, as if the world falls away beneath them and they are suspended in a bewildering unknown space/time that is not hallucinatory but a dreadful reality. Richard Holmes writes: "Wonder leads you into both places: into the beautiful and beneficial, but also into the terrifying and menacing" ("Preface" x). That describes the experience of reading Caitlín R. Kiernan. Her stories and novels are beautifully written but also unsettling and disturbing.

Two of her novels are markedly disquieting. In the next chapter I focus on a close reading of *The Red Tree* and *The Drowning Girl: A Memoir*. These novels seem to be haunted themselves.

Seven

Spectral Confessions
The Red Tree *and* The Drowning Girl: A Memoir

"Tell us a story [...]. A ghoststory."—James Joyce, *Ulysses*, 32

Ravens and crows portend hauntings from the past in Caitlín R. Kiernan's *The Drowning Girl: A Memoir*. The narrator of the novel, India Morgan Phelps (familiarly known as Imp[1]), feels uneasy at the sight of these related corvids. They prefigure an episode of her schizophrenia. Or is it the return of her ancestral ghosts? Crows, black birds and ravens appear frequently in the novel, alerting us to Imp's shifting perceptions. Related phrases occur throughout the book, for example, "ravenous lupine devil" (214) and "raving mad" (287) reminding readers of the dual nature of Imp's experiences. Corvids do not appear as frequently in Kiernan's *The Red Tree* (I discuss the ecoGothic aspects of this novel in Chapter One). But the protagonist of that narrative, Sarah Crowe,[2] feels haunted by her environs. Isolated in a lonely farm house, Crowe senses inner and outer danger. The phrase "a murder of crows" (20) comes early in the book, warning readers of Crowe's trauma. These are two of Kiernan's finest novels.

The Drowning Girl: A Memoir and *The Red Tree* present as confessional fictions. But they are not traditional. The two novels also exhibit aspects of postmodernist literature.[3] For example the novels deploy such postmodern features as a fragmented narrative, intertextuality, a challenge to straightforward realism and metafiction (Brian McHale and Barry Lewis).[4] This chapter argues that Kiernan draws on confessional and postmodern literary techniques to illustrate that writing one's life story works to reveal the ghosts that shape one's destiny. Such stories confront the problem of knowing the real past and understanding the effect of that past on one's experiences in an unruly present. In doing so one confronts the trauma of one's personal history—trauma expressed in the form of hauntings in Kiernan's novels. Julian Wolfreys contends that all stories are ghost stories, that is, all stories tell of encounters with the unknown (3). Kiernan's two novels tell of her central characters' encounters with their pasts and their attempts to salvage or recreate their life through writing. Such attempts at writing about one's personal traumas (that is, to listen to one's specters) might lead to liberation but not always, which is what Julia Kristeva contends.

Confessional Fictions

Kiernan's use of a confessional fiction narrative in these two works is a deliberate strategy.[5] That is because such writing discloses a person's innermost thoughts, inner turmoil and motivations. With this style, a person or a character expresses what it is like to struggle with the meaning of what happens to her, especially those things that are often kept secret or that are dangerous. Confessions are thought of as testimonies of truth, yet they are often found to be fraudulent.

Kiernan's novels are confessional fictions narrated by the protagonists in the first person about webs of personal emotional, physical and social trauma that ensnare them. Such fictions frequently presented a character at a particular point(s) in her life as she relives parts of her past and becomes engulfed by her inmost thoughts (Axthelm 8). Confessional fictions are often structured as a journal, diary, letters or the thoughts and words of a confessant expressed to a listener. Historically confessions have been thought of as a truthful expression by an individual, for example, St. Augustine's *Confessions* (397–400). His confessions seemed an appeal to God, but the book was also aimed at Augustine's critics inside and outside the Catholic Church.[6] Jean-Jacques Rousseau's *Confessions* (1781) was different. He did not appeal to God but to himself and his readers. Readers become entangled in an interplay of truth and lie in the book because the text concealed as much as it revealed, setting the stage for modern confessional writing (see Veliki).

Reliability and authenticity are basic challenges with confessions. Peter Brooks documents how historical and literary confessions are inherently unreliable. That is because they are based on false assumptions. He argues that confessions, either real or fictional, are rarely "products of a free and rational will" (Brooks 63). He contends that confessions arise in situations of either physical or psychological constraint or coercion, that is trauma. Kiernan's two novels represent traumatized writing. Jo Gill ("Introduction") shows that explorations of confessional writing challenge the notions of reliability, authority and truthfulness of all such works. Gill suggests this fragmentation or incoherence in an authorial voice leads to a failure of forgiveness or reintegration. This highlights the uncertainty of any undertaking to express the truth about oneself.[7] Autobiographical memory[8] is hazy and not precise.

And there may be repressed memories caused by traumatic events, according to Sigmund Freud,[9] which the person herself cannot recall. Such repressed memories of trauma sometimes surface through mental instabilities.[10] Kiernan's two novels speak to this disquieting impact of trauma.

Kiernan deploys the literary style and techniques of confessional writing in *The Drowning Girl: A Memoir* and *The Red Tree* to unveil the mental states of the main characters as they find or lose themselves. Both novels expose emotions of loss and fear within a world of loneliness and dread, depicted at the margins of society. The narratives alter normal temporal and spatial sequences because the characters are in a maze of true and false memories while attempting to maintain a sense of reality. There is an awful intimacy in these novels, where readers experience the raw emotions of the lead characters.

Although fraught with challenges, confessional novels allow for candor about the private anguish which afflicts characters. This anguish often arises from a repeated encounter with trauma. *The Drowning Girl: A Memoir* portrays the multiples of Imp, as she experiences, re-experiences, and writes and re-writes the multitude of hauntings from her past and present. In *The Red Tree*, Sarah Crowe cannot escape her narrative of despair, dread and death in an isolated, seemingly alive farm house. A house that broods over an enormous, demonic cellar which is uncannily linked with an ancient, giant red oak that rules the landscape. Sarah Crowe's identity is under siege from the past of that tree, the underground cellar of the haunted house, and a haunted text found in that cellar. In *The Drowning Girl: A Memoir*, Imp's identity is also under siege. Although the novel is generally from a first-person voice (Imp's), a third-person voice (also Imp's) will enter to comment, critique or add to the narrative. Indeed, the opening of the novel features both voices.

Peter M. Axthelm argues that the modern confessional novel focuses on a heroine confronting her life in all of its dark terror (perhaps also its wonder). In both *The Red Tree* and *The Drowning Girl: A Memoir* the narrative channels the experiences of the protagonist as she examines her life, her past and her thoughts in an effort to gain insight or perception into her current circumstances, which seem to hold more terror than wonder. Crowe calls her journal a "coward's confession" (39). Several key elements of the confessional form appear in both novels.[11]

Kiernan uses the characters' confessional writings as the means through which Imp and Crowe attempt to recover from their trauma. All such works explore the problem of memory and how we are haunted by our past, a remembered past, which may not reflect the reality of that past. Richard Ford in his "Author's Note" to *Between Them: Remembering my Parents* (2017) says "entering the past is a precarious business" (n.p.). That is because the past works to make us who we are, but "always half-fails" (n.p.). "Half-fails" is an odd phrase, which expresses the ambiguity of the real impact of the past on our lives and our failure at comprehending what that impact is or is not. Both of Kiernan's novels express this challenge from the past, how it affects us, how it controls us, but also how we try to rewrite our pasts.

Postmodern and Meta-Fictional Facets of The Red Tree and The Drowning Girl

The Red Tree and *The Drowning Girl: A Memoir* are dense with intimations to history, to literature, to science and to popular culture. There are few pages in *The Drowning Girl: A Memoir* without some obvious or oblique reference.[12] For example, Sean Moreland ("'Not Like Any Thing of Ours'") chronicles the hauntings of the text by H.P. Lovecraft and Edgar Allan Poe. Yet the novel is uniquely Kiernan's. She creates a unique voice for Imp, who tries to write her way to an understanding, or rather a reconciliation and coping with a series of uncanny events that haunt her. Kiernan also packs *The Red Tree* with allusions. Agnieszka Magdalena Kotwasińska argues the novel overflows with references to other works and writers (98).

Kiernan presents both novels as constructs. Crowe's journal is a "found" piece of the structure of *The Red Tree*. Crowe is a writer with a severe case of writer's block. But she does keep a chronicle of her experiences at the Wight farm in rural Rhode Island, where she fled to complete her overdue novel. This journal inexplicably finds its way to the desk of the fictional editor, Sharon D. Halperin, who readies it for publication. She pens a lengthy scholarly preface[13] to the book. Crowe's journal, "a suicide's long ordeal and confession" (*The Red Tree* 5) according to Halperin, includes long interpellations from a manuscript, also titled *The Red Tree*. It contains the secret history of the house and its environs, and is printed in a different typeface. Crowe found it in the cellar of the Wight Farm House. The writer of the manuscript, Dr. Charles L. Harvey, hanged himself. The journal contains a short story, "Pony," found and/or written by Crowe and dedicated to Amanda Tyrell, Crowe's former lover, who had also committed suicide. The novel ends with an Editor's Postscript, which provides an excerpt from a novel by Sarah Crowe.

The Drowning Girl: A Memoir is a more considered expression of meta-fiction. Kotwasińska says *The Drowning Girl* is an "intricate web of literary references, styles and textual devices" (139). The novel is presented as Imp's journal. She paints, but the book contains two of her short stories: "The Mermaid of the Concrete Ocean" and "Werewolf Smile."[14] Chapter One reads as if it is an overture to the entire book, indeed, pages 26–27 articulate the key images of the novel. Although divided into ten chapters, Imp says chapters in a book are meaningless. The novel mixes internal monologues, fragments of conversations (that Imp says may not be entirely accurate), streams of consciousness, notes from Imp's researches, telephone messages left for Imp, and sketches from fairy tales. Throughout the text Imp reminds us of its artifice. She repeats a refrain that what she tells may not be true. The reader is never able to lose sight of the fact that what she is reading is a construct. It is a warning not to get lost but also to recognize the interplay of reality and construct. Many of Kiernan's works have self-aware narrators, who are writing the events as if compelled to do so by an internal or external force. It suggests that writing is part revelation and part subterfuge. *The Drowning Girl: A Memoir* welds psychological, supernatural and meta-fictional elements into a modern gothic tale. The novel is Imp's ghost story.

Trauma in The Red Tree *and* The Drowning Girl

David Punter suggests the gothic arose in the late eighteenth century and returned in the nineteenth century as a response to social trauma. He also contends that gothic motifs and themes resonate in today's literature because they speak to contemporary crisis issues, especially personal, social and environmental trauma (2–3). Patrick McGrath suggests this trauma is related to the violence and "destructive tendencies" (153) of the modern world.

Kiernan's fiction depicts individuals in trauma. For example, Crowe and Imp take medications for mental disturbances. Crowe was diagnosed with a chronic neurologic disorder that manifests in seizures. Such episodes leave Crowe sick, disoriented and dazed. Yet she continues to drink bourbon. Imp was diagnosed as a paranoid schizophrenic and her family history is plagued with mental illness. Imp takes a variety of medications (for example, Risperdal, which is an antipsychotic medication used to treat schizophrenia). Imp's schizophrenia[15] symptoms include auditory and visual hallucinations, as well as suicidal thoughts.

They are both artists: Crowe is a writer and Imp is a painter, but they are troubled in their work.[16] Crowe fails at writing the expected novel for her publisher but keeps a journal of her experiences at the house, its environs and her shifting perceptions of them. Imp is writing her ghost story that is not for publication. They see similar apparitions. A vision of a black-haired, naked girl haunts Crowe. That girl moves through the waters of a quarry pond towards Crowe until sinking away all at once. Imp is haunted by a painting, titled "The Drowning Girl," of a young, naked girl at the edge of a pool. Amanda Tyrell's suicide traumatizes Crowe, who is besieged by nightmares of her drowning. The suicides of her mother and grandmother haunt Imp.

Fictional artists trouble the novels. The outrageous art of fictional painters Phillip George Saltonstall in *The Red Tree* and Albert Perrault (in both novels) haunt the characters. Perrault paints disturbing works of wolves and girls, realized especially in his *Fecunda ratis* in *The Drowning Girl: A Memoir*. In *The Red Tree* Amanda Tyrell creates photographic morphologies of humans and mythic beasts engaged in sex, violence and killings. These art works graphically represent the violence and destructive tendencies of the modern world, which produces social and personal trauma. This is depicted towards the end of *The Red Tree*. Crowe finds or thinks she finds Bettina Hirsch's seven grotesque paintings in the attic studio of her rented house. These traumatic paintings seem to trigger Crowe's final misery. Bettina Hirsch committed suicide. She used a straight razor to slice her wrists (272) or she hanged herself (363). Hirsch's lover Joseph Olney hanged himself. Violence and death surround the two main characters.

Doubles traumatize the novels. Constance Hopkins, a painter, moves into the attic of Crowe's rented farm house. They may or may not have been occasional lovers. Constance Hopkins has her own double in Bettina Hirsch, the artist. Abalyn Armitage, a reviewer of video games, moves into Imp's apartment. Abalyn is Imp's on and off lover. Imp's doubles include her mother and grandmother, as well as the manifestations of Eva Canning, which are confounding. Imp finds or imagines finding (perhaps twice) Eva, a spectral stranger, walking naked along a road next to a forest or next to a river. Eva stalks Imp. But there is more than one Eva Canning. Eva Canning's mother Eva May Canning committed suicide by walking into the sea along with other members of The Open Door of Night Cult.

Specters, many of whom committed suicide, haunt both novels. Early in *The Drowning Girl: A Memoir* (3) Imp recalls a conversation with her mother, Rosemary Anne, about the suicides of Diane Arbus,[17] Anne Sexton[18] and Virginia Woolf. Woolf filled her pockets with stones and walked into River Ouse.[19] Death by water dominates in *The Drowning Girl: A Memoir*. Eva Canning came from the sea and returns to the sea. Abalyn rescues Imp when she attempts suicide in a bathtub.[20]

Those who committed suicide stalk the novels. That seems to be a question asked throughout the novels: is life worth living? This is the fundamental question about life, according to Albert Camus. In *The Myth of Sisyphus* (1955), Camus claims the core philosophical question is whether to commit suicide or not in the face of the absurdity of life (3), where the "strangeness of the world is the absurd" (*The Myth of Sisyphus* 11). The absurd means that what we hope to get from the universe, be it meaning, order, or acceptance, is not to be found in an indifferent universe of chaos and trauma. Humans have to create their own meaning of life. Julia Kristeva says one way of creating purpose and to overcome trauma is to write about one's life. That appears to be what Imp and Crowe are trying, writing their way out of their traumas.

In *The Red Tree*, Crowe's madness seems a radical and logical alienation from a traumatic world. When Constance Hopkins leaves the farm house,

Crowe breaks. The shape-shifting underground and the giant red tree will not let Crowe escape. Nature seems hostile to Crowe, as if she is an intruder. There seems little of the wonder in nature in *The Red Tree* that Algernon Blackwood found. For Crowe the nature surrounding her is dangerous and uncanny, it is a primeval terror. There is no grandeur just fear. A fear similar to that expressed by such American Gothic writers as Charles Brockden Brown and Nathaniel Hawthorne, for whom the woods in America were the abode of the devil and witches. Those evil beings seem to be underneath the red oak in Kiernan's novel. But does that wild nature want her soul, as is hinted at in the novel? Or are the terrors in Crowe's head? Either way Crowe is caught "in the jaws of the wilderness" surrounding that isolated farm house (Blackwood, "The Wendigo" 163). The cellar in *The Red Tree* presents the outmost trauma. It is where Crowe finds Harvey's haunted book, it is where she crosses a stone boundary and with Constance Hopkins becomes lost in space and time shifts, mirroring her disintegrating grasp of reality. The question about this shifting cellar space is whether it represents one of Crowe's psychotic episodes or a supernatural phenomenon. That underground (an underground that extends below the red oak) is a vision of dread and despair, where all hope is lost and there is nothing but nightmare.

In *The Drowning Girl: A Memoir*, Imp struggles against traumatic currents from her past, some from a far past, others from a much nearer past, that engulf her present. Her mother (Rosemary Anne) and her grandmother (Caroline) return to speak to her. "The Drowning Girl," that painting by the fictional Saltonstall, keeps reappearing. She also experiences several encounters with the mysterious Eva Canning, who may be a mermaid, a wolf, a ghost, an ordinary young woman, or none, or all of these. These hauntings metastasize throughout the novel disordering Imp's sense of identity and her perceptions of the world. Imp keeps writing to maintain her contact with reality (a connection that is helped by her lover, the transsexual Abalyn Armitage[21]).

Sean Moreland ("'Not Like Any Thing of Ours'") points out that readers find themselves in Imp's mind. After a fashion, Kiernan's novel is a phenomenological study of the structure of Imp's consciousness as experienced from Imp's first-person and third-person points of view. Kiernan says *The Drowning Girl: A Memoir* "is a story about the human mind, and how it shapes reality, how those perceptions of reality are constantly shifting their shapes" (DeRose). And that is the view that readers experience. At times it is baffling, but beautiful, at other times Imp's experiences are terrifying and the world seems a chaos of strangeness.

Clearly the novels are linked. In an interview, Kiernan said, "*The Red Tree* and *The Drowning Girl: A Memoir* are meant to complement each other. Both truly are fictionalized autobiographies dressed up as fantasy, my own self-administered psychotherapy" ("Pernicious Thought Contagions").

Kiernan may agree with Elaine P. Miller when she argues that writing (along with other forms of artistic expression) expresses a type of "survival therapy" after trauma (12). But as Julia Kristeva argues such therapy does not always work.[22]

The Literature of Ghosts: Writing About Hauntings

Janet M. Ellerby agrees with Kristeva's notion that writing (for Kristeva all forms of artistic expression) can give meaning to one's life. It holds some hope of salvaging oneself from trauma. Confessions and memoirs are attempts to understand ourselves and how our pasts shape our destiny. But writing, Ellerby argues, can be a "pluralized, fragmented, conflicted, divergent undertaking" (34). Yet to communicate, writing needs some order, logic, and coherence. Coherence suggests writing that reflects a mind with a set of mental structures operating rationally that fashion, order and adjust performance to meet the goals of an individual, according to Ellerby. But a writer may be "overwhelmed by unconscious drives" and the writing may become "psychotic babble" (Ellerby 34). *The Drowning Girl: A Memoir* provides a narrative that registers Imp's mind. There are times when the narrative is coherent and logical. But other sections of text are fragmentary, confusing and ambiguous. These represent hallucinatory experiences, as well as represent where coherence is inadequate (see Ellerby 38) to convey Imp's trauma. It might be the only way those experiences of Imp, or anyone, can be communicated.

The novels end differently. We know the ending of *The Red Tree* from the editor's preface. Moreover, the excerpt from Crowe's fictional novel *A Long Way to Morning* in the "Editor's Postscript" provides a "foreshadowing," so the editor says of *The Red Tree* (16). Andrea, the heroine of that novel, keeps thinking about the "straight razor in the pocket[23] of her coat" (378). *The Red Tree* is Crowe's long suicide note. A suicide note that seems coerced by the Dr. Harvey manuscript, the Wight farm house and the red oak tree, abetted by Crowe's mental disorder. But the note also records Crowe's long, valiant efforts to fight the torments and disorders that haunt her. Disorders that are internal and external. At the end Crowe is isolated in the Wight farm house and alone with her trauma. That trauma materializes in a large, dark dog at the foot of her bed. She visits the attic room one last time and finds it thick with dust and cobwebs. Nothing remains from Constance's stay in that room. And Bettina Hirsch's seven deadly paintings are gone. Caught like an innocent in the crossfire of her mental instability, her isolation and the haunted environment around her, Sarah Crowe writes her last words, telling Amanda she needs to rest.

But in *The Drowning Girl: A Memoir* Imp says goodnight to hauntings in her final diary entry. No crows or ravens appear, because she has reconciled with her specters. She finds a meaningful creativity, which arises from her encounters with those specters. Imp creates meaning in her life through writing.[24] Despite her psychotic episodes, Imp continues her ghost story. This intense personal engagement with writing expresses her efforts to reconcile with her trauma and her hauntings. Hauntings that she sees as existing separate from her as they struggle on their own to persist. Yet through her imaginative recuperation of her past, her integration of her ancestral ghosts, Imp recovers her identity.

"Hauntings are memes, especially pernicious thought contagions," Imp writes (12). She notes the connection between hauntings and memes several times in her ghost story (for example 27, 33, 87, 88, 90, and 329). Kiernan uses "meme" in the sense that Richard Dawkins defines it in *The Selfish Gene* (1979), that is, a meme "conveys the idea of a unit of cultural transmission, or a unit of imitation" (249). Dawkins identifies human behaviors that seemed useless from an evolutionary perspective, yet they persist, for example, committing oneself to one's art or sacrificing oneself for a cause. Dawkins postulates memes as a way to understand how some ideas persist and spread, while others do not. He suggests that these memes persevere in complete indifference to their hosts. In the novel Imp uses "meme" to name and categorize her ghosts. Ghosts conceived as memes become part of our knowledge. Thinking of her hauntings as memes, Imp writes to recover from her trauma. Yet a tension remains in the novel.

That is because a meme is loosely related to the concept of the phantom as theorized by Nicolas Abraham and Maria Torok, and to Jacques Derrida's concept of the *spectre*. Abraham and Torok suggest that trauma experienced by a parent can be transmitted to their children and beyond. It begins an intergenerational haunting.[25] Abraham ("Notes on the Phantom") says that the phantom represents, "the burial of an unspeakable fact" (288). The phantom strives to keep the initial cause of the trauma a secret but cannot stop the trauma's disquieting effects on subsequent generations. These generations are in distress, but they do not know the secret cause of the trauma. To be healed this secret must be uncovered. The notion of the phantom suggests that both Crowe and Imp (as literary characters) and the novels themselves harbor deeper, unspeakable secrets, which remain hidden. But Abraham and Torok's phantom (as Colin Davis argues) represents a sense of "shame and prohibition" (378), which is not what the ghosts in Kiernan's novels represent. Kiernan's ghosts seem more akin to Jacques Derrida's specters. Her ghosts are "figure[s] of uncontrollable and uncanny repetition," which keep recurring to her (Schultz 281). Derrida says that part of the meaning of a specter is "frequency" (125) because "it returns to see us" (126).[26] Imp's specters are found throughout her story, so much so that her memoir becomes a ghost itself. It is a haunted book filled with ancestral and modern haunting voices from Imp's fictional memories and from the fiction of dead authors.

The psychic disturbances that rattle Imp and Sarah Crowe arise from the presence of ghosts. Such ghosts may lead one to what is needed or missing, as Schultz suggests. That is, the specter may help reconstitute "mis-rememberings, mis-perceivings, and the 'necessary falsification' of the past" (Schultz 285). By delving into her autobiographical memory Imp writes her ghost story and thereby her ghosts cease to be frightening and hostile, because they are her maternal ghosts, or ghosts of female writers. Her book borrows from the past so she can reclaim her identity while reconciling with those ancestral ghosts. Imp's narrative completes (what Crowe's does not) the full integration of her own ghostly past into her personal identity.

Sarah Crow in *The Red Tree* represents the failure of this revisiting of the past. That happens because the specters in the novel do not arise from her past, but from the past of the haunted Wight House, its cavernous cellar, the Harvey manuscript and the ancient red oak. Sarah Crowe fails to find what is missing in her identity through the specters from her own past, for example, Amanda. Instead the past of the haunted house and the red tree appropriate her identity. For Sarah Crowe the repetition and reenactment of that past brings no solace from her trauma, because it is not her past. Kotwasińska argues Sarah Crowe's journal mixes and jumbles "real" event memories and dreams to such an extent that it is "impossible to differentiate between visions of the past, hallucinations, elaborate metaphors and pure fiction" (92). This describes Sarah Crowe's chaotic new identity. A devastated identity because Crowe is pulled back into an archaic chaos represented by the Wight House environs, which intensifies her trauma. She loses her personal identity and becomes possessed. There is no escape from her phantoms.

Davis argues Derrida's *spectre* represents a figure caught between life and death that makes accepted truths vacillate. Imp's prime ghost, Eva Canning, hovers between life and death, and she shatters Imp's sense of certainty in her world. As well, Imp listens to and speaks with her ghost, as Derrida urges. He says that even though it may seem impossible, it is essential "to speak *to the* specter" […] and "*to make or* to *let* a specter *speak*" (11, emphasis in original). This is critical because the specter is outside the order of knowledge, according to Davis. This differentiates it from the notion of memes, which are part of the order of knowledge. Specters are outside our current comprehension of the world. Kiernan's novels push readers into spaces where specters return. Encountering a specter means bumping up against the unknown. Such encounters can be deadly, as Crowe experiences in *The Red Tree*. The distress in Crowe's life is too overwhelming, too dangerous, for one in such a fragile condition. But the novel as literature expresses that tension between the impossible and our ache to make it knowable.

Following a sketch of Imp watching Eva Canning walk into the sea, *The Drowning Girl: A Memoir* concludes with a sequence of dated diary entries. This shift in narrative structure signals an end to the spatial and temporal trauma of Imp's experience in the novel. Now, Kiernan characterizes Imp writing in an open and direct style. This more intimate or revealing style of the diary form mirrors Imp's reclamation of her identity. But she has not exorcised her ghosts, rather she has accepted them as part of her identity.

One of the diary entries starts: "We weave necessary fictions, and sometimes they save us" (319). These fictions include the stories we tell about ourselves. The inserted stories in both novels highlight the nature of confessional fictions. The characters' stories underscore their continuing attempts to cope with their illusions and their fright in an unruly reality. The writing is an attempt to recover from their lifelong trauma. The stories suggest that creative expression may work as a form of survival therapy, but not always. It works for Imp because, to express it slightly differently from Kotwasińska: "suicides and her foremothers' madness are not shameful secrets, threatening Imp's integrity" (145) but they are her specters, from whom Imp reconstitutes her identity.

The novels, as fictions, accentuate the link between hauntings and the work of literature overall. Julian Wolfreys argues that the specter is at the heart of any modern narrative. All stories call forward or provide a space for the return of "something other," a something that haunts the text (3). And that arises from the impossibility of ghosts yet their presence everywhere. Stories tell about encounters with the unknown, the strange, the unspoken and the other. And this encounter is not a mystery to be solved, but rather, as Davis suggests, a call for an openness to all those voices calling from the past. Voices that may speak from or about personal or social trauma. Kiernan's two novels explore our relationship to the dead—how the dead keep interrogating us and how we are fashioned by the dead.

In Summation

The challenge of Kiernan's writing arises from the ambiguity and allusiveness in her work, as if there are things that are impossible to tell, as if reality, madness, and the supernatural are not easily separated. She says, "I'd rather leave as many questions as possible unanswered and let the reader consider the possibilities" ("Interview: Caitlín R. Kiernan"). *The Red Tree* and *The Drowning Girl: A Memoir* challenge readers with the chaotic inner and outer experiences of the central characters. Part of that effect is produced through the narrative structures of the novels, for example, their fragmentation and intertextuality. But completing that effect requires her use of confessional techniques, such as unreliable narrators, doubles, and interior monologues. Yet more is needed and that comes from Kiernan's prose style that is at times lyrical, at others, gritty, and most tellingly, deliberately inchoate at times. This style gives life to the experience of turmoil and terror a character suffers in the unknown space between aberrant perceptions and deadly hauntings, between the known and the unknown. This is a central device in these two novels, to capture readers in the text and have them feel the characters' shudder of confusion and terror nearly as a direct experience. Kiernan's readers may feel at sea about the non-linear narrative flow and the inexplicability of some scenes in both novels. This happens because Kiernan's postmodern, confessional fictions blend in the modern gothic and weird traditions to induce in readers an experience of awe and terror of the other, of the unknown. That other her characters witness, but which seems "immune to the faculties of human reason" (*The Drowning Girl* 201).

Confessionals are traditionally viewed as asking forgiveness or reintegration. Some recent analyses of confessionals suggest they are more likely to be unreliable or purposefully deceptive. But confessional techniques that blur fact and fiction and reconstruct memories may be a way for a story to show how a person, suffering from trauma, can lose or salvage herself. Kiernan's confessional novels are fictional and her writing develops the characters. Although in reading the novels it seems the characters develop themselves (differently it is true) through their own writing. Kiernan achieves the illusion of her characters writing their own confessions, yet also illustrates the problematic nature of confessional fiction. In *The Red Tree*, Kiernan highlights this confusion of authorship when Crowe does not remember that she wrote "The Pony." Jaime Weida says this is because Crowe didn't write it; Kiernan wrote the story. Yet Kiernan wrote the entire novel in Crowe's voice. Readers know the books are fictional, but feel they speak the truth about the characters' inner and outer life with all of its hurt, pain and fright. This is the "experience of the spectral," where one experiences "being touched by that which is other" (Wolfreys 140). Readers know the novels are constructs but feel a sense of unease, because these narratives animate genuine uncanny experiences. In other words, the texts themselves become haunted.

Eight

Dark Futures

Surveying Kiernan's Science Fiction

> "I hear the ruin of all space,
> shattered glass and toppling masonry."
> —James Joyce, *Ulysses*, 43

Alieka Ferenczi drags herself across the rusty wastes of Mars to rescue Muirgheal Hemingtrust from the Maafa in Kiernan's "Slouching Towards the House of Glass Coffins" (2011). It is a hopeless quest expressed through an inventive Martian/English vernacular. Another Martian quest story is found in Kiernan's novella *Bradbury Weather* (2005), where Councilor Dorry tracks Sailor Li across a desolate and plague stricken Mars to Lowell Crater, where both of their pilgrimages end in horror. In the novella *Dry Salvages* (2004), Kiernan captures the voice of an elderly woman with a fading memory, who is trying to comprehend her harrowing encounter on Piros. An alien presence seems on a quest in "Hydrarguros" (2010), as a mysterious silver closes in on the cranked-up narrator, who is just trying to crime-survive in a near future Philly and Jersey.

In addition to her dark fantasy, weird and neo–Gothic fiction, Kiernan has written numerous science fiction (hereafter sf) works. Indeed, her first professional fiction sale was the sf short story "Between the Flatirons and the Deep Green Sea" in July 1993. She collected many of her sf stories in *A Is for Alien* (2009), while others have appeared in sf anthologies and in Kiernan's short fiction collections. A novella, *The Dry Salvages*, was published in 2004, and *Black Helicopters*, another novella, in 2013 (an expanded version was published in 2018). Some of Kiernan's stories express anti-colonialism, several imagine dystopias, a few are quest narratives and others explore the mutability of mind and body, often expressed through encounters with the alien. Kiernan is writing within the sf tradition, but she enriches it with her gothic sensibility. Indeed, sf itself is linked to the Gothic according to Brian W. Aldiss.

Most of Kiernan's sf stories are not straightforward; rather they have digressions and flashbacks as Merrick writes in her journal in "Galápagos" (2009). There are many examples of Kiernan's complex sf narratives, for example, "In View of Nothing" (2007), "Tidal Forces" (2011) and especially *Black Helicopters*. Allusions abound in this dark science fiction/fantasy novel. Kiernan's scenes are akin to puzzle pieces, crisscrossing time from 1966 to 2152, I think. And they hip-hop among various locales, including Ireland as I note in Chapter One. It is a challenge for readers to put the kaleidoscopic puzzle together. But there are strange and menacing linkages across the story's characters, events and locations.

Kiernan probes the psychology of paranoia, madness and alienation in a world under siege from a perplexing invading infection, while caught in a web of combating espionage organizations. Her fictional world is a confusing mystery and this is because not every mystery is solvable. Does the title give us a clue? The phrase "Black helicopters" is a key phrase in a conspiracy theory that a world government is plotting to take over America. The phrase is also used as a term of ridicule about such claims. Of course, there are the real Sikorsky UH-60 Black Hawks.

Kiernan writes often of feeling out of place, of being exiled. In her dark sf, she sketches this feeling in a future which seems infected by the past. Kiernan's characters are brought to life with narrative brushstrokes, as befits her primary sf short story form. Her characters are not of the super-heroic version found in some sf, but seem more real, as they are confused, suffer and wonder at their predicament in the universe. As well, Kiernan's aliens seem truly strange, often only hinted at, or their effects noted. They seem a monstrous rhapsody on otherness, and an attempt to express a sense of the truly alien. Most of all, Kiernan is unflinching in her portrayal of desire, despair and degradation in her created space and times. While her sf takes on a variety of narrative forms, imagines new worlds and explores strange societal relationships, it is not disconnected from reality.

In this chapter I survey Kiernan's sf works through four lenses. Her sf steampunk stories are reviewed separately in Chapter Nine. Her sf de-myths colonization, especially the colonization of the American West. Her future-oriented vision is anti-colonial and speaks to unacknowledged crimes at the heart of modernity (see Gerry Canavan). Specifically, her stories work against the American frontier myth and the glorification of space colonization in sf, which Carl Abbott suggests are one and the same. According to Abbott waves of space exploration are similar to the waves of colonization of the American West. Many of Kiernan's sf stories expose that underlying violence, which Ned Blackhawk argues is the key characteristic of the colonization of the Americas. Kiernan depicts this violence through images of alien biotic invasions, as if a counter-colonization from space. Stephen D. Arata suggests using "reverse colonization" as the term to describe this type of sf story where the center of the empire is under siege by something from the outlands or outer space. As Rob Latham argues such stories reveal the anxieties underlying the expansion of imperialistic power and its fundamental contingency. Kiernan's stories unveil the exploitation, violence and fear at the heart of European colonialism.

Other Kiernan sf stories are dystopian, although she might challenge that description. But I see her dystopian sf revealing dangerous tendencies in the present. She heightens these in her imagined futures. Her stories present as forms of cognitive maps following Fredric Jameson ("Cognitive Mapping"), as a way to understand how contemporary geopolitical, economic and environmental realities may shape the future. In her stories, Kiernan pictures an imaginary, future world in which current trends are realized. She draws these futures from today's inequalities, climatic destruction, religious fantasies, surveillance, technological advances and xenophobia. As well, her dystopian stories reveal the danger behind some utopian imaginings of the future.

In addition, some of Kiernan's sf stories are heroic quests, which reframe the traditional male hero story into a tale of female struggle in alien environments. Kiernan's work illustrates the false mythology of such traditional stories. In her stories there are no mythic male heroes, who overcome every challenge and conquer all through their marvelous super powers (which, in fact, represent the power of the ruling forces in society). Rather her protagonists are marginalized individuals who are lost and bewildered as they struggle against ruling forces.

Fourthly, Kiernan's sf fiction illustrates the vulnerability of the body and the mutability of identity. These stories also reflect the political, that is power, responses to differences between people, be it class, gender, color or sexual orientation. Essentially Kiernan writes of revolt against the tyranny of the normal.

Reverse Colonization

Several scholars have argued that the roots of much sf can be found in imperialism and colonialism.[1] In *Colonialism and the Emergence of Science Fiction*, John Rieder documents how sf arose during the peak of Western imperialism in the late nineteenth century. He argues sf and colonial history are incontestably linked because the conditions for sf's emergence were established by imperialism and reinforced by advancing technology, both in colonial conquest and administration (3–6). Confirming this, Patricia Kerslake contends that the theme of empire is deeply ingrained in sf. She says that empire can be found in the basic attributes and purposes of the genre (3–7).

Furthermore, Istvan Csicsery-Ronay, Jr., argues sf (that is, American, British, German, French, Japanese and Soviet sf) supported the expansion of empire and is a creature of imperialism and inspired by a techno-scientific worldview (243–245). These authors and others argue that part of sf recreates and propagandizes colonialism and the expansion of a globalized, technologically based empire, controlled by Western powers. What is more, by doing so, sf immunizes readers to continual violence, advanced weaponry and technological control. Several other authors, for example, David Mogen, Gary K. Wolfe (in his "Frontiers in Space"), Greg Grewell and Ursula K. Le Guin (in her "A Non-Euclidean View of California as a Cold Place to Be") suggest part of American sf glorifies the conquest and colonization of America. Gerry Canavan suggests this view sees sf as "empire's propaganda arm, its R&D lab, prototyping the weapons of the future and accommodating us to tomorrow's genocides today" (494–495). From an Indigenous perspective, Nalo Hopkinson maintains that the sf theme of space travel and colonizing the natives is not an adventure story, rather it is non-fiction for indigenous peoples.[2] Grace L. Dillon suggests that much of sf still rewrites colonial atrocities into space adventures.[3]

Of course, not all sf glorifies colonialism and imperialism. For example, the early sf work, H.G. Wells's *The War of the Worlds* (1898), can be understood as an anti-colonization narrative, as is true for Ray Bradbury's *The Martian Chronicles* (1950). Jack Finney's *Invasion of the Body Snatchers* (1955) depicts Earth invaded by spores from space. More recently, Michael Moorcock's *Warlord of the Air* (1971) seems a critique of imperialism and Le Guin's *The Word for World Is Forest* (1972) reflects the historical facts of European and Native American conflict. On the other hand, the very recent film, *Avatar* (2009) depicts Indigenous peoples as standing in the way of progress or needing guidance from "civilized" invaders to survive. The film uses the traditional sf trope of humans going into space to mine needed resources. The moon, Pandora, holds unobtanium. On that moon, a physically challenged, white Marine goes native and saves the Na'vi, the people of blue color, from a marine assault, as if they are incapable themselves.

Kiernan's sf works against the adulation of empire and technological hegemony. She demystifies the narratives of the victors and ruling authorities through her sf. One such story is "Black Ships Seen South of Heaven" (2015). Ostensibly a Lovecraftian Mythos tale, I see it as portraying colonization and genocide from an Indigenous perspective. The story is told through the voice of a fatalistic survivor, who knows she and her entire culture are in their last days. Trapped in a stronghold surrounded by fungal forests, which are the ghosts of her dead ancestors, she takes her turn on the fortress walls. Those ancestors fell to a plague (similar to smallpox that killed so many of the Indigenous peoples of America), a plague that infects Susannah. There is no hope for Susannah or the other remaining warriors in the fortress, because Kiernan pictures the end of their culture as a gigantic dark wave submerging their world. It is a metaphor for genocide.

Kiernan depicts the initial trauma of colonization in "Riding the White Bull" (2004). In the story, Earth is a planet of endless wars, climate disruptions, human mutations, surveillance and secret exobiology missions, all ruled over by a controlling Agency. The Agency uses space exploration to advance colonization and exploitation. But in this imagined future, space exploration brings more suffering, not utopian contact. Nor does it discover a habitable world as a safe haven for the rich.[4] Deet Paine, a male empathic detective, and his cyborg handler, Sarah, are on the front lines of an alien incursion. It is an incursion by an alien presence brought back to Earth from a probe to Europa. Everyone is baffled by the alien's nature and intentions, but more so, they are terrified at the seeming power of the incursion and the threat to everyone. The invaders here do not seem to be technologically superior, rather they spread a biological contagion.

Kiernan writes detailed character studies of Deet and Sarah. She depicts the effects of colonization on individuals not on entire populations to personalize the trauma. Deet is an addict, haunted by his mental contact with the alien presence and his experience of the agony of infected humans. Sarah was once only human, but Kiernan shows her opting to become a cyborg to express the current fantasy for technological immortality. The human hosts of the alien things in Kiernan's story dissolve slowly, agonizingly. It seems to attack the interior of humans first and works slowly to dissolve their bodies. It is a dreadful, wasting type of disease that emphasizes the fragility and mortality of the newly infected. This alien-based infection or contagion suggests the initially unknown and destructive power of HIV/AIDS and the fear and ostracism it spread across countries.

Although more complex and multi-layered, Kiernan's 2004 novella, *The Dry Salvages*, also works against the fantasy image of the glory of colonization. The story is an anti-space opera, which depicts a weary, bleak and claustrophobic future. The story takes the form of a memoir through which Dr. Audrey Cather recalls the defining event of her life: a harrowing experience on Piros, a moon of Cecrops around Gliese 876.[5] Kiernan sets this in a future where Earth is a ruin, run by the mysterious and all-powerful ANSA, which watches everyone with synths (advanced androids with human characteristics) and other means. Cather rewrites the voyage of the space ship, *Montelius*. Her writing seems an act of therapy to overcome her trauma and might be a form of revolt against authoritarian rule. Commenting on the work of Julia Kristeva, Elaine P. Miller argues that writing can be a form of "survival therapy" (12). Dr. Cather recreates the past to recover her memory and recover herself.

Dr. Cather and her crewmates on the *Montelius* space-travel to Piros to check out the fate of the silent *Gilgamesh,* which was commissioned to explore the geology and mining potential of the moon. Kiernan uses a trope Abbott argues was lifted into space by sf writers from the American West. This notion of exo-world mining is found in such American sf works as Robert Heinlein's *The Moon Is a Harsh Mistress* (1966), Jack Williamson's *Seetee Ship* (1951) and the early Edmond Hamilton's novella, "A Conquest of Two Worlds"[6] (1933). David Spurr identifies this as following from the European colonial attitude that the natural resources of colonized territory belonged to them not to the Indigenous populations (28). In Kiernan's novella the *Gilgamesh* turns out to be run by synthfolk and machine droids. Four of the human crew had disappeared while on Piros exploring the abandoned mining operation. The two remaining humans on the ship have been mentally infected by something from the moon and end up dead.

Of course, Dr. Cather and her crewmates follow the path of the crew from the *Gilgamesh* and shuttle down to the surface of Piros. When they land it seems we are in the backcountry of nineteenth-century Colorado with its dust storms and its abandoned mines and quarries (on Piros the mining operations were abandoned centuries in the past by previous colonizers—not from Earth). But the moon is much deadlier than Colorado. And the open pit quarry is vaster—seven kilometers across. The four crew members of the *Montelius* find the lander from the *Gilgamesh* next to the deep quarry, but find no survivors. They do find an unfathomable presence in that sinister flooded quarry. A native Piros dark specter that is never precisely described in the story. It is only hinted as something like a shadow or a darkness. Across the oil-dark pool, Dr. Cather sees a "darkness folding or unfolding, coiling or uncoiling"[7] (*Dry Salvages* 119). This darkness may be her only way to express the experience of terror of that alien phantom-like being on Piros. Its effects are shown in its impact on the crew of the *Montelius*, who become disoriented, confused and terrified on the moon. They feel they are "inside a ghost story" (*Dry Salvages* 115) which is reality and from which there is no escape. One dies in quarantine, another commits suicide and a third is in and out of psychiatric wards until he dies.

Did the Earth explorers on Piros contract a "virus of the conscious mind" (*Dry Salvages* 82)? Did Cather contract it as well, but her virus has a longer incubation period than her crew-mates and the crew of the *Gilgamesh*? Is it a weapon of the life-form on Piros, modeled on Bradbury's "The Third Expedition" where the crew is fooled by Martian "telepathy and hypnosis" and die (60)? The retaliation by that alien life force seems an infection that spreads with a kind of intelligence. The nature of this intelligence is unclear, its effects are shown, but what it really may be is not known. Is it one, or several intelligences, or is it a group intelligence, like an ant colony? Or perhaps it is something like the sentient ocean in Stanislaw Lem's *Solaris* (1970), which torments the researchers on Solaris Station with reified images of their fear and guilt. It is the experience of an "unexplainable dread of outer, unknown forces" as Lovecraft called it (*Annotated Supernatural Horror* 28).

The narrative structure of the novella shifts between Dr. Cather's ancient, small apartment on *la rue Linné*[8] in a frozen Paris and the action of the space mission. Cather's writing contradicts the media story of the contact on Piros, which portrayed the events on that moon as a feel-good story about joyous contact with alien life. A fake news story because no one is allowed to disrupt the extrasolar expeditions that industry depends on. Down the hall from Dr. Carter, lives Zora, a synth, who now has rights and is not just property anymore, so she claims, but is a snitch just the same, even though she seems a friendly, concerned artificial intelligence. In the story, Zora is able to lie and ruse, as well as any human.

Dr. Cather writes the memoir with archaic pens, as if it is an act of desperate subversion because any electronic form of writing would be immediately known by the ANSA. But does she really believe that her jottings might escape its attention, which controls all things, and knows all things, and kills when it wants to ensure that space exploitation continues for the benefit of corporate industry? Such actions are the same as those of imperial colonization. But the writing, the actual physical writing, is Cather's attempt at a recovery from trauma and a telling of truth in a world where manufactured truth rules. It is similar to the "return of memory" Julia Kristeva contends may lead to a "subjective rebirth" ("Dialogue with Julia Kristeva" 6). But Dr. Cather lives in a carceral world, confined to her small apartment. So many of Kiernan's female characters are confined to constricted places, as Kiernan pays homage to that traditional Gothic motif.

Moreover, the story illustrates the estrangement of Dr. Cather from her own dark experience. She encountered an extreme otherness, an otherness that resisted colonization, an indigenous force that fought back. She seems to feel it nearing her on Earth. At the end of the novella, Dr. Cather writes of rumors of odd signals emanating from Piros, deaths on space stations, and fresh sightings of sinister, shadow shapes beyond the Kuiper Belt.

Dr. Cather travels deep into her memory of anguish and trauma in an attempt to heal her wounds. In a sense, the title of the novella reflects Dr. Cather's writing as an attempted salvaging of her memory and salvaging of herself. She writes from a memory that may or may not be accurate, but it is the only intermediary between her past and her future. It is a memory she can control, a memory not yet controlled by the totalitarian state, or so she thinks. It is something she can reclaim from her experience. Her writing is an act of resistance to reclaim a traumatic remnant of the past as hers and as a tribute to her crewmates. Dr. Cather remarks she is akin to Ishmael of *Moby*

Dick (1851) because she is the sole survivor left to tell the tale, and hers is similar to Ishmael's, as both articulate an encounter with an unknowable force, an incarnate dread and all their crewmates are dead.

Kristeva in *The Crisis of the European Subject,* writing of Hannah Arendt, suggests that telling the story of one's life may give it meaning. She contends that forgetting or suppressing memory forms the core of modern culture. But Elaine P. Miller argues writing can be a form of revolt and an act of resistance to silent acquiescence to authority. Writing the truth expresses a hope that perhaps one day things may get better.

There is a hint of revolt in the novella. A student, Jedda Callahan, who accosts Dr. Cather, asks her if she had been followed back from Piros and urges her to be forthcoming about her experiences. That student is later found dead; it is labeled suicide. Revolts are always deadly. But the ANSA allows Dr. Cather to continue her secret memoir. Does her writing become merely another aspect of the control of that future society over people and what passes for facts and truth? Because if writing is left merely as a narrative, with no action, it may be an empty meaning, as Julia Kristeva suggests (*Crisis of the European Subject* 85). But I think that Dr. Carter's writing in this story is a subversive act. It is dangerous to ANSA because it threatens its system of command and control. Elizabeth Ammons argues this is what happens in Charlotte Perkins Gilman's "The Yellow Wallpaper." Explicitly in that story the threat is to the male dominated society. Ammons says "[t]o write is to be active" (263). As Gilman's narrator was radical so is Dr. Cather for she violates the silence that the ANSA imposed upon her and everyone in that future world. Through writing Dr. Cather is no longer a victim, but a witness and rebel.

Dystopias

Kiernan's sf does not imagine technological marvels, but rather imagines future economic, sociological and environmental impacts on individuals. She depicts a ruined Earth in *The Dry Salvages*, "Riding the White Bull" and other stories. There are continuous wars, climate disruptions, human and animal mutations, constant surveillance, discipline and authoritarian rule.

The backdrop to Kiernan's "The Pearl Diver" (2006) is an Earth of suicide camps, biologic weaponry, wide spread tyranny and 10 billion people—a broken world. It is the epitome of the Anthropocene epoch, that is, the epoch where humans colonize nature and all things are assigned an exchange-value (their market value). In Kiernan's story the main character, Rarasha Kim, seems incarcerated in her coffin-like apartment, watching shows on her small screen, eating her dismal meals, always afraid, always alone. In that near future human intersubjectivity ends.[9]

Confined in her personal cell Kim finds a strange refuge in elaborate dreams surfacing from her young encounter with a fantastic painting of a pearl diver. But she opens a forbidden email and is doomed to be fired, because the government knows all, and the company enforces compliance.

Kim survives her daily work routine by using "stimugel" every morning (*A Is for Alien* 92). In the Anthropocene, human rhythms earn no place in the globalized space-time of the corporate/government nexus of power over information, capital, commodities, people and nature. The story exhibits what Ruth D. Weston calls "the closed-in quality of life in a carceral society" (10). That is, the story shows the cultural and economic binds that limit individual, especially female, development. This imagined future may be the embodiment of Michel Foucault's study, *Discipline and Punish,* of the transference of punishment from public spaces into more threatening, private, enclosed spaces. These enclosed places are erected to monitor and control all aspects of an individual's life, including interior life, so they can be directed and manipulated for the purposes of conformance to the norms and needs of the production and consumption cycle. In the story, Kim experiences the forces of discipline (as Foucault would have said) deployed by the power structures of work places and government to normalize everyone. She lives in a prison society, where small and punitive spaces keep one's suffering away from the view of others, who also suffer.

That mass surveillance society focuses on process optimization, which means to correct business processes to deliver higher productivity, more quantity, or higher return from systems or people. In Kiernan's story an Artificial Intelligence links government and business to ensure process optimization through surveillance and discipline. Kiernan brings to life that future tyranny through the psychological and physical agony of a single individual.

Kim works in a hive[10] office, where one must not smile or interact in any way with fellow drones. Kim works in fear until fired by a Mr. Binder, a male boss, for reading an unauthorized electronic message. Back at her cell, Kim finds a manila envelope left at her door—an envelope that hints at resistance and rebellion in that future tyranny. By merely opening the package, Kim revolts against her imprisonment. As Weston might suggest, Kiernan's protagonist opposes the tyranny of the dominant technological society.[11] Here as in most of Kiernan's fiction, the oppressed and rebellious characters are female.

Yet the story paints a future dystopian, carceral world, that may offer a glimpse of hope that Tom Moylan argues modern dystopias often do. There is a strange undercurrent of revolt against authoritarian rule in this story as in *The Dry Salvages*. But in the end Kim suffers the deleterious effects of her confinement. Kiernan writes a diagnostic and critical account of oppressive societies combined with elements of resistance, that might be futile or victorious at a personal level.

The envelope that Kim finds contains some papers, a metal disk and a stoppered vial of black powder. The vial breaks, and soot fills the air of her cell, spreading a contagion that alters her body. Kim becomes "infinitely mutable" as the soot divides "polypeptide chains" and inserts new "amino acids" throughout her body (*A Is for Alien* 138). Kim deforms and reforms, dissolves and condenses. The ending of the story challenges readers as though Kiernan intends to show how the rational mind is unable to understand the infinite processes of biological transformation that Kim experiences. But what comes from her metamorphosis? In the story, she enters an alterity where "there is no longer loneliness or fear, boredom or the dread of whatever is coming next. [...] [as] 'her soul fills up with pearls'" (*A Is for Alien* 110). These pearls are metaphors for Kim's physical and psychological collapse from solitary confinement.[12]

But thinking of the old Gothic, this is a story of feminine capture and escape. Here Kim individually acts against the tyranny of her world, and in her act of solitary defiance unleashes a new vision of wonder from her past. Admittedly Kim asserts her self-autonomy in a strange way, but her self-expression through transformation is a restorative act of civil disobedience.

A more catastrophic future is portrayed in Kiernan's apocalyptic story "John Four"[13] (2010). The central image in the short story is a towering Temple in the darkness that has flooded the world. Pools of greater darkness spring forth here and there in the Temple. A central character is a nameless woman, who is welded to the dark stone floor of the Temple. Human pilgrims, now mutated and deformed, lurch forward to pay homage to her, or some form of god, bearing alms. The best alms are remnants (relics of a consumer society) from the world before the apocalypse.

The main action begins when a beautiful, normally bodied woman (who is also nameless) separates herself from the throng to offer alms. Although the nameless woman rebuffs her at first, eventually she takes the naked woman's offering. The nameless woman switches on that flashlight. When the light beam chases away the gloom, so it also banishes the nameless woman. The flashlight falls, rolls into black waters of a pool and the darkness returns. It seems the waters are death, extinguishing all light. The pilgrims cry out and flee the Temple, running down its five thousand steps. The naked woman kneels in despair at the loss of her flashlight (perhaps this signals her loss of identity). As she does, the Temple sends stone tendrils around her body, merging her into itself. She becomes the dark priestess of stone. This story depicts a grim dystopian future, where humanity returns to a dark age of religious rule.

Kiernan's story alludes to Nathaniel Hawthorne's (1804–1864) "The Man of Adamant" (1837). Richard Digby flees into the forest to escape contact with other people, as he alone knows the true faith. There he creates his tabernacle.

It is a cave, as cold as his religious beliefs. He dwells there alone, drinking the water dripping from the roof. Over time Digby turns to stone, as does the woman in Kiernan's story.[14] In a related fashion to Hawthorne, Kiernan's story depicts the outcome of some religious beliefs. Such religions espouse the last days and apocalypse when believers will ascent to an otherworldly brightness and the earth descends into darkness and chaos. They long for that final utopia. But the world they long for is a "world in which all [...] things and experiences—positive as well as negative—will have been obliterated" (Jameson, *Archaeologies of the Future* 97—to misuse a phrase of Frederic Jameson), including the death of billions.

Kiernan's dystopian stories say something is wrong today that could result in future disaster. Andrew Milner argues that Jameson is correct about what the key question for sf is: "did it sufficiently shock its own present as to force a meditation on the impossible?" But Milner, contrary to Jameson, says this applies to dystopias as well as utopias (117). There is clear evidence today of existential threats: threats from climate change, from increasing surveillance, from the increasing domination of a controlling technology, from the exploding violence of spectacle in social media, from religious intolerance, from anti-science, from continuous wars and from increasingly excessive and unequal production, distribution and consumption. If we ignore these threats, then we seem sentenced back into a dark age.

Anti-Quest Narratives

A dark age that was forecasted in William Butler Yeats's apocalyptic poem, "The Second Coming" (1919). The poem is a possible source for Kiernan's short story "Slouching towards the House of Glass Coffins" (2011). Alieka Ferenczi, a factory worker on Mars, slouches across "sands of the desert" (Yeats, *Collected Works* 187)[15] on her hopeless quest to rescue Muirgheal (an Irish name meaning sea-bright or fair one of the sea) Hemingtrust from the Yellow House. It is a Gothic house of confinement, cannibalism and torture—a great house of the dead. Alieka lives with her parents in a new Annapolis on Mars.[16] The Maafa routinely raid Annapolis from their Yellow House deep in the wasteland. They capture young people and bind them away to their stronghold, akin to the slave trade raids on African towns from the 1600s into the 1800s.[17] The Yellow House is a place of misery, torture and death for those taken away, as happened to those taken by the Atlantic Slave Trade.

Joseph Campbell describes the journey of the hero:

> A hero ventures forth from the world of common day into a region of supernatural wonder: fabulous forces are there encountered and a decisive victory is won: the hero

comes back from this mysterious adventure with the power to bestow boons on his fellow man [30].

There are three phases: Departure, Initiation, and Return.[18] What takes Alieka out of her known world towards an unknown world is her love for Muirgheal. Alieka is tested in her quest by a harrowing journey across the desert, until she almost miraculously finds herself before the high mustard walls of the Yellow House. The Initiation into the unknown continues inside the Yellow House where guards accost her. Everything is dark. She thinks the rusty doorway slamming behind her sounds like "Sheol" (*The Ape's Wife* 176) ("sheol" is the place of deep darkness, the unknown or the abode of the dead). As in many tales of the hero, it is in the land of the dead where the hero is fully tested, where she must overcome her greatest fear. The Maafa of the Yellow House seem the dead. The guards march her into a round room, past a fire pit where a human is being roasted, to a dais where the bony headman, with orange eyes, squats.

The final test is what the hero most dreads. If the hero meets the test, she is transformed, because she overcomes her great fear of the unknown. The headman orders the guards to take Alieka to the room of glass coffins. Left alone, she finds Muirgheal in a tube being rendered alive, dissolving slowly. It is agonizing. So many are trapped inside the glass tubes unable to die, but yet not to live; it is the reimagined agony of African American slaves. This story seems an allegory about Annapolis, Maryland, which grew to wealth and status due to its role as a port and center of the slave trade to North America. And the Yellow House in its depravity is a metaphor depicting the truth behind the genteel depictions of plantations in the American South.

Now inside the Yellow House, Alieka is at a crossroads. At this stage in the monomyth, as Campbell suggests, the hero must decide what action to take. The story ends with Alieka staring at the remnants of Muirgheal. To her chest, Alieka hugs a bomb, as if it is Muirgheal who "once wore blue ribbons in her hair" (*The Ape's Wife* 178). It is a phrase of love and heartbreak. Alieka sees herself as lost and forsaken, like so many of Kiernan's characters. Alieka ponders her choices: join the Maafa, as the strange leader offered, or blow up the room, and save Muirgheal from her endless torture? There is no resolution, as in Yeats's poem.

Kiernan's sf works do not predict the future or offer utopian solutions, rather it proposes questions about possible consequences of current trends. *Bradbury Weather* (2005) is another quest story which unmakes traditional heroic narratives of voyage, discovery and conquest. In the novella, a plague rages on Mars. Plagues are a familiar trope in dystopian sf. Mary Shelley gave the plague feminine characteristics in her apocalyptic novel *The Last Man* (1826), or at least the narrator Lionel Verney does. The deadly and unknown scourge kills all, well, nearly all. The plague on Mars is also a mysterious and insidious force. It killed off all the men on the planet, as did the plagues in Joanna Russ's "When it Changed" (1972), Nicola Griffith's *Ammonite* (1992), and on Earth in James Tiptree Jr.'s (pen name of Alice Bradley Sheldon) "Houston, Houston, Do You Read?" (1976).

In Kiernan's novella the plague transforms victims into something more hideous than death, "something hardly human" (*A Is for Alien* 189). The whole planet seems infected. Kiernan calls it the Fenrir contagion (Fenrir is a monstrous wolf in Norse mythology). In the midst of this unknown invasion a religious cult movement arises, where adherents seem to worship the disease or to worship the source of the disease. The cause of the plague is unknown to scientists. They had found a serum to stay the disease, not a cure. But now the serum is losing its effectiveness, because the contagion appears to have mutated.

The novella is Dorry's story, perhaps it is her confession. After beating up her household servant, Sailor Li, whom she loves after a fashion, she starts her trek across Mars. Dorry's love turned to rage when Sailor Li came home with the mark of the mystery religion; a sign that she had joined the mystery contagion cult. Sailor Li flees and Dorry tracks her across Mars. This quest story consists of, as do most quests, an outward journey and an inward journey.

To paraphrase Thomas Pynchon, Kiernan's story suggests "everyone has a Mars,"[19] that is, someplace everyone seeks to find answers about herself. Mars is that empty canvas in which Dorry tries to find, not just Sailor Li, but herself. Dorry's quest is one of loss, a quest based on rage and despair, and an expression of self-loathing at her own physical and mental decay, because she is likely infected. Along the way Dorry encounters perilous trials that are more psychological than physical.

The story chronicles Dorry's journeys into her own psychological heart of darkness. One of her quests is to go deep under the Hope VI dome. There Dorry follows Mikaela underground, down into a pit. It is Dorry's journey into hell. There she sees hers and Sailor Li's spawn, a "pale thing," a "wad of hair and mottled flesh, bone and scabby shell of half-formed exoskeleton" (*A Is for Alien* 179). She flees that nightmare baby, that Martian. It is a thing infected and transformed, because on that Mars there is no future for humans. Is this strange creature a radical posthumanism? This creature seems to be a new Martian where human cells are completely transformed into something utterly alien. The Fenrir contagion biologically transforms humans into the image of the indigenous life force, admittedly a monstrous life force, but yet a generative life force. This is a strange and dark posthumanism stranger than that suggested in Octavia Butler's *Clay's Ark* (1984) where an extraterrestrial virus so modifies human cells they propagate beast-like quadruped children.

Kiernan's story disrupts the idealized family because the monster baby hidden in a dark cellar represents the failure of colonization and the victory of the indigenous forces on Mars.

Kiernan's story disrupts the traditional tale of heroism and conquest. Across Mars, Dorry chases Sailor Li to Lowell Crater. Arriving there Dorry sees or dreams of seeing the thing that was Sailor Li. It opens slits that were eyes. Eyes that are now "wet orbs like pools of night" (*A Is for Alien* 199). Dorry watches Sailor Li being absorbed into a monstrous thing below the surface of Mars. Sailor Li becomes a Martian.

Encountering the Alien

The humans on Mars in *Bradbury Weather* encounter an alien presence (although humans are the aliens on Mars) expressed through a plague that transforms them. In Kiernan's story, Dorry tries to kill the alien (she guns down a Fenrir priest), which is one of the most frequent results of encountering the alien in sf. Perhaps that is because that otherness seems unknowable or threatening. How should one respond to the encounter with the other? Dorry's quest across Mars expresses our longing to know the alien, but also our insularity as human. Many of Kiernan's stories grapple with this loneliness and isolation that we experience. *Bradbury Weather* depicts an alien contagion altering humans into something alien. But sometimes this alienness is part of one's being.

According to Patrick McGrath, Gothic motifs, such as the double, monsters and madness, represent the "instability of identity" and question what the human is (155). Kiernan shows this instability using such sf motifs as an alien encounter, interspecies morphology and the rise of cyborgs to address issues of gender, race and identity and the social constructs of being human. Kiernan says her sf explores the "idea of the alien […] and the loss of self, mutability of identity, insanity" ("Interview: Caitlín R. Kiernan"). Indeed, much of her writing examines change, becoming something else, often through a strange contact with an otherness, sometime sought for, but not always.

In Kiernan's "I Am the Abyss and I Am the Light" (2008), Titisa Fitzgerald subjects herself to an experiment in metamorphosis: a human transforming into an alien, or rather, merging with a shhakizsa to create a new being. Rosemary Jackson says one of the two kinds of myth in the modern fantastic is where fear originates in a source external to the subject, a sort of fear of merging with the other. In this story, Kiernan celebrates that merging; she turns a fear into ecstasy. Jackson argues such merging eliminates the difference from the other and it is frightening. Kiernan uses this motif as an experiment in euphoria for Fitzgerald, who aches because she feels so alone within her imposed identity. Fitzgerald thinks that that aloneness is unbearable. She feels alienated from her given identity. It may be that her volunteering for the experiment is an expression of that alienation and a type of suicide. The title of the story comes from a group of six paintings by Charles Sims, which were exhibited shortly after he committed suicide. But it is more likely that it is a story of findings one's true self or selves.

Frederic Jameson seems to argue that the other is unknowable always, because that is what otherness means. Jameson suggests that the point of contact with an alien in a sf story is to illustrate that we ourselves are unknowable (*Archaeologies* 117–118). In part, Fitzgerald's loneliness is that feeling each of us experiences as we try to work through the complex construction of self-identity. Then the encounter with the alien is a metaphor for an encounter with ourselves. Kiernan's story illustrates how we can be estranged from our authentic self within our current societal systems. Such systems often prescribe our beliefs, ideals and our relationships with others. Some people are also estranged from their real gender or sexuality and recover themselves by becoming transgender or transsexual. Other individuals discover within themselves another self and recognize that they are two-spirited. I think this is what Kiernan shows in the story, that is, she illustrates the tranny of the normal, as described by Leslie Fiedler, and the challenges individuals face when they try to overthrow that tyranny.

There are at least three voices in the story, including an "it," a "she" and a "we" (*Confessions* 157). They are all from one source. Fitzgerald says she was not completed by her human lover Theodore, who was born Theodora on a Mars colony. But she finds an emerging wholeness from the ongoing experiment. And that is the core of the story. The construction of identity is an ongoing project. The three voices suggest a recognition of how we do not know ourselves. Fitzgerald, or that which was formerly called Fitzgerald, is an amalgam of personality traits. And the alien she merges with is herself. Kiernan refashions the sf motif of confrontation with the other in this story. It does not cause fear and does not culminate in the killing of the alien (in this story it would mean Fitzgerald commits suicide, which does not happen). Rather the story has Fitzgerald recognize that identity is a construct and a work-in-progress always. She welcomes all of her identities and is no longer alone, because she has reconstructed herself to match her real, multiple being. Moreover, Fitzgerald does not define herself against something alien or different, no, she merges with that other.

Cyborgs or synthetic humans are sf motifs exploring the concept of otherness and the fragility of identity. Kiernan's "Zero Summer" (2007) explores this issue. In the story two androids are devastated when they discover they are not human, but artificial. They know they have been deceived by humans with implanted memories. Yet, these androids find their true self. They represent how we are often estranged from our true selves within the technologies and institutions of our current societal environments. These systems prescribe our beliefs, our ideals and our buying and voting habits. Akin to androids we have been constructed within a web of societal institutions. Escaping from those prescribed norms is dangerous but also liberating.

In Summation

Most of Kiernan's sf stories are not straightforward. At the start of Kiernan's novella *Bradbury Weather*, the character Dorry mulls over an aphorism from a Gyuto monk: "No story has a beginning, and no story has an end" (*A Is for Alien* 161),[20] as if expressing a Kiernan writing tenet. Many of her sf stories lack a beginning hook, a linear exposition and clear ending. The stories leave questions not answers. But there are key themes in her fiction.

Earth in many of Kiernan's sf stories is a ruin, with continuous wars, climate collapse, regimentation, industrial control and mass surveillance. Part of the point of this is, that it is happening today, through the toxification of the planet by chemicals and plastics and the overconsumption by "first-world countries" and the rich. Kiernan's stories provide lenses to see more clearly our present troubles. Indeed, Kiernan, in an interview, says her sf is "how the world and human society might be reshaped by the consequences of the present, and the past" ("*A Is for Alien* in 60 Seconds"). She sees dangerous tendencies in contemporary economic, political and societal trends and intensifies these in her sf to illustrate the perils ahead. During another interview she said "certain outcomes seem almost inevitable, given the present course of our civilization. [...] I'm referring to stories that focus on more realistic threats—ecological collapse, global warming and climate change, bioweapons, nuclear war, and so forth" ("Exclusive Interview: Caitlín R. Kiernan on *After*"). As Peter G. Stillman writes about Octavia Butler, Kiernan sees dangerous trends in today's world and intensifies them through imagined futures to alert us to the dangers growing in the present to prod readers to thought and action.

It is not cleverness in dreaming up new technology that interests Kiernan in her sf, rather it is the physical, economic, psychological, and social effects on people, usually individuals, of not only changing technology, but also cultural norms, economic systems, and political power. Her sf aligns more with John Rieder's contention in *Science Fiction and the Mass Cultural Genre System* that modern sf is not defined by writing technical fictions about the future course of science, rather sf is more an instrument of social and cultural criticism (168–169). Kiernan's ordinary, often outcasted, characters, are caught up in imagined futures that depict the genocide of colonization, the destructive effects of rampant consumerism and consumption and the loss of individual freedom through authoritarian, surveillance and command governments.

NINE

Retruthing Steampunk
Kiernan Rewrites American West Steampunk

"Blight and death alone./No Summer shines."—James Clarence Mangan, "Siberia," *Selected Poems of James Clarence Mangan*, p. 234

The previous chapter surveys Kiernan's science fiction (sf) works. Although not as numerous as her dark fiction works, she has contributed much to the genre. Kiernan writes within the sf tradition, but she enriches it with her gothic sensibility. Her sf stories critically reimagine the past and present through dystopian futures, female quest narratives and encounters with the alien. Kiernan also de-myths colonization, especially the colonization of the American West. Here I explore a selection of Kiernan's stories set within the steampunk sf subgenre. Her steampunk stories work against the glorified colonization of the American West, which appears in many steampunk fictions.

Steampunk is a form of science fiction notionally set in the "nineteenth-century characterized by technologies extrapolated from the science of that era, but which were not invented at that time" (*Brave New Worlds* 221). This subgenre of sf originated during the 1970s and 1980s. In an April 1987 letter to *Locus*, K.W. Jeter invented the term "steampunk" to characterize some of his Victorian fantasy works and similar ones by Tim Powers and James Blaylock that explored alternative outcomes for steam based technologies. Most, but not all, steampunk works engage with the nineteenth century in setting, technology or theme, and such works often pose an alternate history. But the term "steampunk" now connotes more than that expressed in the literary definition. Rachel A. Bowser and Brian Croxall (2016), Brian J. Robb, Jeff VanderMeer, David Beard and Christine Ferguson explore the many manifestations of steampunk in popular culture as a fashion trend, musical expression, a design aesthetic and as a DIY enterprise. Role-playing steampunk games, steampunk how-to books, video games, cosplay and steampunk conventions, some focusing solely on American West steampunk, continue to proliferate.

Steampunk literature arose from the fantasy and science fiction works of the Victorian time period in Britain and the Gilded Age in the United States. British steampunk stems from H.G. Wells and Jules Verne's classic novels. American steampunk roots are found in the "Edisonade" (a term coined by John Clute in *The Encyclopedia of Science Fiction*). Originally, an Edisonade told the story of a young American male hero who invents a new form of transportation or other mechanical marvel and travels to "uncivilized parts of the American frontier" (Nevins, "Introduction: The 19th Century Roots of Steampunk" 4), or other alien places to punish the enemies of the United States, for example, the Indigenous people of the Americas. *The Huge Hunter: Or, The Steam Man of the Prairies* (1868) by Edward S. Ellis is likely the first Edisonade. The novel refers to American "Indians"[1] as demons[2] and depicts them as savages. It features technology embodied in a steam powered machine man, as do many Edisonades. In most such works women are accessories, if seen at all.

In its many forms, steampunk is the subject of increasing scholarly scrutiny. Patrick Jagoda maintains steampunk is evident across many creative media. He claims it helps to rethink Victorian literature and history. Jagoda focuses his analysis on *The Difference Engine* (1990) by William Gibson and Bruce Sterling. As well, Cynthia J. Miller and Julie Anne Taddeo suggest steampunk is subversive as it examines race, class and gender politics both in the past and the present. Margaret Rose examines the short stories in *Extraordinary Engines: The Definitive Steampunk Anthology* (2006) edited by Nick Gevers, and concludes the stories emphasize historical accuracy. Moreover, she claims the stories within her sample do not undermine the importance of the reality of the past. Ken Dvorak sees steampunk inspiring debates on current day social, economic and cultural issues. Similarly, but more specifically, Catherine Siemann argues steampunk offers a vision of how to avoid or face current and future urban crises. Moreover, steampunk artists, according to Lisa Hager, along with Victorian era scholars present different but essential critical understandings of Victorian literature and culture.

On the other hand, scholars also question steampunk's fictional portrayal of the nineteenth-century. Mary Anne Taylor contends steampunk mythologizes the industrialized nineteenth-century. Reviewing steampunk's narratives on women, she argues it distorts gender equality and builds a false empowerment for women in its depictions of female economic and political roles, styles and sexual relationships. Amanda Stock says steampunk perpetuates aspects of Victorian culture as a conservative agenda where men express their longing for past times when gender roles where clearer for them. Examining the rhetoric of steampunk style, Kristin Stimpson concludes it reproduces the ideology of empire, either under Britain or in the American West. Steampunk novels such as Harry Harrison's *A Transatlantic Tunnel, Hurrah!* (1972) and K.W. Jeter's *Morlock Night* (1979) envision a mighty and continuing British Empire. Marie-Luise Kohlke and Christian Gutleben see steampunk as nostalgically enamored with imperial aesthetics, including elaborate weapons meant for conquest, for example, in such works as Scott Westerfeld's *Goliath* (2011), which fictionalizes Nikola Tesla's "teleforce" weapon, and in Greg Broadmore's Dr. Grordbort's series, where Lord Cockswain employs retro-futuristic guns to murder aliens across the solar system. China Miéville ("Having a Higher Bar") critiques steampunk as part of a recent ideological trend he sees as working to rehabilitate British and American empires. David Beard argues steampunk generates a false nostalgia, that is, it portrays a dreamworld of how the past might have been but offers no vision for how the present or future might change, because it distorts the past. Very recently Bowser and Croxall (2016) scan the history, context, and impact of steampunk, while both identifying its significance and its need for more study. They suggest at least two critical perspectives on steampunk. One is that the subject matter and time period of much steampunk allows for a progressive analysis of past and future social conditions. But steampunk can also be nostalgic for empire, ignore the historic reality of the Victorian era for women and the working class, and fetishize technology.

This chapter centers on a close reading of five of Kiernan's short stories, which create an American steampunk world centered in the fictional city of Cherry Creek,[3] Colorado in the 1890s and early 1900s. In these stories Kiernan works against four steampunk themes: the status of women, industrialization, technology and colonization, especially as portrayed in American West steampunk.[4] First, Kiernan's stories rewrite the role of women within the steampunk genre's envisioned power relationships. Lead female characters populate her stories.[5] No longer secondary, or helpless victims, or complete dependents, they confront the demands of industry, prescriptive societal mores and confining gender roles. Originating steampunk works, such as James P. Blaylock's "The Ape-Box Affair" (1978) depict Victorian women fainting at the slightest peril. The lead characters in K.W. Jeter's *Infernal Devices* (1987) are males, while the character, Miss McThane, seems always subordinate to Mr. Scape.[6] The two lead females in *The Difference Engine* seem to be under constant surveillance. Kiernan also includes children's authentic experiences in her steampunk world. Secondly, Kiernan's story sequence illustrates the destructive effects of conquest on the Indigenous peoples of the American West. Her steampunk stories are haunted by their absence. Rather than glorify empire, as some steampunk does, for example, S.M. Sterling's *Peshawar Lancers* (2002), her stories illustrate the destructive effects of colonization. A third signature of normal steampunk ideology is the idolization of industrialization, while often ignoring its harmful impact on workers and the environment. Kiernan writes about the experience of ordinary people in an industrializing city in the West, which reveals steampunk's valorization of industrial power and its productive capacities. Fourth, Kiernan reworks the impact of steampunk technology. It is alluring, intrusive and dangerous in her stories. Signature steampunk technologies appear in her stories, such as airships, steamworks, clockwork mechanisms, prosthetics and goggles. But she uses them to disrupt conventional steampunk narratives. For example, "Goggles (c. 1910)" transforms that central image into a vision of the ultimate outcome of steampunk's historical distortions into apocalypse.

Kiernan dates each of her steampunk stories, as if they chronicle a history of the fictional town of Cherry Creek. "Derma Sutra (1891)" (2008) introduces the steampunk city with its polluting industrialization and vanquished American Indians. Using fantasy as a narrative technique, the story also explores the Victorian perspective on gender roles. "The Collier's Venus (1893)" (2011), continues the imagery of the devastation of Indigenous peoples and illustrates the deadly impact of coal mining. As an engine mechanic, Dora Bolshaw experiences the mining world of colliers. She cross-dresses in defiance of prescribed gender roles, but it does not protect her from black lung disease. In "The Steam Dancer (1896)" (2007) Kiernan traces the life of Missouri Banks. No mechanical man rules the story line, but Banks's lover, the mechanic, keeps her alive and dancing with steamwork prosthetics. Another female character in a so-called man's job in the late nineteenth century, Cala Monroe Weatherall in "The Melusine (1898)" (2008), faces the insidious use of a steampunk technical marvel. In Kiernan's story bedrooms, dreams and diaries are not private in a steampunk surveillance state. David Spurr shows how an empire rules its colonies in part through surveillance. The final story, and last written, in the sequence is "Goggles (c. 1910)" (2012). Turning an iconic image of steampunk safety, goggles, into an image of historical distortion, Kiernan writes the final outcome of steampunk technology as an apocalyptic destruction of Cherry Creek. Each of Kiernan's stories works against the four key steampunk themes, but each story also has a unique emphasis.

Liberating Steampunk Women from Their Prescribed Gender Roles

The first story, "Derma Sutra (1891)," features two female characters, Stephanie (Tess) Brockett and the nameless woman, who is only referred to as such throughout. The story's narrative takes place in a small garret. Outside, Cherry Creek bustles with industry. Inside the room Brockett moans and screams, while the nameless woman's "words drip poisonously from her claret tongue" (*Confessions* 195), as she attacks Brockett. The technology of steampunk reigns over Cherry Creek with foundries, trains and airships thrumming to the modern age of industry and commerce.

Towering smokestacks cloud the Cherry Creek sky, hiding the blue during the day, the stars at night. The streets buzz with citizens, but only rarely do "red Indians" (*Confessions* 191) drift through, like ghosts, who are scarcely to be seen in Kiernan's steampunk tales, and deliberately so, to illustrate the effects of the historical conquest in the American West. And farther out "vanished herds of shaggy bison" (*Confessions* 203) haunt the prairies, a tragedy Russell Thornton says was likely the most calamitous for the Indigenous peoples of the American West. He estimates the North American Buffalo population as 60,000,000 in Aboriginal times, 20,000,000 in 1850; but by 1875 1,000,000, and then in 1895 less than 1,000 (52). This resulted from increasing numbers of pioneers into the West, deliberate actions to reduce the bison population, weapons technology, and the advance of the railway (so exalted by steampunk). Articulating a prevailing attitude in the nineteenth century, the German nineteenth-century ethnologist Oscar Peschel proposed the railroads leading to California would lead to the "extinction of the Bison tribes and other remnants of the Indian race" (150) and used this as an example of the process of natural selection. There was no extinction, but Thornton concludes the collapse of the American Indian population after 1492 was a "long holocaust" resulting in "millions of deaths" (xv).

Brockett and the nameless woman are doubles, that is, they reflect both sides of the Victorian Era view of women. Kiernan's story illustrates the contradictory image of women in Victorian times, as well as the constructed nature of gender. Elaine Showalter examines the internal contradiction in the concept of women's gender roles (as well as men's roles) in the late Victorian Age. During the *fin de siècle*, women on the one hand were viewed as ethereal, angelic creatures, while their bodies were seen as dangerous due to their sexual power, that is, they were saintly and demonic. The relationship of "Derma Sutra (1891)" to *fin de siècle* Decadent writers and artists is discussed briefly in Chapter Two.

In the beginning of the story Brockett is cast as an angel, while the nameless woman is the demon. Arousing from a drug coma, Brockett finds her body completely tattooed. But her makeover is just beginning. The garret becomes a torture scene with the unnamed woman repeatedly sexually attacking the holy body of Brockett, who once killed witches, werewolves and tribades (lesbians)—those outside the norm. Kiernan pens the attack on the angel in clinical, gynecological detail. The nameless woman deconstructs Brockett and remakes her identity. After her metamorphosis, Brockett peers from eyes "as black as colliers' fingernails" (*Confessions* 200). Now outside the classificatory systems defining Victorian identity, Brockett is transformed into a construct or an abomination in the tradition of Frankenstein's monster to terrorize Victorian morality.

Showalter documents how the Victorian era defined female same-sex relationships as morbid and sexually perverse. In "The Steampunk That Dare Not Speak Its Name," Nisi Shawl critiques steampunk literature for avoiding meaningful lesbian stories. Kiernan writes such a story. Brockett welcomes the awful physiological agony and euphoria of change from the angelic, that is, she awakens to her material sexuality. The doubles, Brockett and the nameless woman, resolve their contradiction in lesbian ecstasy. For this explicit story ends with the nameless woman and the thing once known as Tess Brockett in endless lovemaking, as if to mock the Cherry Creek world of "purpose, commerce and progress" (*Confessions* 191) and the false modesty of the American Victorian West.

This story runs counter to steampunk, which draws upon a tradition found in as early a work as Villiers de l'Isle-Adam's decadent, proto-steampunk and misogynistic novel, *L'Ève future* (1886). The novel features Thomas Edison creating an ideal woman, the automaton Hadaly. He fantasizes on populating the world with his android Eves, for the pleasure of men. Jay Lawrence takes up this theme in "The Perfect Girl" (2011). She turns out to be a clockwork mechanism, named Victoria. In Paul Di Filippo's "Victoria" (1991) Cosmo Cowperthwait, sick about real women, creates a Queen Victoria stand-in with a humanized newt done up in a corset and wig. Such stories fantasize real women out of existence entirely. Gail Carriger's steampunk and fantasy novel, *Prudence* (2015), replays Victorian high society and fashion in the carefree airship adventures of the upper class. By far most Victorian women did not live in luxury and travel the world in pomp and ceremony. They had few rights. Kiernan's steampunk is different in that she does not glorify conformity to predicable female norms. This is important because Kiernan's stories illustrate the truth about the condition of women in the American West and the historic reality of the societal constrictions on women in the Victorian era.

Depicting Nineteenth-Century Industrialization Effects on the Working Poor

Stimpson points out that much of steampunk does not feature the nineteenth-century industrial working class but seems focused on the upper classes. Kiernan's characters differ. Coal helped fuel the industrializing West. Kiernan's "The Collier's Venus (1893)" explores the world of the American West coal miners, who worked to feed factories, trains and steel works. Cherry Creek is again depicted as a city consumed by industry, where the "night skies

[…] glow an angry orange from the dragon's breath of half a hundred Bessemer converters" (*The Ape's Wife* 77), while "starving guttersnipes […] haunt Colliers' Row" (*The Ape's Wife* 82). In the story, Dora Bolshaw brings news of a find in a mine, the shocking discovery of a living thing deep in Shaft Number Seven. The thing is portrayed as a coal dark woman, but she is a metaphor for the dangers of mining and for the discovery of deep time in the Victorian Era. In that Colorado mine, two men died after they cracked open a rock wall and the dark woman, or what they took for a woman, emerged. That woman ends up locked in a cell in a hospital for the bodily and mentally infirm. Professor Jeremiah Ogilvy, who runs a natural history museum, confronts her in the cell. The dark lady speaks as if she is the endless stretch of geological time within which humans are specks, mere coal dust soon drifting away into nothingness. Then she vanishes in a swirl of coal dust. Ogilvy is drained by the confrontation, as if he has experienced deep time, or perhaps ingested the black dust. Later the lungs of the two dead men in the mine are found to be filled with that black coal dust.

Bolshaw is a strong independent woman in Kiernan's American steampunk West. She represents the Victorian New Woman who eschewed marriage and sought life opportunities not normally open to women (Showalter 38–58). Kelly Hurley suggests the Victorian Era male-dominated culture felt threatened by the New Woman of the late Victorian time not only due to her aim to learn and work, but also to have rights to sexual freedom. As an engine mechanic for the Rocky Mountain Reconsolidated Fuel Company Bolshaw represents Patricia Nelson Limerick's discussion of women as active participants in the history of the American West. She cross-dresses, perhaps as camouflage in that patriarchal work world. But more so, Kiernan subverts gender dress codes "to represent rebellion and resistance against dominant and pervasive gender norms" (43), as Mary Anne Taylor thinks more of steampunk needs to do. Moreover, Taylor sees much of steampunk misappropriating Victorian female fashions as empowering, when they were in fact constraining and embedded in a patriarchal hierarchy.

Bolshaw and Ogilvy are contraries. He manages the "Ogilvy Gallery of Natural Antiquities," which exhibits marvels from across the world, including a clockwork and steam Mastodon. Magnanimously, Ogilvy offers a free day monthly to the city's "negroes, coolies, and red Indians" (*The Ape's Wife* 77), the impoverished, shunned underclasses. Technology fascinates Ogilvy; he is dazzled by the docking airships. Ogilvy represents the ruling male society, while Bolshaw represents women and the colliers. Ogilvy also represents the impact of the discovery of deep time. "The Colliers' Venus (1898)" articulates the awe and terror at the notion of deep time in the Victorian Era. James Hutton initiated the discovery in the 1700s, which was extended by Charles Lyell in the 1800s through his geological work, and confirmed by Charles Darwin in his revolutionary work on evolution. Kiernan is acutely aware of deep time through her paleontological work.[7] During an era when Biblical time was the prevailing belief, the notion of a past hundreds of millions of years long (not to speak of billions) seemed unfathomable. Bowser and Croxall (2010) claim Lyell's work stunned the Victorians imagination. And as Stephen Jay Gould argued deep time is still difficult to comprehend, because it is so outside our ordinary experience. The invisible depths of time became visible in Kiernan's story, and Ogilvy's illness represents the shock of deep time.

Cora Bolshaw works with the colliers and knows the sense of terror deep in the mines that colliers experienced as they worked there. The mining conditions in Colorado were the subject of repeated strikes and battles between miners and the owners, who often enlisted the help of government and private forces. Elizabeth Jameson and George G. Suggs Jr. document how political and business interests brutally battled emerging labor unions in Colorado at Leadville, at Cripple Creek and in the Ludlow Massacre in 1914. Labor was dangerous in the confined mine drifts, in poor light, often in strangling rock dust. Every strange noise could foretell a cave-in and death. Bolshaw suffers the hacking cough of those with the advanced chronic lung disease caused by exposure to coal dust. That dark woman, found in the mine, reifies the lurking and prevalent danger of pneumoconiosis. Kiernan writes about the effects of industrialization on workers, including the dreadful working conditions, meager living quarters and, for coal miners, black lung disease. As well, abandoned children trouble this story. Such effects are not common in most steampunk, because they do not fit into a Victorian re-imagined fantasy world. Kiernan's stories depict the real effects of the industrial machine on ordinary people in the American West.

The Difference Engine tells of the rise of an industrial, technocratic aristocracy over the traditional British royalty starting in 1855, but seems to adulate triumphant industrialization over the working class. Jay Clayton argues that the novel affirms the alliance between technology and the Victorian attitudes toward empire, female sexuality and the need for police (190). It is a fantasy of the Victorian past when male supremacy and female sexual subservience were the norm and the police kept the working-class in their place through surveillance and superior weapons.[8] Jeter characterizes Tom Clagger in his *Morlock Night* as a tosher (a Victorian sewer-hunter), but Clagger seems to live a fine, retired life earned from the supposed riches to be found in the sewers. Mike Perschon contends this is a romanticized view of the Victorian London poor. Bolshaw differs from the aristocratic heroine of Emilie P. Bush's *Chenda and the Airship Brofman* (2009), who is gifted with release from her household by the death of her wealthy husband, which bequeaths her the resources to partake in a life of travel and adventure. Bolshaw works for her living and will die from it. She is not a ruling aristocrat like Alexia

Tarabotti (to be Lady Macon) in Gail Carriger's *Soulless* (2009), the first book of the *Parasol Protectorate* series. In that romance steampunk novel, Lady Macon becomes an adventurer, serves the British Empire and is a member of Queen Victoria's Shadow Council.

Working Against Steampunk Technology That Fetishizes Violence

I reviewed Kiernan's steampunk story, "The Steam Dancer (1896)" earlier in Chapter Three of this book. There, the character Missouri Banks's need for prostheses foregrounds the fallibility of the human body, but also presents the variability of the body and works to disrupt the idea that all bodies are the same and uniform. I also show how the story illustrates Banks confronting standard views of what it means to be a person with physical challenges. She represents all of those who are different, those who are marginalized by their physical differences and those sidelined economically. Yet Kiernan also tells of the power of the experience of someone with physical challenges who overcomes those challenges.

Here I will illustrate how "The Steam Dancer (1896)" disrupts the standard steampunk view of technology. Banks bears a prosthetic arm and leg and an artificial eye. Kiernan paints a much different "mechanical woman" in this story than in standard Edisonade based American steampunk, which always seem to depict mechanical men. Not a killing machine, Banks is an artist, who succeeds in creating a meaningful life in the old West. Moreover the male mechanic in Kiernan's story made and repairs Banks's steam prostheses. But the real hero is Missouri Banks who overcomes her disabilities through mechanized prosthetic limbs, which she uses for artistic expression in a bordello.

Kiernan begins the tale with a lush description of the landscape leading up to Cherry Creek: "the endless yellow prairie laps gently with grassy waves and locust tides at the exposed bones of the world jutting suddenly up towards the western sky" (*The Ape's Wife* 15). After her mother and father died Banks scrapped out a short life on the streets and alleys of Cherry Creek. Banks is not a common character type in steampunk. In order to survive, she found food in trashcans, wore rags, went barefoot and ended up "among the spoil piles and the rusting ruin of junked steam shovels and hydraulic pumps and bent bore-drill heads" (*The Ape's Wife* 15–16), awaiting death. Nineteenth-century industrial technology displaced and discarded people like Banks. On that mattress Banks dreams of when she was a little girl, of the "shaggy herds of bison" (a nearly identical phrase is used in "Derma Sutra [1891]") and other bygone things (*The Ape's Wife* 21).

Kiernan's steampunk fiction varies from much steampunk in that it features ordinary, often marginalized, people. This story plays out in the underworld of the late nineteenth century in the American West, where Chinese laborers were shunned and eventually excluded from immigrating to America by the Chinese Exclusion Act of 1882,[9] where abandoned children fended on their own and where Banks does what some women were at times fated to do in the West: get a man, dance in a saloon, or be a prostitute. But Banks survives and flourishes through technology. Kiernan writes Banks in the role of a female artist, who is mechanical but who is other to the norms of steampunk American West while embedding Banks in real history.

Banks celebrates her form through art, for her dancing is art, not a sordid display. She overcomes disability. At Madam Ling's brothel, The Nine Dragons, she is a steampunk, stripping woman seemingly safe with the immigrant Chinese male audience. Made of muscle and steel, skin and artifice, Banks merges art and technology into a wondrous being. She takes her dancing cues from the "metronome rhythms of the engines that drive her metal leg and arm." The smell of steam is as "sweet [...] as rosewater," and her piston rods pump "something more alive than blood" (*The Ape's Wife* 18–19).

In the story, Kiernan illustrates the strange connection between technology and eroticism expressed through a steam-powered performance artist, who revels in the fact that she has been crafted. "The Steam Dancer (1896)" creates an ordinary but extraordinary pair. Although she has few belongings, Banks earns a small living and shares it with the mechanic, who also makes a small living at a foundry. Kiernan creates an alterity of technologically enhanced life within a time of colonial militarism, social constriction and gross industrialization. Differing from much steampunk, Kiernan's prosthetics mean art and love, not death and destruction. As Crowther points out prosthetics are ubiquitous in steampunk.[10]

The steampunk films *Wild Wild West* (1999) and *Steamboy* (2004) feature bodily enhancements used by protagonists to wreak havoc in the world. In Jeffrey Ford's story "The Seventh Expression of the Robot General" (2008) prosthetics also lead to destruction. The story tells of a man remade as a robot to slaughter the alien Harvang discovered on the Moon. This may be a brutal satire, but it continues the tradition of technology being used primarily for killing. An important variant from many steampunk works, "The Steam Dancer (1896)," portrays the lived experience of a disabled person using the steampunk style, but within the context of historical realism.

Decolonizing American West Steampunk: The Facts of Conquest

In "The Collier's Venus (1898)" Kiernan exposes "Indian-hating" in the nineteenth-century American West. Proud of his role in the city, Professor

Ogilvy boasts of "the small part he has played in birthing this civilization from the desolate wilderness fit for little more than prairie dogs, rattlesnakes, and heathen savages" (*The Ape's Wife* 87), articulating the prevalent attitude at that time of even the educated about American Indians. "The Melusine (1898)" also voices this theme. This story references the near extinction of the American Bison, here called the "Great Depredations" (*Confessions* 114). The opening scene describes the parade of Othneil Z. Bracken's Transportable Marvels, a carnival of amusements and beguilements, through the red dusty streets of Cherry Creek. Kiernan evokes the atmosphere of steampunk technology as the parade features prairie schooners and Bollée steam-powered carriages, along with an automaton mastodon, and clockwork doves, while in the distance moored zeppelins squint under the bright summer sun. The parade barker calls the Indigenous peoples "savages" (*Confessions* 114), but they are largely absent, just like the bison.

At the carnival, another independent female protagonist, Cala Monroe Weatherall, encounters something that may be a mechanical fake or perhaps the real thing. The story tells of the conflict between reason and emotion, a conflict with nineteenth-century sexual mores and the false promise of technology. Weatherall works as an engineer in a man's world, even though it separates her from imagination and wonder. She graduated from the "Missouri School of Mines and Metalliferous Arts," is economically independent and is "disinterested in [...] men" (*Confessions* 116). She manages the production of valves and is good at her job, as she keeps trains running and the zeppelins flying. Weatherall visits the carnival set up near the colliers' shacks, which are next to the towering piles of mining debris. Kiernan contrasts the fantasy of the carnival with the real life experience of mine workers. Inside a large tent, Weatherall scoffs at the bogus displays. The supposed white marble slab from the fabled Lemuria does not evidence wear from "the sea's abyssopelagic plains or hadopelagic trenches" (*Confessions* 119), with Kiernan's distinctive flair for scientific phraseology. She shakes her head at the fake mermaid, cannot believe people will accept a fossilized whale vertebra for a sea serpent, and tries to explain to others the barnacles on a supposed ancient Greek vessel are of a genus not found in the Mediterranean. They shush her, caught in the magic land of illusion, of false history. In this scene, Kiernan deconstructs steampunk's adoration of technical marvels. Cynthia J. Miller and A. Bowdoin Van Riper argue the steampunk aesthetic features technology as spectacle and as the prime focus of stories. Standard steampunk fetishizes technology, imagining technology as the core wonder of fantasy and a worthwhile obsession. "The Melusine (1898)" exposes the illusions perpetrated by steampunk, as such marvels serve to entrance individuals away from reality, such as the destruction of the world of the Indigenous people.

In the carnival tent, a steam-powered, mechanical melusine (a melusine

Nine. Retruthing Steampunk

is an equivocal being, a female water spirit akin to a mermaid) nearly beguiles Weatherall. At first, she believes it is a melusine, because she dreamed of loving such a being. But no melusine swims in the steampunk tank, just a steam-powered automaton. Weatherall bewails being taken in by fakery, as if any carnival technology could fulfill her imaginative wonder. She thinks she is so alone in an American steampunk world that glorifies male hegemony and eccentric technologies designed to enthrall people. "The Melusine (1898)" ends with Weatherall alone in her small room, hiding her lesbian longings, her trans–species longings. But her room is not safe. Spies have invaded her room and taken her diary.

"The Melusine (1898)" reveals the unresolved contradictions in steampunk stories of the American West. In myth it was the populating of empty spaces and the expansion of freedom. But in reality, it meant the founding of industrializing cities that forced people into repetitive work and colonization that killed most Indigenous people. That American colonial society, like the core from which it emanated, also repressed the sexual expression of women and those not cis-gendered. Technology did not liberate but reinforced existing power relationships and shaped individuality into normative behavioral and consumption patterns. In Kiernan's story, steampunk technology transforms an old fairy tale of the melusine into commoditized entrapment. The real symbols of danger here on this steampunk frontier are not the Indigenous peoples, but industrialization, empire and the tyranny of the normal. Weatherall's world is no steampunk utopia but a surveillance state.

American West steampunk often glosses over the devastating impact on the Indigenous populations by Western colonization. This started with such early Edisonades as *Frank Reade and His Steam Man of the Plains* (1876) written by Harry Enton.[11] More recent steampunk such as the television programs *The Wild Wild West* (CBS, 1965–69) and *The Adventures of Brisco County, Jr.* (Fox, 1993–94) also gloss over the real effects of empire. Joe R. Lansdale's story "The Steam Man of the Prairie and the Dark Rider Get Down: A Dime Novel" (1999) stars a large steam driven mechanical man. In the story the stereotype Indigenous character is named "John Feather" and is, of course, an "Indian guide" decked out in "breechcloth and headband" to aid Bill Beadle in pursuit of the Dark Rider (108). Lansdale's story is an over-the-top parody but it shows the stereotypical depiction of American Indians is long-lived. In Cherie Priest's "Addison Howell and the Clockroach" (2011) an historical exhibition notice states: "much can be said about Native traditions and myths, this exhibit focuses on the rural homesteaders" (36), suggesting a continuation of the history of overwriting Indigenous peoples. As well, Priest's *Boneshaker* (2009) includes an Indigenous character called an "Indian princess" (124). Although not intended, this expression suggests the rule of European values over Indigenous beliefs and values. As Joseph Weakland and Shaun

Duke argue such steampunk works as Mike Resnick's *The Buntline Special* (2010) and *The Doctor and the Kid* (2011) are embedded in early American imperialism and manifest destiny. These novels feature "Geronimo" using magic not technology against the steampunk technology of Edison and his cohorts. Felix Gilman's *The Rise of Ransom City* (2012) repurposes American Indigenous people as the "Folk," who are outside of human civilization, as Indigenous peoples were viewed in the Americas. Kiernan's stories are important because they express the truth about the devastating impact of conquest and colonization on the Indigenous people of the American West, a fact that many steampunk works ignore.

Steampunk Apocalypse

The dystopian result of American steampunk technological fantasy is the theme of "Goggles (c. 1910)." On August 22, 2012, Kiernan wrote in her Online Journal that she nearly titled this story, "The Last Steampunk Story." Kiernan goes on to say she "wrote [it] with the intention of demolishing the paradisal and revisionist Victorian Era of the sub-genre" (Kiernan, "And far away behind their lines [...]").

Eleven-year-old Samuel narrates the story. Samuel and several other children, along with a woman, who is only referred to as "Miss," have survived a steampunk apocalyptic war. Miss tries to keep the children alive. But the only food is out there in the ruins and dangers of Cherry Creek. She sends the children out in threes. They each bear a pistol with one bullet to protect themselves from the ravaging deformed wolves, as they navigate through the city of dreadful night, fraught with the dangers of collapsing buildings and raging storms bringing acidic rain and death. Many have died out there, maybe by mutant wolves, maybe through an accident, maybe by shooting themselves. It is a colony of survivors slowly, but inexorably, dying out in their bunker, to leave the planet to the raging storms, the sizzling rain and the deformed monsters. Samuel leads two other children out to find food, but it ends in disaster with his two companions killed and Samuel alone in a downed airship hugging his Colt pistol.

The airship crashed when the city was first hit with the leading "wave of blowbacks from Tesla's teleforce mechanism" (*Beneath an Oil-Dark* 462). Kiernan's fictitious war has crippled the planet, poisoned the atmosphere, killed nearly all, but not the packs of mutated dogs and deformed wild predators ravaging the ruined streets of Cherry Creek. Accompanying Samuel on the scavenging mission are nine-year-old Patrick Henry, who bears a keloid scar on his chin, and eight-year-old Molly, missing one pinkie bitten off by a feral dog, which killed her sister. They are physically and psychologically scarred.

Samuel acts the tough kid whose nightmare world is haunted by dreams of plenitude and fresh air. Out of the bunker, he leads the way to a fallen dirigible to scavenge for cans of food, because it is the rummaged leftovers of the past that yet nourish the present.

At the broken airship, its steel skeleton like bones, Patrick Henry hesitates and will not go in. Molly defends Patrick. Samuel leaves them out in the ruins as he goes for provisions. Inside the airship, he hears wolves tearing his friends apart. Creeping away deeper into the airship, he waits in the darkness. Kiernan reshapes that iconic image of the steampunk dirigible away from grandeur and travel into Samuel's coffin. Cynthia J. Miller says airships are the exemplar icons of steampunk as they represent "the magic of possibility and the possibility of magic—and embody a promise that, somewhere, frontiers still exist" (159). In Kiernan's story the airship symbolizes the end of steampunk fantasy. Alone in that ruined airship, Samuel thinks of Miss telling him the realities of the late nineteenth century. It was a reality of harsh working conditions, of colonization where "Red Indian reservations" (*Beneath an Oil-Dark* 466) incarcerated the Indigenous peoples, armament build-up, and oppression of immigrants. Miss told him of how it all led to war. The woman's litany sounds schoolmarmish and preachy, but deliberately so. This is a grim, unrelenting, dystopian story. The dark ruins of Cherry Creek illustrate the final destiny of steampunk's false narratives.

Kiernan collapses the illusory notion of the safety of goggles when Samuel tears his off at the end, as if to remove the distortions of the American West steampunk myth. Bowser and Croxall (2010) argue that goggles in steampunk stories are meant to keep the steampunk hero safe, but not in this story. Kiernan explores what might have arisen in an era with steampunk weapons; the "Great War" would set fire to the sky and kill all. Samuel tries to survive with his own delirium of smarts and arrogance, and now he has lost his two friends to the wolves. Only the monsters survive in this dystopia. A small boy waits to die. And all those other little ones starve back in the bunker. This story uses goggles as a metaphor for the distortion steampunk gives to history. The children's mutilated, mauled bodies are the reality of the violence of the American West. Kiernan works against steampunk by re-imagining the Victorian era based on a sense of the actual, not fantasy, history of the American West. Kiernan's steampunk apocalypse is out of step with the standard dream-logic of typical steampunk, but it re-historicizes American actual history into steampunk.

In Summation

Set within a fictionalized American West in the 1890s and early 1900s, Caitlín R. Kiernan's Cherry Creek, Colorado, stories work against signature themes of steampunk. Rather than whitewash the history of the Victorian era as some steampunk does, Kiernan writes with attention to historic realism. As David Beard suggests, if steampunk is set in a re-imagined Victorian background, then the real historical issues need to be addressed (xxv). In doing just this, Kiernan disrupts four key steampunk themes (the status of women, colonization, industrialization, and technology), to illustrate the distorting effects of steampunk, especially American West steampunk. No fabulous male inventors of large mechanical devices or fabulous weapons, which turn out to be mostly killing machines, inhabit her stories. Kiernan's stories provide no sweeping plot lines across the American plains and exhibit no wild wonder at the age of steam grown big in the American West. Rather, factories darken the skies of Cherry Creek, homeless children wander the mean streets and miners live in slums. The stories highlight the impact of industrialization on the environment and workers. Indigenous peoples are phantoms in her stories reflecting the facts of conquest and violence in the colonization of the American West. Their fleeting appearances reflect the deliberate attempt by some to write them out of existence.[12] Each story presents a strong woman in struggle with her time, although in "Goggles (c. 1910)" a young boy is the main character. Technological apocalypse ends the story sequence. Just a dystopian ruin remains, where a lone woman and ragamuffin children struggle to survive, but are doomed to suffer and die under an oily, sizzling sky.

Kiernan brings American West steampunk to its logical conclusion through a counter-fiction. Her steampunk stories express what Leslie Fiedler suggested when he wrote of science fiction as the "last Victorian genre" (*In Dreams* 287). He might have considered steampunk as the last gasps of the Victorian foundations for science fiction. Steampunk then exemplifies "the used-upness of certain forms or the felt exhaustion of certain possibilities" in artistic expression (64), as John Barth writes in "The Literature of Exhaustion" (1967). An exhausted literature returns to well-known classics, as steampunk does with the works of H.G. Wells and Jules Verne and the Edisonades.

Steampunk exhibits a sense of literary fatigue as it morphs into a multiplicity of cultural expressions, as if it is a search for meaning in our era of endless wars, environmental change, surveillance, ruthless economics and alternate facts. Kiernan's steampunk stories inform that genre with a sense of reality of the past, which we must know to understand the present and the shape of possible futures. Kiernan's steampunk story sequence illustrates the importance of attending to historical realism within the steampunk imagined nineteenth century, especially the reality experienced by people who were powerless, marginalized, dispossessed, disenfranchised or outside the norm. Spurr argues that ignoring the colonial reality of the nineteenth century not only reproduces the ideology of imperialism, misogyny and exploitation, but also preserves current political and economic structures of power. As Mary

Midgley comments on the Morlocks in H.G. Wells's *The Time Machine* (1895), it is not that "there might be Morlocks somewhere, some day. It is that there are Morlocks here now" (24). It is not that those outside the norm will be persecuted in the future; they are now, as they were in the past.

This is a key theme of much of Kiernan's fiction. Her characters are outsiders, estranged from the norms of society and constrained by societal power structures. They are mostly women who struggle against enforced roles. Kiernan does not focus on dreaming up new technology or extravagant space quests in her sf. Rather she writes about the physical and psychological effects on people, usually individuals, of not only technology, but also cultural norms, economic systems and political power. Her sf aligns more with Rieder's contention in *Science Fiction and the Mass Cultural Genre System* that modern sf is not ruled by technological or scientific musing, rather it provides a framework for the creative explorations and projections of today's ascendant societal developments. Kiernan's sf steampunk stories portray characters in historically accurate pasts in the American West and her future oriented sf depicts characters in projected futures based on current trends. These reimagined pasts and imagined futures alert readers to the concerns, problems and dangers in the present and they may inspire us to thought and perhaps to action.

Conclusion: Caitlín R. Kiernan's Modern Dark Fiction

"'What are you doing in the dark?' asked a voice"—James Joyce, "Ivy Day in the Committee Room," *Dubliners*, 120

Since beginning to publish her fiction in the early 1990s, Caitlín R. Kiernan has now established herself at the forefront of modern dark fiction and science fiction literature. She writes within the tradition of the Gothic, the ghost story and the uncanny tale. The original European Gothic was initiated by Horace Walpole's publication of *The Castle of Otranto: A Gothic Story* in 1764 and continued by Anne Radcliffe, Matthew Gregory Lewis and Charles Robert Maturin through to Mary Shelley and others. Kiernan's work also reflects the American Gothic pioneered by Charles Brockden Brown in his novels *Wieland* (1798), *Arthur Mervyn* (1799–1800) and *Edgar Huntly* (1799); and continued by Nathaniel Hawthorne, Washington Irving, Edith Wharton, Ambrose Bierce and others. The female Gothic[1] has also affected Kiernan's fiction. She writes in the tradition of such authors as Emily Brontë, Rosa Mulholland, Gertrude Atherton, Charlotte Perkins Gilbert, Olivia Howard Dunbar, Octavia Butler and many others. In her online journal, interviews and in her published works, Kiernan has noted the many influences on her fiction.[2] Throughout this book I explore the relation of Kiernan's fiction to the tradition and themes of dark and science fiction. More importantly, I explore how her stories and novels adapt traditional dark fiction themes and motifs to modern conditions and concerns. At her best, Kiernan channels the psychological intensity of Edgar Allan Poe and Shirley Jackson, the awe and wonder of Algernon Blackwood and the cosmic emptiness and biological fear in H.P. Lovecraft's work.[3] Kiernan also writes with a social and political edge akin to Angela Carter and Ursula K. LeGuin. Many of Kiernan's characters face that nightmare void of existential loneliness found in Carson McCullers. But her fiction is her own; her characters, her sentences and her story lines are uniquely of Caitlín R. Kiernan.

Judith Wilt writes, "Dread is the father and mother of the Gothic" (5). More than that dread breeds fright and terror, but also awe and worship. Our search for the meaning of existence always stumbles upon dread. That is, we search for the meaning of the human condition in the material world and in our imagination, which includes the supernatural or the unknown. Dark fiction shows characters in situations of dread. This experience of dread occurs when you stumble upon "an unknown world which had just broken" in on you (Eliot, *Middlemarch* 720). Or to take another line from George Eliot's great novel, you hear that "great roar which lies on the other side of silence" (173). Kiernan's characters know dread. They experience that gothic dread, which Mario Praz saw as an awful metaphysical anxiety from an awareness of an "ultimate nothingness" (9). Kiernan writes how dread shreds her characters' identities. She writes of our existential estrangement from ourselves and from our fellow humans. And this is articulated within a sense of the violence, inequality and despair that infects our current society. A society that enforces cultural and identity chains that engender estrangement, fear and then heroic rebellion, which may be without hope.

Kiernan's fiction confirms Wilt's argument that dark literature is important not only because of its exploration of dread but also because of its sexual and political concerns and its moral and aesthetic vision. This is what Praz saw as the pointed original Gothic critique against a "bigoted, pompous and decadent society, with debauched ecclesiastics […] demented sovereigns" (15). The original European Gothic can be thought of as an expression of rebellion against the obscenities of perverse power. Wilt says the gothic reveals the hidden truth about gender, trauma and power. According to John C. Tibbetts in his *The Gothic Imagination* (2011), the gothic is "transgressive" writing which strives to overcome prescribed social, cultural and gender roles enforced by the standards of current science and culture (5). Teresa A. Goddu thinks the same way. She argues the gothic shows a culture's contradictions by writing a distorted but revealing version of reality. Dark fiction contests conventional depictions and roles within society and releases what is buried away or tabooed.

Kiernan writes within the long tradition of the gothic and dark fantasy. And she acknowledges the influence of many authors, artists, scientists, composers and musicians on her work. In an interview with Jeremy L.C. Jones, Kiernan says she is haunted by the specters of authors who have influenced her development ("A Complex Web of Influence with Campbell, Kiernan"). These seem more like inspiring ghosts than terrifying ones. Nonetheless, Kiernan goes beyond all of these influences and grounds her work in an original and recognizable voice with distinctive themes and artistic motifs.

Kiernan is powerful at creating mood and atmosphere, bringing her characters to life through dialogue and action, and using a variety of points-of-view in her fictions. She paints sensitive word-portraits of settings and landscapes, such as the blasted hill in the story "One Tree Hill (The World as Cataclysm)" and the ruined Devonian trackway on a windswept Irish island in "Valentia." Her narratives are rich in sentence variation; they are often cinematic in structure (see her "The Prayer of Ninety Cats") and her word choice and phrasing match the events and characters in her stories. Part of this is how her scientific education provides a sense of objectivity and distance within the inmost private terrors in her stories ("In the Water Works [Birmingham Alabama 1888]"). Her stories often favor mood and atmosphere over plot (the plots are the puzzles readers put together, as in the short story "Tidal Forces"). Her fictions are constructs of tone and emotion, where the power of language is foremost. This is shown most clearly in her vignettes, which provide a fleeting glimpse into the unusual and strange experiences of her characters (see "Madonna Littoralis").

Many of Kiernan's non-linear stories leave questions for readers, sometimes explicitly as in "Slouching Towards the House of Glass Coffins." Revelations for readers come from an intense engagement with her fiction. Yes Kiernan has a rich imagination (she is prolific in her writing output) grounded in science, and enriched by myth and folklore, but expressed in the reality of today. Yet there is an ambiguity and allusiveness in her work, as if there are things that are impossible to tell. Kiernan's stories are sometimes challenging for a reader. In his review of *The Very Best of Caitlín R. Kiernan* (2019), Gary K. Wolfe says, "Kiernan's writing does often demand close attention, but she's earned it, and it pays off."

Her novel *Black Helicopters* calls for a reader's careful attention. There are dozens of allusions to Lewis Carroll, W.B. Yeats, the Little Red Riding Hood fairy tale, James Joyce, T.S. Eliot, chaos theory, quantum physics and more. She mentions many of these in her "Acknowledgments" at the end of the novel. The novel seems a puzzle akin to a chess problem (there is chess in the novel). At times, Kiernan ignores traditionalist dictates about clarity and plotting. You find many nameless characters (in "Derma Sutra [1891]," "John Four," "Houses Under the Sea" and many others) and complicated narrative structures (*Agents of Dreamland*).[4] As well, sometimes her stories are replete with digressions. Her science fiction story, "Galápagos" (2009), presents as the journal kept by Merrick, who is a space anthropologist back from exploring a spaceship inexplicably rerouted around Mars. Merrick writes her journal in switchbacks and meanderings while in a psychiatric ward; she writes it to please those doctors who give her meds. Kiernan's plots may be relaxed, as in "The Cryomancer's Daughter (Murder Ballad No. 3)" (2006). She writes that way to give readers insight into the experiences of characters in an unruly and still mysterious world.

Throughout this book, I provide brief examples of Kiernan's distinctive literary style. In Chapter Three, I discuss "The Ammonite Violin (Murder Ballad No. 4)" as an example of Kiernan's gothic body motif. But the story is also a paradigm of her versatility with language. Elegantly structured with the voices of three characters and a conductor, the story's lyrical language sounds musical. The fat man, who is a serial killer and is sometimes called the Collector in the story, is the first voice. He loves the sea and ammonites. A second voice enters, Ellen. She dislikes the sea in counterpoint to the fat man. And then the violin speaks, or rather, Ellen's dead sister speaks in the notes Ellen plays. Kiernan's story contains repeated melodic lines. The fat man says, "language is language is language" (*Beneath* 102), as he yearns to talk more, but Ellen muses, that same phrase, as she strings her violin chords counterpointing mere words. While Ellen plays the fat man mutters, "*Don't let it end* [...] *Let it never end*" (*Beneath* 106). And she thinks the same phrases, while she listens to her sister's voice.

Another word sequence acts as a musical phrase expressing the anguish of telling such a story. At the beginning of the story, the narrative voice, the conductor of the piece, suggests of the fat man that "if he were ever to try to write this story, he would not know where to begin" (*Beneath* 95). Later that narrative voice says the violinist would not write the story. Finally at the very end of the story, the music returns to its beginning words with the conductor saying that Ellen would never "put this story into words [...] and like the violin, the story has become hers and hers alone" (*Beneath* 109).

"The Ammonite Violin (Murder Ballad No. 4)" is a reinvented ghost story, from its narrative styling to its haunting language. At times Kiernan leads us inside the minds of the characters themselves, blending the narrator's voice and the characters' voices. But at other times the narrative voice disappears behind the conversations of the characters. Kiernan is adept at various forms of weird literature. In this story she reconstructs the psychology of the diseased mind of a serial killer. And she illustrates the grief and joy of a sister connecting with her murdered sister through music.[5]

Many of Kiernan's first-person narrators describe events as if compelled to do so. The characters, Sarah Crow in *The Red Tree* and Imp in *The Drowning Girl: A Memoir*, repeatedly call attention to the fact that they are writing. Many of her stories are not linear; they are written in scenes, but the scenes seem like puzzle pieces, as she probes the psychology of identity, madness and alienation. But these self-reflective narratives show the internal struggles of her characters; they are not written to express anguish with traditional narrative forms. Rather it is a way to express the way people actually experience the current modern world with its emphasis on spectacle and consumption and divisive cultural politics. She writes about outsiders and it is not just grief or fear, it is also social and personal trauma that beat up on these people.

Kiernan's writing style has matured over her writing career. Her aesthetic power has always been there. Although rich in imagery, with well-drawn characters and lyrical in diction, her early stories overused compound adjectives and luxuriated in a virtuosity of word choice and phrasing. Today her lyricism remains, as do her arresting descriptions of the real world and the imagined world. But her voice is now her own, even her Lovecraftian stories belie their origin through her dark lyrical fictions set in worlds of her own making and with striking female characters linked to the hurt in the real world. Kiernan says this shift started with her 2003 dark fantasy story "Andromeda Among the Stones" (*Two Worlds* 340). Appropriately it is a coming of age story.[6] Meredith, the daughter of Machen[7] and Ellen Dandridge, finds the strength to cross the threshold between the known and unknown and experience a metamorphosis into something strange, powerful and dangerous. It is an act of extreme heroism as she sacrifices her identity to protect others. And it is a story written by Kiernan to assert her identity within the dark fiction tradition.

The story shifts between the fantastic and the real, or perhaps more accurately depicts the intersections of the two realms. One appears on the California coast. There the Dandridge family members face the gateway to the unknown, or the dark depths of the sea where the deep ones of Lovecraft or the ancient Irish sea gods, the *fomor* or *fomoiri,* abide. But this strange locale on the pacific intersects with the real time of World War I in the years 1914–1915. There on the coast the crashing breakers sound like cannons, as Kiernan melds the real with the fantastic. The earth on Meredith's mother's grave reeks of death from the French trenches. The distant horizon shines red from the flames of burning cities in Europe. Lightning rattles like mortar shells. And thunder sounds in the attic like explosions. This dark fantasy is haunted by the real world of continuous wars.

That attic is where Avery, Meredith's brother, is locked up (in the original Gothic, women were confined to constricted places[8]). He had attempted to patrol the mysterious gateway. Yet Avery is a sympathetic character, because, akin to Meredith, he revolts against his tyrannical father. In this story, as in others, Kiernan distinguishes among the four characters through their individualized voices and actions. She depicts Avery answering Meredith's plaintive questions by passing penciled notes under the attic door. Kiernan is able to show his pain, fear and deformity but also caring in his scrawled last words of love, loss and despair.

The story is a threshold for Kiernan herself, as if she writes beyond the influence of Lovecraft and the traditional weird, supernatural or ghost story. Her weird as well as science fiction stories feature strong female characters. She reshapes traditional gothic and science fiction motifs. Her females respond heroically to threats. Part of the heroism in this story arises from

Meredith talking with and listening to the ghost of her mother, depicted as a body thrown back by the sea. Her sea wracked body is symbolic of the dying of the oceans through climate change. As Derrida urges, Meredith listens to and speaks with her mother, the ghost.

Meredith undergoes a transgenerational haunting (see Jodey Castricano), which is an outer manifestation of intergenerational trauma. The voice of her dead mother manifests itself in Meredith's rebellion against her father. That is, she responds to that call from her ghostly mother. Castricano says that to be haunted is to be called upon and that we ignore the dead at our peril (16–19). In the form of a haunting, her mother guides Meredith away from the traumatic past of her father's authoritarian rule with his forbidden book of power (this story is replete with motifs from the dark fiction tradition) that brings ruin not redemption. Meredith overcomes her trauma and determines her destiny by listening to her mother, as Imp in *The Drowning Girl: A Memoir* overcomes her trauma by attending to her dead mother and grandmother. Imp and Meredith's ghosts are not frightening and hostile because they are their maternal ghosts. Imp and Meredith integrate their ghostly past and are thus able to make their own future. Meredith's mother, the ghost, is the link between a recovered past and the future. Of course, Meredith's future is a gothic one. Meredith is a reimagined Andromeda, but she does not need to be unchained by Perseus to avoid being devoured by sea monsters. In this dark fantasy, Meredith chains herself to an island and becomes a sea monster.

I have not discussed all of Kiernan's work in this book: it is nearly impossible anyway in light of her large number of publications. She has worked extensively in comics and has produced graphic novels, which were not explored in detail here. Her graphic novels feature the character, Dancy Flammarion, who also appears in a number of her non-graphic works. Flammarion appears to be an avatar of outrage and outlaw justice for all those who are outside, abused and submerged by societal, economic and religious forces of power and discipline. Flammarion challenges readers: who are you that allow these continuing infamies on the poor, the helpless and the different? Flammarion, as imagined in *Alabaster: Wolves*, is part of this narrative outrage. The monsters she battles are reified economic, cultural and social norms that intend to snuff out deviation from orthodoxy. The chaos of her battles is an expression of outrage. This series is also a critique of the pop fascination with violence.[9]

In exploring Kiernan's fiction, I have approached her work through various contemporary critical lenses that are manifested in her work. I have also looked at her place in the gothic and science fiction traditions. The essential themes in Kiernan's stories and novels include our bodily fragility, the conflict between science and mystery, the continuing relevance of the decadence, the devastating effects of trauma, the strange alloy of the cosmic and the personal, spectral hauntings from our ancestors, and the despair, yet heroism of marginalized individuals and groups. Kiernan's fiction explores the corrosive power of the cruelty of the normal, the strange relationship between writing and trauma, and the links between memory and haunting. She expresses the continuing ostracism and oppression of the LGBTTQ+ community. She writes of inherited spectrality, the gothic body and the continuing power of folklore and myth. Her science fiction illustrates such themes as the falsehoods of the steampunk subgenre, the relation between science fiction and empire, and how dystopian science fiction reveals today's dangerous economic, social and political tendencies. Kiernan's fiction brings to life our dread about the unknown, the alien, bodily decay, death, the supernatural, the grotesque and the dark, inherited legacy we all have. Kiernan portrays these with a lyrical expressionism of the dark side of life in urban and in rural environments under a wide dangerous sky and in the ruins of modern culture.

Kiernan is an imaginative and gifted stylist, exploring the dark spaces of life, the illusions of perception, and the vast spaces of awe and hurt that everyone feels, causes and regrets within a world that is impossibly dangerous and beautiful. Her fictions go into the unconscious mind to dredge up our deepest fears and our most outlandish fantasies. She shows the experience of dread. But Kiernan's fictional work is not disengaged from our reality. Part of her work can be seen as sociological in that it is a lens through which to see more clearly our current world and its host of maladies. Kiernan's stories and novels do that. Her characters often confront the tyranny of the normal; they are outsiders shunned and forsaken by society and they struggle in a world of trauma, waste and brutality.

In her fiction, Kiernan responds to Frank O'Connor's call for stories to give voice to the voiceless and to speak for the "submerged population" (O'Conner 40). She creates a literary space where outcast, marginal and diverse voices can be heard. But it is not always a safe space for readers. She writes about loneliness, mental anguish and physical trauma through characters who persist on the fringes of society, for example, street kids, people with mental health challenges and LGBTTQ+ communities. With vivid images of societal confinement and oppression, her stories are psychological descents into the damaged psyches of those persecuted today. These mental states are often depicted through experimental, non-linear narratives that are set within a sense of the indifferent universe we inhabit.

As today's premier author in the gothic, weird and supernatural fiction tradition, Kiernan's body of work uniformly displays artistry, originality and cognitive power.[10] A lyrical writer, she has a gift for characterization and description, and brings an inventive approach to modern supernatural literature. Her stories are rich with visual imagery in a luxuriant yet precise prose.

Her knowledge of literature and science enriches stories through multiple allusions and references. Kiernan's unique fictional vision is a world webbed with terror and wonder, where disparate and strange events are connected in inexplicable and terrifying ways and where everyone gets broken. She writes powerful stories of suffering and inhumanity within an indifferent universe. Kiernan writes of our elemental biology: how at times it seems alien, how fragile it is, and how insignificant and lost we are in the vastness around us. As the narrator in "The Bed of Appetite" puts it, we are "no more than a raindrop against the sea's unfathomable abyss" (*Confessions* 30). In this book I have tried to convey through many examples some idea of the richness, variability and insight in Kiernan's fiction. As well, I have shown how her work fits into the weird fiction tradition through literary exposure of our fragility, despair, wonder and awe as a primal source of the continuing power of supernatural literature.

Caitlín R. Kiernan is now in the prime of her writing career with an extensive and growing body of work. At this stage Kiernan has many distinctive literary achievements in weird, uncanny and dark science fiction literature. Yet more will be forthcoming from her, for she is an author who will be read in the future.[11] Kiernan enriches the gothic by her unsentimental writing, her focus on the trauma of outsiders, her melding of fantasy and the gothic, her appeal to folklore and myth, her scientific sensibility and her exposure of the dread that lurks at the core of dark fiction.

Chapter Notes

A Brief Biography of Caitlín R. Kiernan

1. Kiernan's Irish heritage has and continues to influence her fiction. It is found in her first written novel, *The Five of Cups* (2003), which starts in Ireland during the famine and features an Irish vampire, and in her latest novel, *Black Helicopters* (2018), which opens in Dublin.

2. The online journal is "Dear Sweet Filthy World: The Online Journal of Caitlín R. Kiernan." greygirlbeast.livejournal.com.

3. Kiernan published a chapbook of short stories, *Candles for Elizabeth* (Meisha Merlin) in 1998, dedicated to the memory of Elizabeth Tillman Aldridge, who is also remembered on the dedication page of many of her publications.

Chapter One

1. The colonization of Ireland began nearly one thousand years ago with the Norman Invasions of 1169. Over time the English gradually conquered by force the island. In 1603, the Irish were overthrown and Ireland became an English territory. But the process of colonization continued until the early twentieth century.

2. This story was originally titled "Murder Ballad No. 6" (2008) in *Sirenia Digest* (June #37).

3. The Irish *sí* folklore also appears to be the basis for Kiernan's "Children of the Cuckoo," who are changelings captured and raised underground by ghouls, and who feature in the stories "The Dead and the Moonstruck" (2004) and "The Thousand-and-Third Tale of Scheherazade" (2009), and the novel *Daughter of Hounds* (2007).

4. According to Declan Kiberd, nearly one million people died from starvation and associated diseases during the Famine, while one and a half million emigrated (*Inventing Ireland* 21).

5. Sir Henry Irving was the premiere actor/director of the British stage at the London Lyceum Theatre during the Victorian Era. Stoker was his devoted business manager for 28 years, and he accompanied Irving on several theatric tours. Barbara Belford argues that Stoker modeled Dracula, in part, on Irving.

6. Kiernan ends "Stoker's Mistress" (1996) with a quote from Yeats about the "*Leanhaun Shee* (fairy mistress)," who is the Gaelic muse (Yeats, *Writings* 12). She gives inspiration but is a "malignant phantom" (13), who feeds on a person and brings death at the end.

7. Bram Stoker died in 1912 in London.

8. Quinccy actually bears the names of each of the men of the Crew of Light, although called Quincey after Morris, the American.

9. The French colonial rule in Vietnam began in 1887. Until 1954 it was part of French Indochina. In 1949 the Viet Minh revolted for independence in what some called the First Indochina War of Independence. In 1954 French forces fled Vietnam. But this was not the end of the colonization of Vietnam. The United States had supported France and after its departure took over military support for South Vietnam. This led to the Vietnam War, also called the Second Indochina War.

10. Since the early 1990s, Paul O'Brien points out the vibrancy of the Irish economy has resulted in a growth in population due to the return of Irish emigrants, an inflow of economic migrants from Eastern Europe, and refugees from various countries.

11. At the end of the story, Kiernan adds a quote from the "The Second Coming" of W.B. Yeats.

Chapter Two

1. Craig Gingrich Philbrook points out that queer theory resists definition. But part of queer theory is the notion of the societal privileging of "heteronormativity." Michael Warner says that heteronormativity is a worldview that privileges heterosexuality as the normal/preferred sexual orientation. As a form of power and control, heteronormativity exerts power on straight and gay individuals to conform to accepted social sexual/gender norms.
2. Rachilde was the pen name of Marguerite Vallette-Eymery (1860–1953). Her novel tells the exploits of Raoule de Vénérande, who discards her social and sexual role as a woman and takes on a male gendered identity. She feminizes her lover, Jacques Silvert. He becomes her mistress (in the feminine) and then his wife.
3. Salomé was not officially produced in England until 1931. Its first performance was in Paris in 1896, while Wilde was in jail (Showalter 150).
4. Kiernan's toothed vagina recalls the folk literature of *vagina dentata*, which Stith Thompson categorized as marvel motif F547.1.1. Such teeth may represent a male's fear of a woman's sexuality, or overall cultural anxieties about women's sexual power, or a symbol of sexual passion (Sharon Rose Wilson, *Margaret Atwood's Fairy-Tale Sexual Politics* 17 and 225).
5. Bram Stoker's *Dracula* was published in 1897 and it exhibits homoerotic elements. Christopher Craft in his 1989 article "'Kiss Me with Those Red Lips': Gender and Inversion in Bram Stoker's *Dracula*" reads *Dracula* as a book about gender fluidity, as a means of hiding the novel's homoeroticism. He shows that male interactions pass through a woman. Sedgwick's queer analysis of such Victorian books suggests that male-male relations were hidden by writing them through triangulations with women. Kiernan's story reflects and denies this triangulation by having the boyfriend cross-dress as Marie Antoinette.
6. The name "Salmagundi" comes from the Salmagundi Art Box tins, which Alphonse Mucha designed for Whitman's candies in the 1920s. The figure is derived from his Sarah Bernhardt posters. The Salmagundi Art Club in New York City was founded in 1871 and continues today. Mucha joined in 1921.

Chapter Three

1. Lovecraft uses "biological heritage" to suggest that our biological evolution through the struggle for survival in a harsh world resulted in the "physiological fixation of the old instincts in our nervous tissue" (26). Our instinctual leaps of fear in a hostile or unknown environment demonstrate this heritage. Based on Lovecraft, Jack Morgan argues that horror literature has its source in our "bio-existential situation" arising from "the agonies and exigencies of physical life" (4).
2. Another example of the abject appears in the short film *The Captured Bird* (2012). A young girl wanders away from her family and approaches an enormous, gothic manor. Just outside its dark entrance, mealworms flow out of a drainpipe and writhe in a rising pile. They symbolize our physicality, our destiny. The abject articulates that sense of materiality, of our corporeality. In the film, the mealworms warn, but go unheeded, because the girl enters the dark manor. The blonde-haired girl appears delighted at first with what she finds in the manor, but in the end, she screams in terror because alien, insectoid things engulf her.
3. Garland-Thomson's thesis appears to erase distinctions between audience members at carnivals. They internalize the spectacle of the extraordinary body to help them contemplate and confirm their image of the ideal person, more particularly the ideal American. Garland-Thomson suggests this has a long history in America, citing Ralph Waldo Emerson's use of "icons of bodily vulnerability" (including: "invalids," "minors" the "halt," and "presumably women") to define by opposition his ideal "man" (*Extraordinary Bodies* 42). In other words, the ideal body is established in contrast to the non-normative bodies. The role of the audience in viewing the spectacle of "extraordinary bodies" is to normalize everyone in opposition to the exhibited abnormal bodies. Yet it may be that audience members

are not all the same in their reactions. Stephen T. Asma maintains people do not all have the same experience when confronted by human abnormalities. Some members of an audience may feel sympathy, or concern for such individuals. Or they may feel an anxiety that they may not live up to the concept ideal person.

4. Fiedler points out "how dangerous enforced physiological normality" (*Tyranny of the Normal* 150) can become under dictatorial regimes.

5. Garland-Thomson suggests there may be a limit on the extension of the notion of cyborg to persons with disabilities. Some may not want to be so transformed (*Extraordinary Bodies* 114–15). Fiedler makes a similar point in his discussion of dwarfs fighting against enforced medical treatments (*Tyranny of the Normal* 153–54).

6. Kiernan says that "Faces in Revolving Souls" is "a story about very real prejudices that are with us right now [...] including "sexual orientation, race, sexism, and so on. Also, clearly, I'm addressing the prejudices encountered by people who choose any sort of extreme body modification" (Stokes "Author Spotlight").

7. Paulina Palmer posits a dual usage of the term "queer" in *The Queer Uncanny: New Perspectives on the Gothic* that "challenge[s] the concept of stable sexual identification and problematize[s] the binary division homosexual/heterosexual" (4).

8. "Transgender" generally signifies people who do not conform to accepted gender roles, while "transsexual" denotes persons who identify with a gender different from their biological ones and who may employ sex assignment surgery (Palmer 91). C.J. Gomolka suggests that "transgender" has come to encompass all people whose social presentation of gender challenges social norms. Gomolka goes on to say that such gendered expressions question the entire epistemological framework of gender and sex.

9. The phrase "Tears seven times salt" is one of Ophelia's lines in *Hamlet* (4.5.155). Later in that Act 4, Queen Gertrude laments Ophelia's "mermaidlike" (4.7.177) body in the stream.

10. Haniver's abject body washes into the sea in contrast to those abject bodies in Kiernan's "Salammbô Redux (2007)," "The Mermaid of the Concrete Ocean" and *Murder of Angels* that wash up on shores.

Chapter Four

1. A quarry is also reclaimed with water by nature on an alien moon, Piros, in Kiernan's dark science fiction novella *The Dry Salvages* (2004).

2. Kelly Hurley says she borrowed the term "abhuman" from William Hope Hodgson (1877–1918). The term signifies a "Gothic body" (5), something only vestigially human, or in a process of becoming something monstrous. She claims this is an essential feature of much gothic writing. This is close to Kriteva's notion of abjection. It is also akin to the notion of the "uncanny valley" coined by Masahiro Mori, that he uses in his analysis of people's reactions to humanlike robots. He hypothesizes that a person's response would abruptly shift from empathy to revulsion as the robot neared, but failed to attain, a lifelike appearance. He thought this descent into eeriness may be essential for human beings, perhaps an integral part of our instinct for self-preservation from proximal danger. Mori's "uncanny valley" is similar to Kristeva's concept of the abject in that there is an initial attraction but an ultimate revulsion. Hurley's concept of abhuman means becoming the abject, becoming the alien other and losing one's identity.

3. I discuss *The Red Tree* more fully in Chapter Seven, with an emphasis on trauma and ghosts.

4. Robert Graves says that Persephone prefers the company of Hecate, who is the goddess of witches (1.123). According to Graves, Persephone is Demeter's daughter's name while in the company of Hades, her name out of hell is "Core" (*The Greek Myths* 1.91). Persephone is also mentioned in Dr. Harvey's manuscript. Harvey writes of Joseph Olney comparing Bettina Hirsch to Persephone, because he yearns to bring her out of hell (*The Red Tree* 278).

5. Andrew Smith and William Hughes's edited volume, *EcoGothic*, includes a number of articles exploring the increasing incidence of ecoGothic fiction.

6. The "neo-gothic," or contemporary Gothic, or the New Gothic refers to a literature that redeploys the landscapes, architecture, and characterizations of the original Gothic. In their "Introduction" to the anthology *The New Gothic* (1991), Bradford Morrow and Patrick McGrath call these

settings and props the "*furniture*" (xi) of the original Gothic. The neo-gothic reframes this furniture into a modern or post-modern context, sometimes in parody, but more so in homage to a literature that expressed primal fears, explored psychological disturbances, and critiqued corrupt power structures. Morrow and McGrath contend the New Gothic exhibits a "gothic sensibility" by expressing themes of "horror, madness, monstrosity, death, disease, terror, evil, and weird sexuality" (xiv).

7. Dumbrava says: "These creatures of the underground were called *fairies* in the region of Muntenia, vâlve in Transylvania, *stime* in Muntenia and Southern Transylvania, and *spirits* in Moldavia" (30).

8. The skinwalker is part of Dineh (Navajo) legend and folklore, as S.K. Robisch illustrates. A skinwalker is a malevolent force; it is one who can don an animal pelt and shape-shift into that animal to carry out evil (244–46).

9. Kiernan describes the electricity as if it is alive and dangerous as it is in Fritz Leiber's "The Man Who Made Friends with Electricity" (1962).

10. The young Narcissa Snow in *Low Red Moon* (2003) also keeps a hoard of small treasures, as does the woman in "The Lovesong of Lady Ratteanrufer" (2006).

11. In the story "Bridle" the kelpie has similar webbing between her fingers.

12. "Paedomorphosis" is the resemblance of adult animals to the young of their ancestors.

13. Sharon Rose Wilson examines in depth Atwood's use of fairy tales in her work.

14. Kiernan continually explores the latent content of "Little Red Riding Hood" in such works as "Apokatastasis" (2005), "The Bed of Appetite" (2007), "Werewolf Smile" (2009), "As Red as Red" (2010), "Random Notes Before a Fatal Crash" (2012), *Low Red Moon*, *The Drowning Girl* (2012) and others.

15. See "The Story of Grandmother" in *Little Red Riding Hood: A Casebook*, edited by Alan Dundes.

16. Terri Windling provides an engaging history of the "Red Riding Hood" folktale. There are many suggestions for the two pathways. One is that the pathways reinforce the sexual content of the fairy tale. For example, the two paths in the folk tale can be understood as separate aspects of growing to adulthood, with the way of the pins the time of learning and growing up from child to young woman. The path of needles follows and leads to sexual maturity.

17. Albert Perrault is a recurring character is Kiernan's fiction. His art seems a harbinger of terror in such stories as "The Ammonite Violin (Murder Ballad No. 4)" (2006), "Rappaccini's Dragon (Murder Ballad No. 5)" (2008) and many others. Of course, the name is a reference to Charles Perrault (1628–1703), author of *Histoires ou contes du temps passé* (1697), a set of fairy tales, including *Le Petit Chaperon rouge*.

18. Kiernan's "Pickman's Other Model (1929)" addresses a similar theme. But it is more directly related to Lovecraft's story "Pickman's Model" (1927), which I discuss in Chapter Five.

Chapter Five

1. "Empiricism" is a word used in varying ways. Often it is used in a general manner to suggest the research tools and practices of science (which I think is what Latour means). It connotes observations of the natural world and a focus on experiential data, collected in a standardized and controlled manner, including experiments. Empirically based scientific theories are routinely tested against observations of the world and do not rest solely on a priori reasoning. In epistemology, empiricism means that knowledge of the natural world is based on sense impressions. Empiricism differs from realism. The fundamental premise of realism is that a mind-independent reality exists. Scientific realism holds that it is possible to describe those mind-independent objects, even when they are not directly observable.

2. Dr. Solomon Monalisa is a strange, mysterious scientist. Kiernan says she borrowed Dr. Monalisa from her earlier story "Onion," in her "Author's Note" in the "Afterword" to *Weird Shadows Over Innsmouth* (2005), where the story first appeared. In Kiernan's "Onion" (2001), Dr. Solomon Monalisa is a shadowy character Frank tries to track down, to help him understand the "glimpses of impossible geographies, entire worlds hidden in plain view" (*Two Worlds* 219) that he and Willa are gifted to see. "Onion" is discussed in Chapter Six.

3. Kuhn's "paradigm" roughly means a set

of theories, procedures and practices that guide scientists in their research. "Normal science" is what happens within such paradigms. However, within a paradigm, "anomalies" may arise, these are things that cannot be accounted for within a paradigm. If the anomalies are big enough or there are many of them, they may result in a scientific revolution. Kuhn's theory of scientific change has been challenged. Margaret Masterman interrogates the meaning of Kuhn's "paradigm." S.E. Toulmin and J.W.N. Watkins dispute Kuhn's designation of what happens in "normal science" and the distinction between "normal" and "revolutionary" science. Imre Lakatos suggests that Kuhn's thesis is fundamentally irrational in that the shift from one paradigm to another paradigm, which are by definition incommensurable, cannot be explained or justified by any rational means.

4. The definition and applicability of correspondence rule and correspondence rubrics (bridge rules) are controversial subjects within the philosophy of science. Jody Azzouni summarizes the debates on this issue and proposes a new perspective on scientific theories.

5. Churchland ("A Deeper Unity") engages directly with Feyerabend's central philosophy of science principles and finds them to be insightful, especially in a neuro-computational sense.

6. There is indeed a Devonian trackway located in the northeast region of Valentia Island, which Kiernan shifted to Culloo for the purpose of the story. The trackway, *bóithrín tetrapod* in Irish, bears some of the oldest traces of four-legged vertebrates moving on land—between 350 and 370 million years old.

7. "Valentia" was written prior to *Threshold*, and the import of this strange object receives a grander treatment in the novel, which Kiernan notes (*To Charles Fort* 33).

8. The North Cape spilled 828,000 gallons of home heating oil, resulting in the deaths of millions of lobsters, surf clams, and fish, and billions of invertebrates, as well as, over 2,000 birds.

9. A recent study (M.O. Clarkson, et al.) found evidence that acidification in the oceans through increased CO_2 in the atmosphere was the precipitating event for the mass extinction at the Permo-Triassic boundary. Today's oceans are becoming increasingly acidic (Doney, et al., Fabry, et al., Gruber, et al., and Jeremy B.C. Jackson). Not only that, but M.C. Urban synthesized over 130 published studies to "estimate a global mean extinction rate and to determine which factors contribute the greatest uncertainty to climate change–induced extinction risks. Results suggest that extinction risks will accelerate with future global temperatures, threatening up to one in six species under current policies" (571).

10. "Nor the Demons Down Under the Sea" is one of a trilogy of stories constituting Kiernan's Dandridge Cycle. "A Redress for Andromeda" (2000) is the first story, while "Andromeda Among the Stones" (2003) closes the cycle. This story is reviewed in the Conclusion.

11. The anatomical anomaly of Vera Endicott in Kiernan's story is a tail bone—"a crooked, malformed thing sprouting from the base of the spine and reaching halfway to the bend of the subject's knee" (*Beneath an Oil-Dark*, 211). Pickman's sketches and paintings were not imaginary. In Lovecraft's story Pickman's ghoul portraits are painted from "*photograph*[s] *of life*" (*The Dunwich Horror*, 25 emphasis in original).

12. "In the Dreamtime of Lady Resurrection" is fiction, so it may be overly factual to say that such a research project would not likely meet the ethical standards of an Institution Research Board in the USA (in Canada a Research Ethics Board, one of which I have chaired), which would be charged with ensuring protection for human research participants.

13. Thomas Ollive Mabbott called Poe's poem "an unparalleled evocation of mystery" (Poe *Complete Poems* 409).

14. Among other things, "Concerning Attrition and Severance" is a virtual treatise on the problem of reference in language.

15. Shirley Jackson's *The Haunting of Hill House* (1959) describes an experiment concocted by Dr. John Montague, an anthropologist, although his studies are not strictly scientific. Kiernan references this character in "Nor the Demons Down Under the Sea" as Dr. Jonathan Montague, an anthropologist who writes books on haunted houses.

Chapter Six

1. A more scientific concept, caloric theory, once explained combustion and heat.

Caloric was postulated as weightless fluid that flowed from bodies to other bodies. Roughly, as a fluid it flowed from warmer bodies to colder bodies and as a gas it passed through pores in solids and liquids. Scientists claimed to perceive caloric fluid as they felt it flow from cold to hot (see Churchland, *Scientific Realism* 16–18), but there is no such thing.

2. Many historians of science have documented the shifts over time in scientific understanding of the world and the universe. E.J. Dijksterhuis traced the development of the physical sciences from the ancient Greeks to Isaac Newton. A. d'Abro recounts the changes from Newton to Albert Einstein. J.L.E. Dreyer details the shifts in astronomy from the earliest cosmologies to the work of Johann Kepler (1571–1630). Thomas S. Kuhn studied the Copernican revolution and also wrote an overview of the nature of shifts in scientific explanations in *The Structure of Scientific Revolutions*.

3. Fritz Leiber argues Lovecraft's story works out the concept of hyperspace travel.

4. This scene recalls a similar one in "The Treasure of Abbot Thomas" (1904) by M.R. James, whose stories often feature an antiquarian scholar who discovers a horror through curiosity. Searching for a fabled cache of the disgraced abbot, the Rev. Justin Somerton finds an irregularity in the abbey stonework and unearths a cavity. He puts his arm into the hole and something falls around his neck. A cold face presses against his face and he feels "legs or arms or tentacles or something clinging" to his body (176).

5. "The Long Hall on the Top Floor" also forms part of Kiernan's *Low Red Moon* (2003).

6. *Unaussprechlichen Kulten* is the Latin analogue, created by August Derleth, for Robert Howard's *Nameless Cults*. *De Vermis Mysteriis* was Lovecraft's Latin version of Robert Bloch's *Mysteries of the Worm*, that Bloch created as an analogue to Lovecraft's *Necronomicon*.

7. St John's Catholic Church was the model for the church of the Starry Wisdom in Lovecraft's story, and it was razed in 1992.

8. *Caoimhe* is an Irish language feminine given name derived from *caomh* meaning "beautiful," or "precious." *Colleen* is the generic term for Irish women or girls, from the Irish *cailín*.

9. *Morrígan*, in modern Irish, or *Morrígu* (the Great Queen) is the war-goddess of Irish mythology. The *Morrígu* is present in all wars either as herself or as a carrion crow, so it is told (Squire 52).

10. Dinoflagellates are single-celled organisms and one of the most important components in plankton. Some are bioluminescent.

11. The story also illustrates the insignificance of humans in the face of an omnipotent natural event similar to that in Nathaniel Hawthorne's "The Ambitious Guest" (1835). In Hawthorne's tale, a family is swept away when: "Down came the whole side of the mountain in a cataract of ruin" (*Tales and Sketches* 306), as if we are mere specks in nature's indifferent destruction.

12. This scene is reminiscent of Virginia Woolf walking into the River Ouse with her pockets filled with heavy stones (see Panken 262). Kiernan mentions this action of Woolf in *The Drowning Girl: A Memoir* (2010), which is discussed in Chapter 7.

Chapter Seven

1. Of course, the name "Imp," suggests Edgar Allan Poe's story "The Imp of the Perverse" (1845). The raven image also alludes to Poe.

2. In *The Red Tree*, Sarah Crowe reminisces on her discovery of a trilobite specimen that turned out to be a new species.

3. Defining "modernism" and "postmodernism" is problematic. In *Modernism: Evolution of an Idea* (2015), Sean Latham and Gayle Rogers conclude that it is not possible to offer a tidy definition of modernism. Indeed, the term may be most fruitfully viewed as connotative ether than denotative (James and Seshagiri). Latham and Rogers offer a historiography of modernist studies, which suggests that modernism may be understood as a time bounded (for example first half of the twentieth century) artistic and cultural movement or as a continuing artistic and cultural ethos into the twenty-first century. Views of postmodernism are also complex. Bran Nicol contends that modernist works favor form, realism and innovation while postmodernist works use bricolage, mix styles and genres, integrate high and popular culture, while displaying the artifice of works. These differences are tentative and meant to portray a sense of the

difficulty in drawing an explicit boundary line

4. Kiernan's novels do not, I think, reflect other tenets of postmodernism. Alan Sokal and Jean Bricmont argue that part of postmodernism professes theories disconnected from any empirical test, and cultivates "a cognitive [...] relativism that regards science as nothing more than a 'narration,' a 'myth,' or a social construction" (1). This is not what Kiernan suggests in these two novels. She does not say that science is merely a narrative, a fiction in other words. This sense of postmodernism leads to a post-truth world of the alt-right. The universe may be indifferent to us and our comprehension of it. Our science is a self-improving human enterprise and we do not fully understand the universe, but there are facts we know about our Earth. Moreover, Western Science is increasingly recognizing other research strategies in understanding the universe, for example, Indigenous research methods (see Margaret Kovach and Shawn Wilson). The continuing struggle is to improve our understanding. There are facts; alternate facts are lies.

5. Kiernan uses confessional techniques similarly to Katherine Mansfield. Conrad Aiken called Mansfield's short stories "confession[s]" (490). But C.A. Hankin rightly argues that although Mansfield's stories exhibit confessional techniques and call upon her own experiences, her stories are psychological studies of the inner life of people. Mansfield reworked her own memories into such modernist stories as "Prelude," which was first published by Virginia Woolf's Hogarth Press in 1918 with the title "The Aloe." Many of Mansfield's characters are disillusioned and unfulfilled. She brings these characters to life by writing their thoughts, dreams and memories. Kiernan writes in a similar fashion but adds a character's encounter with something outside normal experience, of something beyond realistic perception.

6. See Henry Chadwick's "Introduction" to Saint Augustine's *Confessions*.

7. Moreover, a writer of a confession may deliberately alter the story of her life. So, confession is an uncertain path to self-understanding, as Michel Foucault argues (*Technologies of the Self*, 18). Foucault also points out the historically critical role of the confessor in confessing, that is, a confession in a sense demands the presence of someone who hears it and demands it and who then punishes or forgives (Foucault *History of Sexuality*, 61). This role in some modern confessional fictions is embodied in a double.

8. Autobiographical memories are those memories about personally experienced events, which extend beyond the factual description of past events to include "personal beliefs, thoughts, and emotions" (Vanderveren, Bijttebier, and Hermans).

9. See Freud's "Mourning and Melancholia" (1917). Nicolas Abraham also discusses melancholia. He sees it as the outcome of the loss of a loved one, followed by a period of unsuccessful mourning, and then the incorporation of the lost loved one inside oneself as a form of psychic tomb ("Notes on the Phantom").

10. Through a meta-analysis, Tom J. Barry, et al. confirmed that compromised memory specificity is an important cognitive consequence of trauma exposure. Their research supported that of J.M.G. Williams, et al. who found that reduced memory specificity might be associated with exposure to trauma.

11. The novels include doubles, unreliable narrators and self-confessing documents, for example, *The Red Tree* is presented as Crowe's found journal.

12. I have selected three consecutive pages in *The Drowning Girl: A Memoir* to illustrate the richness of the allusions. During one of Imp's psychotic episodes, her mind is deluged by such references. For example, on page 211 there are references to tenets of Catholicism (for example, transubstantiation); the Bible, Leviticus 17:11: "For the life of the flesh is in the blood"; Tiresias (who was turned into a woman for seven years—Imp's episodes obsess on seven); and quantum physics, along with black birds. On page 212 there are references to Hieronymus Bosch (c.1450–1516), the Medico Della Peste (the plague doctor mask with its long nose, supposedly to help protect from the plague), crows, and the number seven (which represents Imp's psychotic state). On page 213 Kiernan alludes to T.S. Eliot's (1888–1965) "The Wasteland" (1922); William Blake's "The Tyger" (1794); and "A Visit from St. Nicholas" (1823) by Clement Clarke Moore. It is likely that I have missed others on each of those pages.

13. Jean Paul Sartre's (1905–1980) confessional fiction *Nausea* (*La Nausée*) (1938) also starts with an "Editors' Note" saying the manuscript, a diary, was found among the papers of Antoine Roquentin. Fyodor Dostoyevsky's opening footnote to *Notes from the Underground* (1864) expresses the confounding nature of such notes. He says the author of the work and the work itself are fictitious.

14. "The Mermaid of the Concrete Ocean" was published by Kiernan in *Sirenia Digest* #43 (2009) and *Beneath an Oil-Dark Sea*. "Werewolf Smile" was published by Kiernan in *Sirenia Digest* #45 (2009).

15. Schizophrenia disorders develop through a combination of genetics, brain chemistry and environmental factors (see Austin, et al., 402–414).

16. Kiernan comments that both novels are "fictionalized autobiographies" ("Interview: Caitlín R. Kiernan"). Sarah Crowe's fictionalized short story collection, *Silent Riots*, begins with "The Ammonite Violin," a ghost story of Kiernan's. And the inserted story "Pony" (2006) was published by Kiernan in *Sirenia Digest #2* (2006), *Tales from the Woeful Platypus* (2007), and *Beneath an Oil-Dark Sea*.

17. Arbus was found in an empty bathtub with her wrist slit (Bosworth).

18. Sexton ended her life by carbon monoxide poisoning (Middlebrook).

19. Imp imitates Woolf when she picks up "acorns and chestnuts and rusty bottlecaps and puts them into [...] [her] pockets" (*The Drowning Girl* 143).

20. This is similar to Camus's complex use of water and suicide in *The Fall* (*La Chute* 1956). It also uses confessional techniques, with an unrelenting first-person narration by Jean-Batiste Clamence. A central event is his experience of a young woman, with black hair and dressed in black throwing herself into the Seine. He passed her on the bridge as she stared into the river. On the quay he heard a "body striking the water" (*The Fall* 70) and then repeated cries. He did nothing. Much later in life he hears that cry in the sea from an ocean liner. At the end of the novel he imagines the water "Brr ...! [...] so cold" (*The Fall* 147).

21. Abalyn is a gamer, or rather, a reviewer of video games. She represents the postmodern literary device of hyperreality or technoculture. In today's world we are deluged with information and images mediated by technology. Simulations and media determine our perceptions of reality and our understanding of the world. Guy Debord calls this the experience of spectacle which distorts reality into a false picture determined by controlling social and economic power. In *The Drowning Girl: A Memoir*, Kiernan overcomes this distortion of the spectacle by deploying the gamer as a concrete character in the novel, as a person living with reality, who helps Imp navigate the two (or more) perceptual worlds she inhabits.

22. There are so many writers who committed suicide, for example, John Berryman, Sylvia Plath, Hart Crane, Ernest Hemingway, Primo Levi, David Foster Wallace, and a multitude of others, that one could empirically question Kristeva's notion of the therapeutic value of writing.

23. This reference to a pocket alludes to Woolf, as does Imp's suggestion that her ghost story "might be my pocket full of stones" (*The Drowning Girl* 27).

24. Imp tells a fellow passenger on a city bus that her name came from a character in the novel, *Gone with the Wind*. The woman replies, "It's your name. You're a book" (*The Drowning Girl* 237). This suggests that through writing Imp may be able to heal and recreate herself, that is, she can write her own life story.

25. Another way of explaining the intergenerational effects from trauma comes from the field of epigenetics, which is "the study of heritable changes in gene expression that are not due to changes in the underlying DNA sequence" (Kellermann 34). The *transgenerational transmission of trauma* (TTT) refers to the finding that trauma affecting a first generation may be passed down to other generations. Youseff et al. found an accumulating amount of evidence of an enduring effect of trauma exposure passed to offspring transgenerationally.

26. Derrida writes the "specter is also, among other things, what one imagines, what one thinks one sees and which one projects—on an imaginary screen where there is nothing to see" (125). This could be the definition of a ghost.

Chapter Eight

1. John Rieder defines colonialism as the "process by which European economy

and culture penetrated and transformed the non-European world over the last five centuries, including exploration, extraction of resources, expropriation and settlement of land" (*Colonialism* 25). This definition encompasses the actions of European countries on non-European countries, but does not include all colonialism, for example, Ireland was colonized by England for centuries.

2. Many studies have documented the devastation of the indigenous populations of the Americas, for example, Russell Thornton provides evidence that millions of Indigenous peoples were killed in the Americas as a result of European colonization. Many studies have examined specific aspects of this devastation. For example, M.J. Liebmann, et al. provides evidence that the indigenous population of the Jemez Province in New Mexico declined by 87 percent following European colonization. In this circumstance the reduction occurred nearly a century after initial contact. It was not disease, but the arrival of missionaries that led to the devastation of the Indigenous population. That study provides evidence of the destructive impact of missionary activity in the Americas. More generally, an analysis (2016) of South American skeletons carried out by B. Llamas, et al. indicates that European colonization caused local mass mortality and a substantial loss of pre-Columbian lineages.

3. Ray Bradbury's *The Martian Chronicles* tells of the colonization of Mars but not all with happy results. David Mogen contends Bradbury's novel reworks the old frontier into a new tragic frontier which is being devastated by colonization (*Wilderness Visions* 38). Indeed, Mogen sees *The Martian Chronicles* as reanimating "the ghosts that haunt the American past" (*Wilderness Visions* 77). Several of Bradbury's stories in *The Martian Chronicles* work against the mythic spirit of progress. In "—and the Moon Be Still as Bright," the fourth expedition to Mars discovered that the Martians have been mostly killed by "Chicken pox" (66), which is, of course, an analogy to what happened to many American Indigenous peoples through European diseases, including small pox. The story also notes the destruction brought on the Aztecs. Fritz Leiber in "The Foxholes of Mars" captured the horror of a war against aliens on Mars, actually war in general, and the awful allure it has to some. Of course, on Mars there is a west, "for all planets share a west" (169), as if Leiber is mocking the myth of the American frontier. Of course, not all sf is a retelling of colonization. Gary K. Wolfe ("Frontiers in Space") argues the frontier is one of many themes in sf. But Wolfe seems more aware of the effects of colonization on American indigenous people. He suggests Le Guin's "The Word for World is Forest" reflects the real history of the impact of European intrusion on the Indigenous peoples of America (259) through its depiction of dominated alien cultures.

4. Recently Michio Kaku wrote about the possibilities and necessity of space colonization. Space travel he says is an insurance policy for human survival, but I guess not for all 7.44 billion. He sees terraforming of Mars into a habitable planet for humans fleeing Earth, but not managing climate change on Earth. It seems his fantasy arises from that of billionaires who are looking for more places to exploit. He talks about asteroid mining, which was a staple of sf based on the actual mining of indigenous land in the USA.

5. The red dwarf star, Gliese 876, has a confirmed planetary system and is about fifteen light-years away from Earth.

6. Hamilton's novella is the American West in space. It tells of extermination campaigns against the native populations on Mars and Jupiter, to open the planets' spaces and resources to people from Earth. On Mars, Martians are herded onto "reservations" (59) and the planet sprouts with mining operations.

7. A similar description appears in Kiernan's "In the Water Works (Birmingham Alabama 1888)." Chapter Four explores the mining folklore features of this story.

8. Named after Carl Linnaeus (1707–1778), the Swedish botanist and zoologist who is thought of as a founder of modern taxonomy and ecology.

9. In part Kiernan's story transforms Herman Melville's "The Tartarus of the Maids" (1855). Both portray women trapped in process optimization. But Melville's tale takes place at the beginning of the industrial age, while Kiernan's story is set in a tyrannical, near future and post-information age. Everything is portrayed through the eyes of a man in Melville's story, while a young woman's point of view dominates in Kiernan's story. In Melville's story, a paper mill

is a wonder of industrialization where the "human voice was banished" (74). Rows of pale-faced, young women tend the machines and lead blank lives until death. The language of Melville's story evokes images of hell, where the young women work in suffering, misery and dread, as they service the machines.

10. An early sf dystopian tale is E.M. Forster's "The Machine Stops" (1909). Forster is well known for such novels as *A Room with a View* (1908) and *A Passage to India* (1924). His sf short story depicts a future world of people living alone, each in an underground small room as if they are bees in cells. These are cubicals akin to that of Rarasha Kim. In Forster's future the machine runs everything. People are disconnected from personal contact, and everything is done through the workings and linkages of the machine. The story expresses the fear of technology alongside the fear of the British aristocracy of contagion from common folk.

11. Jacques Ellul characterizes this technological force in society as "technique." He uses this term to cover the strategies, systems and methods that drive the technological and mechanical world in all of its manifestations. It also means, for Ellul, the rule of the quantoid mentality that is behind those systems. He argues that people are forced or seduced into conforming to the needs of technology and that this rots away the individual person. Ellul might say it destroys the human spirit.

12. David Cloud, et al. document the multitude of psychological problems that arise from solitary confinement.

13. The title, "John Four," may allude to the Bible's John 4, wherein Jesus asks the Samaritan woman for water at the Well of Jacob. He speaks of the living water and the villagers act as a Greek chorus as do the pilgrims in Kiernan's story.

14. Religion, as Kristeva argues in the *Powers of Horror*, works to disassociate people from the reality of their decomposing body. Religion and other societal structures create a separation or wall between a person and the abject, helping to repress it. She contends that societal structures can be oppressive and inhumane, built up over time to isolate people from the abject. Art may be one way to face the abject and see one's true identity separate from the shrouds of culture and society.

15. The last two lines of the poem are: "And what rough beast, its hour come round at last,/Slouches towards Bethlehem to be born?" (Yeats, *Collected Works* 187).

16. The rough city on Mars is akin to that portrayed in C.L. Moore's "Shambleau" (1933), which seems patterned on the frontier of the American West. Moore's tale is an updated Medusa legend.

17. David E. Stannard estimates that between 30,000,000 and 60,000,000 African died as a result of the overall effects from the Atlantic Slave Trade (151).

18. Joseph Campbell describes seventeen stages of the hero monomyth distributed across the three phases.

19. In Thomas Pynchon's *V*, it is: "[e]veryone has an antarctic" (255).

20. This phrase is scribbled on a napkin by India Morgan Phelps in Kiernan's Novel, *The Drowning Girl: A Memoir* (6).

Chapter Nine

1. Ned Blackhawk identifies the term "Indian" as problematical (301). Following his practice, in this chapter the terms "Indigenous," "American Indian," and "Native American" will be used to indicate aboriginal communities in the Americas.

2. The demonization of the Indigenous peoples of America started early. Writing of the Indigenous peoples' religion, John Smith (1580–1631) claimed, "their chiefe God they worship is the Divell" (72). Cotton Mather (1663–1728) proclaimed America was once the "Devil's Territories" (14) and the devil resembled a Native American.

3. The fictional Cherry Creek is a recreated Denver. The real Cherry Creek flows through Denver and a neighborhood so named is near the center of the city.

4. Stimpson argues steampunk reflects the fantasies of pioneering the American West (21), for example by Frederick Jackson Turner (1861–1932), who called the American frontier "the meeting point between savagery and civilization" (32). The Indigenous peoples who lived on the other side of the frontier were the "savages," while pioneers (predominantly white male pioneers) were portrayed as strong, optimistic individuals leveraging opportunities of free land to bring freedom, democracy, and industry to the savage wilderness. But Kiernan

writes against that glamorized, Victorian myth expressed in many steampunk works. By doing that, Kiernan seems more tuned into such recent historians as Ned Blackhawk and Patricia Nelson Limerick, who document the inadequacy of Turner's thesis as it ignored the impact of Western industrialization and expansion on Indigenous peoples, the environment, and immigrants and downplayed the role of women in the American West.

5. Margaret Rose suggests an extended examination of the role of gender in steampunk fiction is needed (331n).

6. Dru Pagliassotti argues for this interpretation of *Infernal Devices* in his "Technology and Human Relationships in Steampunk Romance" (2013).

7. As noted in the Brief Biography, Kiernan studied geology and vertebrate paleontology and continues to work in the field.

8. Istvan Csicsery-Ronay, Jr., says *The Difference Engine* focuses on what is imaginatively possible not historically possible, as it avoids historical realism (108–09).

9. Liping Zhu describes in detail the forces leading up to the October 31, 1880, anti-Chinese riot in Denver. Following the invitation of Chinese laborers into Colorado in 1870, anti-Chinese sentiment grew though the decade, in part due to increasingly difficult employment conditions, but also due to racial differences. During the riot much of Denver's Chinatown was sacked by an angry white mob. Zhu argues the 1880 riot ultimately helped lead to the passage of the Chinese Exclusion Act of 1882.

10. Crowther points out the troubling nature of steampunk fans, who are not amputees, donning prostheses as part of their costumes, as it ignores the real obstacles faced by people with real physical challenges.

11. Harry Enton was also known as Harold Cohen.

12. The purported vanishing of the Indigenous peoples was promoted early in American writing, for example William Bradford (1590–1657) wrote that the land where the pilgrims settled was "some of those vast and unpeopled countries of America, which are fruitful and fit for habitation, being devoid of all civil inhabitants, where there are only savages" (26). Philip Freneau (1752–1832) tried to write Native Americans out of reality "to shadows," mere "delusions" (4). George Catlin (1796–1872) also wrote the American Indigenous peoples "are rapidly passing away from the face of the earth" (3). Jean M. O'Brien and Joshua David Bellin document how American literature has worked to distort the lives of American Indigenous people and to write them out of memory.

Conclusion

1. Ellen Moers defines the female Gothic as "work that women writers have done in the literary mode, that since the eighteen century, we have called the Gothic" (138).

2. On April 23, 2013 in her Online Journal, Kiernan said that she "learned to write reading William Faulkner, James Joyce, Virginia Woolf, Gertrude Stein, Joseph Heller, Kurt Vonnegut, Jr., William Blake, T.S. Eliot, Philip K. Dick, William S. Burroughs, Angela Carter, J.G. Ballard, and a hundred other authors" (Kiernan, "A vast light darkens my door [...]"). In addition, she says that "M.R. James, Arthur Machen, Angela Carter, Lovecraft, Poe, Shirley Jackson, and Algernon Blackwood" are writers who played a role in her becoming an author ("A Complex Web of Influence"). In her author's notes at the conclusion of several of her works, such as *The Drowning Girl: A Memoir*, *Black Helicopters* and *The Red Tree*, Kiernan acknowledges numerous authors who influenced the work.

3. S.T. Joshi (*Unutterable Horror*) has explored the influence of Poe and Lovecraft on Kiernan's fiction.

4. *Agents of Dreamland* surfaces as a discourse of chaos. That is, it is not about chaos, it is chaos. Kiernan paces the novel with timeslips through varying points of view, where everything seems conspiratorial and threatening. It imagines biological terror through descriptive passages that show abject, bodily revulsion. But more, the characters, who dissemble any notion of reliability, are lost and alone while they struggle against their awful discoveries. The novel is a science fiction, noir, dark, fantasy novel, grandly written by Kiernan. But it is a narrative without a set of instructions for assembly by readers, just like the world we live in. The final chapter of the novel appears like a parody of the old-fashioned wrapping-up chapter of novels, chiding anyone looking for a resolution, when there is no hope. Most

of all this novel evokes a disquieting feeling of dread in that Kiernanian manner of lonely panic under a too wide open sky.

5. This story is a rare "pure" Kiernan ghost story. As she remarks there are only a few others: "To This Water (Johnstown, Pennsylvania 1889)," "Angels You Can See Through" (2000), "The Madam of the Narrow Houses" (2007), and "As Red as Red" (Kiernan LiveJournal June 5, 2017). She also suggests that *The Red Tree* and *The Drowning Girl: A Memoir* (reviewed in Chapter Seven) are stories about hauntings.

6. "Andromeda Among the Stones" can also be seen as story of an innocent who is asked to be forever a redeemer. This is a theme in the Southern Gothic as exemplified by Flannery O'Connor and Eudora Welty. Some of Kiernan's fiction reflects aspects of the Southern Gothic, for example, *"Les Fleurs Empoisonnées: or, Dans le Jardin des Fleurs Toxiques"* which is reviewed in Chapter Two. Her novel, *Silk*, is also imbedded within that tradition. Alienated young people (musicians, so-called punks and street kids) wander the ragged streets and bars in Birmingham, Alabama. They are estranged from their families, but they form a quasi-family among themselves. The central character is Spyder Baxter, whose abused past returns to transform her family home into a decaying, gothic southern house, where her new family experience the horrors of that past.

7. This seems a deliberate reference to Arthur Machen.

8. In Charlotte Bronte's *Jane Eyre*, Rochester keeps his wife secretly locked in an attic apartment.

9. Flammarion's rage is akin to that expressed in Bruce Cockburn's song, "If I had a Rocket Launcher" (1984), which originated from his experiences in Guatemalan refugee camps.

10. S.T. Joshi says Kiernan has "risen to canonical status in weird fiction" (*Unutterable Horror* 706).

11. From a literary criticism point of view, study in her archives at Brown University will help reveal her compositional techniques, how stories evolve in the drafting process, and how her stories change in subsequent publications.

Bibliography

Primary Sources

For a comprehensive bibliography of Kiernan's works, see "Bibliography (1985–2015)" in *Beneath and Oil-Dark Sea: The Best of Caitlín R. Kiernan*. Vol. 2. (579–600).

Novels

Kiernan, Caitlín R. *Agents of Dreamland*. Tor, 2017
_____. *Beowulf* (film novelization). Harper Entertainment, 2007.
_____. *Black Helicopters*. Tor, 2018.
_____. *Daughter of Hounds*. Roc/NAL, 2007.
_____. *The Drowning Girl: A Memoir*. Roc/NAL, 2012.
_____. *The Five of Cups*. Subterranean Press, 2003.
_____. *Low Red Moon*. Roc/NAL, 2003.
_____. *Murder of Angels*. Roc/NAL, 2004.
_____. *The Red Tree*. Roc/NAL, 2009.
_____. *Silk*. Roc/NAL, 1998.
_____. *Threshold*. Roc/NAL, 2001.
_____. (As Kathleen Tierney). *Blood Oranges*. Roc/NAL, 2013.
_____. (As Kathleen Tierney). *Cherry Bomb*. Roc/NAL, 2015.
_____. (As Kathleen Tierney). *Red Delicious*. Roc/NAL, 2014.

Novellas

Kiernan, Caitlín R. *Black Helicopters*. Subterranean Press, 2013.
_____. *The Dry Salvages*. Subterranean Press, 2004.

Short Story Collections and Separately Published Stories

Brite, Poppy Z., and Caitlín R. Kiernan. *Wrong Things*. Subterranean Press, 2001.
Kiernan, Caitlín R. *A Is for Alien*. Subterranean Press, 2009.
_____. *Alabaster: Pale Horse*. Dark Horse, 2014.
_____. *The Ammonite Violin & Others*. Subterranean Press, 2010.
_____. *The Ape's Wife and Other Stories*. Subterranean Press, 2013.
_____. *Beneath an Oil-Dark Sea: The Best of Caitlín R. Kiernan*. vol. 2. Subterranean Press, 2015.
_____. "Blind Fish." *Searchers After Horror: New Tales of the Weird and Fantastic*, edited by S.T. Joshi, Fedogan & Bremer, 2014, pp. 83–101.

_____. *Confessions of a Five-Chambered Heart: Tales of Weird Romance*. Subterranean Press, 2012.
_____. *Dear Sweet Filthy World*. Subterranean Press, 2017.
_____. *The Dinosaur Tourist*. Subterranean Press, 2018.
_____. *Frog Toes and Tentacles*. Subterranean Press, 2005.
_____. *From Weird and Distant Shores*. Subterranean Press, 2002.
_____. *Houses Under the Sea: Mythos Tales*. Centipede Press, 2018.
_____. "John Four." *A Mountain Walked: Great Tales of the Cthulhu Mythos*, edited by S.T. Joshi, Dark Regions Press, 2015, pp. 493–501. (Also in *Houses Under the Sea: Mythos Tales*. Centipede Press, 2018.)
_____. "A Key to the Castleblakeney Key." *The Thackery T. Lambshead Cabinet of Curiosities*, edited by Ann and Jeff VanderMeer, Harper Voyager, 2011, pp. 225–240.
_____. *Tales from the Woeful Platypus*. Subterranean Press, 2007.
_____. *Tales of Pain and Wonder*. Gauntlet Books, 2000. [2nd ed., Meisha Merlin, 2002; 3rd ed., Subterranean Press, 2008; DIP, 2016].
_____. *To Charles Fort with Love*. Subterranean Press, 2005.
_____. *Two Worlds and in Between: The Best of Caitlín R. Kiernan*, vol. 1. Subterranean Press, 2011.
_____. *The Very Best of Caitlín R. Kiernan*. Tachyon, 2019.

Chapbooks

Kiernan, Caitlín R. *The Aubergine Alphabet (A Fourth Primer)*. Subterranean Press, 2017.
_____. *B Is for Beginnings*. Subterranean Press, 2009.
_____. *The Black Alphabet (A Primer)*. Subterranean Press, 2007.
_____. *Candles for Elizabeth*. Meisha Merlin Publishing, 1998.
_____. *The Chartreuse Alphabet (A Fifth Primer)*. Subterranean Press, 2018.
_____. *The Crimson Alphabet (Another Primer)*. Subterranean Press, 2011.
_____. *False/Starts II: Being Another Compendium of Beginnings*. Subterranean Press, 2015.
_____. *Highway 97*. Subterranean Press, 2006.
_____. *Mercury*. Subterranean Press, 2004.
_____. *Study for "Estate."* Gauntlet Press, 2000.
_____. *Trilobite: The Writing of Threshold*. Subterranean Press, 2003.
_____. *Waycross*. Subterranean Press, 2003.
_____. *The Yellow Book*. Subterranean Press, 2012.

Graphic Novels (hardcover)

Kiernan, Caitlín R. *Alabaster: Grimmer Tales*. Dark Horse Press, 2014.
_____. *Alabaster: The Good, the Bad, and the Bird*. Dark Horse Press, 2015.
_____. *Alabaster Wolves*. Dark Horse Press, 2013.

Scientific Publications

Kiernan, C.R. "*Clidastes* Cope, 1868 (Reptilia, Sauria): proposed designation of *Clidastes propython* Cope, 1869 as the type species." *Bulletin of Zoological Nomenclature*, vol. 49, 1992, pp. 137–139.
Kiernan, C.R., and Schwimmer, D.R. "First Record of a Velociraptorine Theropod (Tetanurae, Dromaeosauridae) from the Eastern Gulf Coastal United States." *The Mosasaur*, vol. 7, 2004, pp. 89–93.
Kiernan, C.R. "Stratigraphic Distribution and Habitat Segregation of Mosasaurs in the Upper Cretaceous of Western and Central Alabama, with an Historical Review of

Alabama Mosaur Discoveries." *Journal of Vertebrate Paleontology*, vol. 22, no. 1, 2002, pp. 91–103.

Schwimmer, D.R., and Kiernan, C.R. "Eastern Late Cretaceous Theropods in North America and the Crossing of the Interior Seaway." *Journal of Vertebrate Paleontology*, vol. 21, no. 3, 2001, p. 99A.

Wright, K.R. "The First Record of *Clidastes liodontus* (Squamata, Mosasauridae) from the Eastern United States." *Journal of Vertebrate Paleontology*, vol. 8, no. 3, 1988a, pp. 343–5.

Wright, K.R. "The Mosasaur *Clidastes*: The Specimens and New Problems." *Journal of the Alabama Academy of Science*, vol. 58, 1987, p. 99.

Wright, K.R. "A New Specimen of *Globidens alabamaensis* from Alabama." *Journal of the Alabama Academy of Sciences*, vol. 56, no. 3, 1985, p. 102.

Wright, K.R. "A New Specimen of *Halisaurus platyspondlylus* (Squamata: Mosasauridae) from the Navesink Formation (Maestrichtian) of New Jersey." *Journal of Paleontology*, vol. 8, no. 3, 1988c, p. A146.

Wright, K.R. "On the Taxonomic Status of *Moanasaurus mangahouangae* Wiffen (Squamata: Mosasauridae)." *Journal of Paleontology*, vol. 63, no. 1, 1988b, pp. 126–127.

Wright, K.R. "A Preliminary Report on the Biostratigraphic Zonation of Alabama Mosasaurs." *Journal of the Alabama Academy of Sciences*, vol. 57, 1986, p. 146.

Wright, K.R., and S.W. Shannon. "*Selmasaurus russelli*, a New Plioplatecarpine Mosasaur (Squamata, Mosasauridae) from Alabama." *Journal of Vertebrate Paleontology*, vol. 8, 1988, pp. 102–7.

Wright, K.R., and Varner, D. "Fleshing-Out the Mosasaurs (Squamata: Mosasauridae)." *Journal of Paleontology*, vol. 8, no. 3, 1988, p. A147.

Online Journal

Kiernan, Caitlín R. "And Far Away Behind Their Lines, the Partisans Are Stirring in the Forest." "Dear Sweet Filthy World: The Online Journal of Caitlín R. Kiernan." *LiveJournal*, 22 August 2012, greygirlbeast.livejournal.com/906780.html.

———. "Dear Sweet Filthy World: The Online Journal of Caitlín R. Kiernan." *LiveJournal*. (April 15, 2004–present). greygirlbeast.livejournal.com.

———. "Howard Hughes and the Day from Heck." "Dear Sweet Filthy World: The Online Journal of Caitlín R. Kiernan." LiveJournal, 15 April 2019, greygirlbeast.livejournal.com/2019/04/15/.

———. "Leeds, One Year Later." "Dear Sweet Filthy World: The Online Journal of Caitlín R. Kiernan." *LiveJournal*, 17 June 2014, greygirlbeast.livejournal.com/2014/06/17/.

———. "A Vast Light Darkens My Door, So I Cannot Cry." "Dear Sweet Filthy World: The Online Journal of Caitlín R. Kiernan." *LiveJournal*, 23 April 2013, greygirlbeast.livejournal.com/971407.html.

Interviews

Kiernan, Caitlín R. "*A Is for Alien* in 60 Seconds." Interview conducted by John Joseph Adams. *Tor.com*, 4 Feb 2009, tor.com/2009/02/04/a-is-for-alien-in-60-seconds/. Accessed 4 April 2018.

———. "Author Spotlight Caitlín R Kiernan." Interview conducted by Erin Stocks. *Lightspeed*, Issue 6, Nov. 2010, lightspeedmagazine.com/nonfiction/author-spotlight-caitlin-r-kiernan/. Accessed 4 June 2017.

———. "A Complex Web of Influence with Campbell, Kiernan, & Others Haunted Legends." Interview conducted by Jeremy L.C. Jones, *Book Life* Interview, 17 Feb. 2011, booklifenow.com/2011/02/a-complex-web-of-influence-with-campbell-kiernan-others-haunted-legends/. Accessed 2 April 2018.

———. "Exclusive Interview: Caitlín R. Kiernan on *After: Nineteen Stories of Apocalypse and Dystopia*." Interview conducted by Charles Tan. *SF Signal*, 6 Nov. 2012, sfsignal.com/archives/2012/11/exclusive-interview-caitlin-r-kiernan-on-after-nineteen-stories-of-apocalypse-and-dystopia/. Accessed 2 April 2018.

———. "Interview: Caitlín R. Kiernan." Interview conducted by Jude Griffin and Paul Descombaz. *Nightmare*, Issue 5, Feb. 2013, nightmare-magazine.com/nonfiction/interview-caitlin-r-kiernan/. Accessed 23 April 2018.

———. "Interview: Caitlín R. Kiernan on Weird Fiction: Deep Time Is Critical…" Interview conducted by Jeff VanderMeer. *Weird Fiction Review*, 12 March 2012, weirdfictionreview.com/2012/03/interview-caitlin-r-kiernan-on-weird-fiction/. Accessed 12 May 2018.

———. "Pernicious Thought Contagions: PW Talks with Caitlín R. Kiernan." Interview conducted by Charlene Brusso. *Publisher's Weekly*, 27 Jan. 2012, publishersweekly.com/pw/by-topic/authors/interviews/article/50378-pernicious-thought-contagions-pw-talks-with-caitl-n-r-kiernan.html. Accessed 18 April 2018.

Secondary Sources

Abbott, Carl. *Frontiers Past and Future: Science Fiction and the American West*. UP of Kansas, 2006.

Abraham, Nicolas. "Notes on the Phantom: A Complement to Freud's Metapsychology," translated by Nicholas Rand, *Critical Inquiry*, vol. 13, no. 2, 1987, pp. 289–90.

Abraham, Nicolas, and Maria Torok. *The Wolf Man's Magic Word: A Cryptonymy*. Translated by Nicholas Rand. U of Minnesota P, 1986.

Adams, John Joseph. "Prefatory Note to 'Ode to Edvard Munch.'" *By Blood We Live*, edited by John Joseph Adams, Night Shade Books, 2009.

Aiken, Conrad. "The Short Story as Confession." *Nation & Athenaeum*, vol. 33, 1923, p. 490.

Aldana Reyes, Xavier. *Body Gothic: Corporeal Transgression in Contemporary Literature and Horror Film*. U of Wales P, 2014.

Aldiss, Brian W. (with David Wingrove). *Trillion Year Spree: The History of Science Fiction*. Victor Gollancz Ltd., 1986.

Alexander, Amir. "Disorder Rules the Universe." Review of *The Quantum Moment: How Planck, Bohr, Einstein and Heisenberg Taught Us to Love Uncertainty*, by Robert P. Crease and Alfred Scharff Goldhaber, *New York Times*, 17 Feb. 2015, p. D3.

Ammons, Elizabeth. "Writing Silence: 'The Yellow Wallpaper.'" *The Yellow Wallpaper, Charlotte Perkins Gilman*, edited by Thomas L. Erskine & Connie L. Richards, Rutgers UP, 1993, pp. 257–275.

Arata, Stephen D. "The Occidental Tourist: Dracula and the Anxiety of Reverse Colonization." *Victorian Studies*, vol. 33, no. 4, 1990, pp. 621–45.

Arendt, Hannah. "Letter to Gershom Scholem." *Encounter*, vol. 22, no. 1, January 1964, pp. 51–56.

Armstrong, Karen. *A Short History of Myth*. Alfred A. Knopf, 2005.

Asma, Stephen T. *On Monsters: An Unnatural History of Our Worst Fears*. Oxford UP, 2009.

Atherton, Gertrude. *The Caves of Death and Other* Stories, edited by S.T. Joshi, U of Tampa P, 2008.

Augustine. *Confessions*. Translated by Henry Chadwick, Oxford UP, 1992.

Austin, Wendy, et al., editors. *Psychiatric & Mental Health Nursing for Canadian Practice*. 4th ed., Lippincott Williams & Wilkins, 2018.

Avatar. Dir. James Cameron. Century City, CA: 20th Century Fox, 2009.

Bibliography 175

Axthelm, Peter. *The Modern Confessional Novel.* Yale UP, 1967.
Azzouni, Jody. "A New Characterization of Scientific Theories." *Synthese,* vol. 191, no. 13, 2014, pp. 2993-3008.
Bacchilega, Christina. *Postmodern Fairy Tales: Gender and Narrative Strategies.* U of Pennsylvania P, 1997.
Bane, Theresa. *Encyclopedia of Fairies in World Folklore and Mythology.* McFarland, 2013.
Barry, Tom. J., et. al. "Meta-Analysis of the Association Between Autobiographical Memory Specificity and Exposure to Trauma." *Journal of Traumatic Stress,* vol. 31, 2018, pp. 35-46.
Barth, John. "The Literature of Exhaustion." *The Friday Book: Essays and Other Nonfiction.* G.P. Putnam's Sons, 1984, pp. 62-76.
Baudelaire, Charles. *Les Fleurs du Mal.* Translated by Richard Howard, David R. Godine, 1983.
———. *Paris Spleen.* Translated by Louise Varèse, New Directions Books, 1970.
Beard, David. "Introduction: A Rhetoric of Steam." *Clockwork Rhetoric: The Language and Style of Steampunk,* edited by Barry Brummett, UP of Mississippi, 2014, pp. xiv-xxxii.
Beauchamp, Tom L., and James F. Childress. *Principles of Biomedical Ethics.* 5th ed., Oxford UP, 2001.
Beizer, Janet. "Venus in Drag, or Redressing the Discourse of Hysteria: Rachilde's *Monsieur Vénus.*" *The Decadent Reader: Fiction, Fantasy and Perversion from the Fin-de-Siècle,* edited by Asti Hustvedt, Zone Books, 1998, pp. 241-266.
Belford, Barbara. *Bram Stoker: A Biography of the Author of Dracula.* Weidenfeld and Nicolson, 1996.
Bellin, Joshua David. *The Demon of the Continent.* UP of Pennsylvania, 2001.
Benton, Michael. J., et al. "Dinosaurs and the Island Rule: The Dwarfed Dinosaurs from Haţeg Island." *Palaeogeography, Palaeoclimatology, Palaeoecology,* vol. 293, no. 3-4, 2010, pp. 438-454.
Benton, Michael J. *When Life Nearly Died: The Greatest Mass Extinction of All Time.* Thames & Hudson, 2003.
Berlant, Lauren, and Michael Warner. "Guest Column: What Does Queer Theory Teach Us About X?" *PMLA,* vol. 110, no. 3, 1995, pp. 343-349.
Birmingham, Kevin. *The Most Dangerous Book: The Battle for James Joyce's Ulysses.* The Penguin Press, 2014.
Blackhawk, Ned. *Violence Over the Land: Indians and Empire in the Early American West.* Harvard UP, 2006.
Blackwood, Algernon. "The Wendigo." *Best Ghost Stories of Algernon Blackwood,* edited by E.F. Bleiler, Dover, 1973, pp. 158-89.
———. "The Wood of the Dead." *They Walk Again,* edited by Colin de la Mare, Dutton, 1942, pp. 453-469.
Blaylock, James P. "The Ape-Box Affair." *The Adventures of Langdon St. Ives.* Subterranean, 2008, pp. 11-25.
Bosworth, Patricia. "Diane Arbus, Her Vision, Life, and Death." *New York Times,* 13 May 1984, p. 41.
Botting, Fred. *Gothic.* Routledge, 1996.
Bowen, Elizabeth. *The Last September.* Jonathan Cape, 1948.
Bowser, Rachel A., and Brian Croxall. "Introduction: Industrial Evolution." *Neo-Victorian Studies,* vol. 3, no.1, 2010, pp. 1-45.
———. "Introduction: It's About Time: Reading Steampunk's Rise and Roots." *Like Clockwork: Steampunk Pasts, Presents, and Futures,* edited by Rachel A. Bowser and Brian Croxall, U of Minnesota P, 2016, pp. xi-xlvi.
Bradbury, Ray. *The Martian Chronicles.* Simon & Schuster, 2012.
Bradford, William. *Of Plymouth Plantation 1620-1647.* 1856. The Modern Library, 1981.

Briggs, Katherine. *The Fairies in Tradition and Literature*. Routledge Classics, 2002.
Broadmore, Greg. *Dr. Grordbort Presents: Victory*. Dark Horse, 2009.
Bronner, Simon, J. "The Analytics of Alan Dundes." *The Meaning of Folklore: The Analytical Essays of Alan Dundes*, Alan Dundes and Simon J. Bronner, Utah State UP, 2007, pp. 1–35.
Brooks, Peter. *Troubling Confessions: Speaking Guilt in Law and Literature*. U of Chicago P, 2001.
Brown, Charles Brockden. *Edgar Huntly; or Memoirs of a Sleepwalker*. Edited by Philip Barnard and Stephen Shapiro, Hackett Publishing, 2006.
Brown, Nicola. *Fairies in Nineteenth-Century Art and Literature*. Cambridge UP, 2006.
Bruhm, Steven. *Gothic Bodies: The Politics of Pain in Romantic Fiction*. UP of Pennsylvania, 1994.
Butler, Judith. *Gender Trouble: Feminism and the Subversion of Identity*. Routledge, 2006.
_____. *The Psychic Life of Power: Theories in Subjection*. Stanford UP, 1997.
Campbell, Joseph. *The Hero with a Thousand Faces*. 2nd ed., Princeton UP, 1968.
Camus, Albert. *The Fall (La Chute)*. Translated by Justin O'Brien, Vintage, 1956.
_____. *The Myth of Sisyphus and Other Essays*. Translated by Justin O'Brien, Vintage, 1955.
Canavan, Gerry. "Decolonizing the Future: Review of Jessica Langer's Postcolonialism and Science Fiction and Ericka Hoagland and Reema Sarwal's Science Fiction, Imperialism and the Third World." *Science Fiction Studies*, vol. 39, no. 3, 2012, pp. 494–499.
The Captured Bird. Directed by Jovanka Vuckovic. Osaka Sunset Pictures, 2012.
Carriger, Gail. *Prudence*. Orbit, 2015.
_____. *Soulless*. Orbit, 2009.
Carrott, James H., and Brian David Johnson. *Vintage Tomorrows: A Historian and a Futurist Journey Through Steampunk Into the Future of Technology*. Maker Media, 2013.
Carter, Angela. *The Bloody Chamber and Other Stories*. Vintage Books, 2006.
Castricano, Jodey. *Cryptomimesis: The Gothic and Jacques Derrida's Ghost Writing*. McGill-Queens UP, 2001.
Catlin, George. *North American Indians*, edited by Peter Matthiessen, Penguin, 1989.
Cevasco, G.A. *The Breviary of the Decadence: J.K. Huysmans's "A rebours" and English Literature*. AMS, 2001.
Cheng, Vincent J. *Joyce, Race, and Empire*. Cambridge UP, 1995.
Churchland, Paul M. "A Deeper Unity: Some Feyerabendian Themes in Neurocomputational Form." *On the Contrary: Critical Essays, 1987–1997*. Paul M. Churchland and Patricia S. Churchland. MIT Press, 1998, pp. 257–279.
_____. *Scientific Realism and the Plasticity of Mind*. Cambridge UP, 1979.
Clarkson, M.O., et al. "Ocean Acidification and the Permo-Triassic Mass Extinction." *Science*, 348, 10 April 2015, pp. 229–232.
Clayton, Jay. "Hacking the Nineteenth Century." *Victorian Afterlife: Postmodern Culture Rewrites the Nineteenth Century*, edited by John R. Kucich and Dianne F. Sadoff, U of Minnesota P, 2000, pp. 186–210.
Cloud, David, et al. "Public Health and Solitary Confinement in the United States," *American Journal of Public Health*, vol. 105, 2014, DOI: 10.2105/AJPH.2014.302205
Clute, John. "Edisonade." *The Encyclopedia of Science Fiction*, edited by John Clute and Peter Nicholls, St. Martin's Press, 1993, pp. 368–370.
Clute, John, and Peter Nicholls. *The Encyclopedia of Science Fiction*. St. Martin's Press, 1993.
Cornwell, Neil. "European Gothic." *A New Companion to the Gothic*, edited by David Punter, Blackwell, 2012, pp. 64–76.
Craft, Christopher. "'Kiss Me with Those Red Lips': Gender and Inversion in Bram

Stoker's *Dracula.*" *Speaking of Gender,* edited by Elaine Showalter, Routledge, 1989, pp. 216–242.

Crane, Tim. "What Is the Problem of Perception?" *Synthesis Philosophica,* vol. 20, 2005, pp. 237–64.

Crosby, Sara, L. "Beyond Ecophilia: Edgar Allan Poe and the American Tradition of Ecohorror." *Interdisciplinary Studies in Literature and Environment,* vol. 21, no. 3, 2014, pp. 513–525.

Crow, Charles L. *American Gothic.* U of Wales P, 2009.

Crowther, Kathryn. "From Steam Arms to Brass Goggles: Steampunk, Prostheses, and Disability." *Like Clockwork: Steampunk Pasts, Presents, and Futures,* edited by Rachel A. Bowser and Brian Croxall, U of Minnesota P, 2016, pp. 73–96.

Csicsery-Ronay Jr., Istvan. *The Seven Beauties of Science Fiction.* Wesleyan UP, 2008.

d'Abro, A. *The Evolution of Scientific Thought from Newton to Einstein.* 2nd ed., Dover, 1950.

Davis, Colin. "Hauntology, Spectres and Phantoms." *French Studies,* vol. 59, no. 3, 2005, pp. 373–379.

DeBord, Guy. *Society of the Spectacle.* Translated by Ken Knabb, Rebel Press, 1983.

Dejasu, Barry Lee. "Review of *Agents of Dreamland.*" *New York Journal of Books.* www.nyjournalofbooks.com/book-review/agents-dreamland. Accessed 15 May 2018.

de la Mare, Walter. "Introduction." *They Walk Again,* edited by Colin de la Mare, Dutton, 1942, pp. 9–32.

Delarue, Paul. "The Story of Grandmother." *Little Red Riding Hood: A Casebook,* edited by Alan Dundes, The U of Wisconsin P, 1989, pp. 13–20.

Dempsey, Aoife. "Hyphenated States: Joseph Sheridan Le Fanu and Settler Gothic Fiction." *Inspiring a Mysterious Terror: Years of Joseph Sheridan Le Fanu,* edited by Jarlath Killeen and Valeria Cavalli, Peter Lang, 2016, pp. 117–137.

DeRose, Christopher. "Caitlín R. Kiernan." *Scribes of Speculative Fiction II.* BearManor Media, 2015, pp. 26–31.

Derrida, Jacques. *Specters of Marx: The State of the Debt, the Work of Mourning, and the New International.* Translated by Peggy Kamuf, Routledge, 1994.

Di Filippo, Paul. "Paul Di Filippo Reviews Caitlín R. Kiernan." *Locus Magazine.* 22 March 2017, locusmag.com/2017/03/paul-di-filippo-reviews-caitlin-r-kiernan/

———. "Victoria." *Steampunk,* edited by Ann and Jeff VanderMeer. Tachyon, 2008, pp. 241–294.

Dickinson, Emily. *The Poems of Emily Dickinson,* edited by R.W. Franklin. The Belknap Press of Harvard UP, 2003.

Dijksterhuis, E.J. *The Mechanization of the World Picture.* Oxford UP, 1961.

Dillard, Annie. *Teaching a Stone to Talk: Expeditions and Encounters.* Rev. ed., Harper Perennial, 2013.

Dillon, Grace L. "Imagining Indigenous Futurisms: The Native Slipstream." *Walking the Clouds: An Anthology of Indigenous Science Fiction,* U of Arizona P, 2012, pp. 1–14.

Dimitriadis, Greg. "The Sexuality Curriculum and Youth Culture." *Counterpoints,* vol. 392, 2011, pp. 279–287.

Dodds, E.R. *The Ancient Concept of Progress and Other Essays on Greek Literature and Belief.* Oxford UP, 1973.

Doney, Scott C., et al. "Ocean Acidification: The Other CO_2 Problem." *Annual Review of Marine Science,* vol. 1, no. 1, 2009, pp. 169–192.

Dorney, John. "The Big House and the Irish Revolution." *The Irish Story.* 21 June 2011, www.theirishstory.com/2011/06/21/the-big-house-and-the-irish-revolution/#.WwwW Wi-ZP-Z. Accessed 11 August 2015.

Dreyer, J.L.E. *A History of Astronomy from Thales to Kepler.* 2nd ed., Dover, 1953.

Duhem, Pierre. *The Aim and Structure of Physical Theory.* Atheneum, 1962.

Dumbrava, Gabriela. "Mining Folklore: Beliefs and Taboos Related to the *Vâlva Băii*—The Fairy of Transylvanian Mines." *Revista Minelor/Mining Revue,* vol. 16, no. 3, 2010, pp. 29–31.
Dundes, Alan. *Analytic Essays in Folklore.* Mouton, 1975.
Dundes, Alan, and Simon J. Bronner. *The Meaning of Folklore: The Analytical Essays of Alan Dundes.* Utah State UP, 2007.
Dunn, Ben. *Steampunk Palin.* Antarctic Press, 2010.
Dvorak, Ken. "Foreword." *Steaming Into a Victorian Future: A Steampunk Anthology,* edited by Cynthia Miller and Julie Anne Taddeo, Scarecrow Press, 2013, pp. ix–xi.
Dyke, Gareth. "The Dinosaur Baron of Transylvania." *Scientific American,* vol. 305, no. 4, 2011, pp. 80–83.
Einstein, Albert. *Autobiographical Notes.* Open Court, 1996.
Eliot, George. 1871–1872. *Middlemarch.* Folio Society, 1999.
Eliot, T.S. *Four Quartets.* 1944. Faber & Faber, 1970.
Ellerby, Janet M. "Julia Kristeva and the Psychological Dynamics of Writing." *Journal for Expanded Perspectives on Learning,* vol. 3 (Winter), 1997–1998, pp. 32–39
Ellis, Edward S. *The Huge Hunter, Or, the Steam Man of the Prairies.* Project Gutenberg. www.gutenberg.org/files/7506/7506-h/7506-h.htm. Accessed 1 May 2018.
Fabry, Victoria J., et al. "Impacts of Ocean Acidification on Marine Fauna and Ecosystem Processes," *ICES Journal of Marine Science,* vol. 65, Issue 3, April 2008, pp. 414–432. doi.org/10.1093/icesjms/fsn048.
Fairhall, James. *James Joyce and the Question of History.* Cambridge UP, 1993.
Ferguson, Christine. "Surface Tensions: Steampunk, Subculture, and the Ideology of Style." *Neo-Victorian Studies,* vol. 4, no. 2, 2011, pp. 66–90.
Feyerabend, Paul K. *Against Method.* Verso, 1978.
_____. *Problems of Empiricism,* vol. 2, Cambridge UP, 1981.
Fiedler, Leslie. *Freaks: Myths and Images of the Secret Self.* Simon & Schuster, 1978.
_____. "Introduction." *In Dreams Awake,* edited by Leslie A. Fiedler, Dell, 1975, pp. 1–23.
_____. *Love and Death in the American Novel.* Criterion, 1960.
_____. *Tyranny of the Normal: Essays on Bioethics, Theology and Myth.* David. R. Godine, 1996.
Flannery, Eoin. "Irish Cultural Studies and Postcolonial Theory." *Postcolonial Text,* vol. 3, no. 3, 2007, pp. 1–9.
Ford, Jeffrey. "The Seventh Expression of the Robot General." *Steampunk III: Steampunk Revolution,* edited by Ann VanderMeer, Tachyon, 2012, pp. 317–324.
Ford, Richard. *Between Them: Remembering My Parents.* HarperCollins, 2017.
Forster, E.M. *Howards End.* Vintage, 1989.
Foucault, Michel. *Discipline and Punish.* Translated by Alan Sheridan, Vintage, 1995.
_____. *The History of Sexuality, Volume 1: An Introduction.* Translated by Robert Hurley, Random House, 1990.
_____. "Technologies of the Self." *Technologies of the Self: A Seminar with Michel Foucault,* edited by Luther H. Martin, Huck Gutman, and Patrick H. Hutton, U of Massachusetts P, 1988, pp. 16–49.
Fowler, Karen Joy. *What I Didn't See and Other Stories.* Small Beer Press, 2010.
Frayling, Christopher. "Introduction: Lord Byron to Count Dracula." *Vampyres.* Faber & Faber, 1991, pp. 3–84.
Freneau, Philip. "The Indian Burying-Ground." *The Little Book of American Poets: 1787–1900,* edited by Jessie B. Rittenhouse, Houghton Mifflin, 1915, pp. 3–4.
Freud, Sigmund. "Mourning and Melancholia." *The Collected Papers.* Vol. 4. Translated by Ernest Jones, The Hogarth Press, 1950, pp. 152–170.
Ganz, Shoshannah, "Margaret Atwood's Monsters in the Canadian EcoGothic." *EcoGothic,* edited by Andrew Smith and William Hughes, Manchester UP, 2013, pp. 87–102.

Garland-Thomson, Rosemarie. *Extraordinary Bodies: Figuring Physical Disability in American Culture and Literature*. Columbia UP, 1997.

———. "The Politics of Staring: Visual Rhetorics of Disability in Popular Photography." *Disability Studies: Enabling the Humanities*, edited by Sharon L. Snyder, Brenda Jo Brueggemann, and Rosemarie Garland-Thomson, Modern Language Association, 2002, pp. 56–75.

Garrard, Greg. *Ecocriticism*. 2nd ed., Routledge, 2012.

Gautier, Theophile. *One of Cleopatra's Nights*. Translated by Lafcadio Hearn, Wildside Press, 1999.

Gibson, William, and Bruce Sterling. *The Difference Engine*. Gollancz, 1990.

Gill, Jo. "Introduction." *Modern Confessional Writing*, edited by Jo Gill, Routledge, 2006, pp. 1–10.

Gilman, Felix. *The Rise of Ransom City*. Tor, 2012.

Gingrich-Philbrook, Craig. "Queer Theory and Performance." *Journal of Homosexuality*, vol. 45, no. 2-4, 2003, pp. 353–356.

Glotfelty, Cheryll. "Introduction: Literary Studies in an Age of Environmental Crisis." *The Ecocriticism Reader: Landmarks in Literary Ecology*, edited by Cheryll Glotfelty and Harold Fromm, U Georgia P, 1996, pp. xv–xxxvii.

Goddu, Teresa A. *Gothic America: Narrative, History and Nation*. Columbia UP, 1997.

Gomolka C.J. "Hushed Bodies, Screaming Narratives: The Construction of Trans-Identity in 19th-and 20th-Century French Literature." *Romanica Silesiana*, vol. 1, no.8, 2013, pp. 115–128.

Gould, Stephen Jay. *Time's Arrow–Time's Cycle: Myth and Metaphor in the Discovery of Geological Time*. Harvard UP, 1987.

Graves, Robert. *The Greek Myths*. Penguin, 1966–68.

Grewell, Greg. "Colonizing the Universe: Science Fictions Then, Now, and in the (Imagined) Future." *Rocky Mountain Review of Language and Literature*, vol. 55 no. 2, 2001, pp. 25–47.

Grimm, Jacob, and Wilhelm Grimm. *The Annotated Brothers Grimm*, edited by Maria Tatar, W.W. Norton, 2004.

Gruber, Nicolas, et. al. "Rapid Progression of Ocean Acidification in the California Current System." *Science*, vol. 337, 13 July 2012, pp. 220–223.

Hager, Lisa. "The Alchemy of Aether: Steampunk as Reading Practice in Karina Cooper's *Tarnished* and *Gilded*." *Like Clockwork: Steampunk Pasts, Presents, and Futures*, edited by Rachel A. Bowser and Brian Croxall, U of Minnesota P, 2016, pp. 179–197.

Haggerty, George E. *Queer Gothic*. U of Illinois P, 2006.

Halberstam, Judith. *In a Queer Time and Place: Transgender Bodies, Subcultural Lives*. NYU Press, 2005.

Hamilton, Edmond. "A Conquest of Two Worlds." *The Best of Edmond Hamilton*, edited by Leigh Brackett, PhoenixPick, 2010, pp. 48–75.

Hankin, C.A. *Katherine Mansfield and Her Confessional Stories*. MacMillan, 1983.

Haraway, Donna. "A Manifesto for Cyborgs: Science, Technology and Socialist-Feminism in the Late Twentieth Century." *The Cybercultures Reader*, edited by David Bell and Barbara M. Kennedy, Routledge, 2000, pp. 291–324.

Harris, Jason Marc. *Folklore and the Fantastic in 19th-century British Fiction*. Ashgate, 2008.

Harrison, Harry. *A Transatlantic Tunnel, Hurrah!* Faber & Faber, 1972.

Hawthorne, Nathaniel. "The Man of Adamant." *American Gothic Tales*, edited by Joyce Carol Oates, Plume, 1996, pp. 45–51.

———. *Tales and Sketches*. Library of America, 1982.

Heaney, Seamus. *Opened Ground: Poems*. Faber & Faber, 1998.

Hillard, Tom, J. "Gothic Nature Revisited: Reflections on the Gothic of Ecocriticism." *Gothic Nature*, vol. 1, 2019, pp. 21–33.

Hollinger, Veronica. "Contemporary Trends in Science Fiction Criticism." *Science Fiction Studies,* vol. 26, no. 2, 1999, pp. 232–262.
Holmes, Richard. "Preface." *The Gothic Imagination: Conversations on Fantasy, Horror, and Science Fiction in the Media* by John C. Tibbetts, Palgrave, 2011, pp. ix–xii.
Hopkinson, Nalo. "Introduction." *So Long Been Dreaming: Postcolonial Science Fiction and Fantasy,* edited by Nalo Hopkinson and Uppinder Mehan, Arsenal Pulp Press, 2004, pp. 7–9.
Hurley, Kelly. *The Gothic Body: Sexuality, Materialism and Degeneration at the Fin De Siècle.* Cambridge UP, 2004.
Hustvedt, Asti. "The Art of Death: French Fiction at the *Fin-de-Siècle*" the Decadent Reader: *Fiction, Fantasy and Perversion from the Fin-de-Siècle,* edited by Asti Hustvedt, Zone Books, 1998, pp. 10–29.
Huysmans, Joris-Karl. *Against Nature,* edited by Nicholas White and translated by Margaret Mauldon, Oxford UP, 1998.
———. *The Damned* (*Là-Bas*). Translated and edited by Terry Hale, Penguin, 2001.
Irwin, W.R. *The Game of the Impossible: A Rhetoric of Fantasy.* U of Illinois P, 1976.
Jackson, Jeremy D.C. "Ecological Extinction and Evolution in the Brave New Ocean," *Proceedings of the National Academy of Sciences (PNAS),* vol. 105 (Supplement 1), August 12, 2008, pp. 11458–11465. doi.org/10.1073/pnas.0802812105.
Jackson, Rosemary. *Fantasy: The Literature of Subversion.* Routledge, 1981.
Jackson, Shirley. *The Haunting of Hill House.* Penguin, 2013.
Jagoda, Patrick. "Clacking Control Societies: Steampunk, History, and the Difference Engine of Escape." *Neo-Victorian Studies,* vol. 3, no. 1, 2010, pp. 46–71.
James, David, and Urmila Seshagiri. "Metamodernism: Narratives of Continuity and Revolution." PMLA, vol. 129, no. 1, 2014, pp. 87–100.
James, M.R. *The Collected Ghost Stories of M.R. James.* Edward Arnold, 1931.
Jameson, Elizabeth. *All That Glitters: Class, Conflict, and Community in Cripple Creek.* U of Illinois P, 1998.
Jameson, Frederic. *Archaeologies of the Future: The Desire Called Utopia and Other Science Fictions.* Verso, 2005.
———. "Cognitive Mapping." *Marxism and the Interpretation of Culture,* edited by Cary Nelson and Lawrence Grossberg, U of Illinois P, 1988, pp. 347–60.
———. *The Political Unconscious.* London: Methuen, 1981.
Jamieson, H.E. "The Legacy of Arsenic Contamination from Mining and Processing Refractory Gold Ore at Giant Mine, Yellowknife, Northwest Territories, Canada." *Reviews in Mineralogy and Geochemistry,* vol. 79, no. 1, 2014, pp. 533–551. https://doi.org/10.2138/rmg.2014.79.12
Jarvis, Timothy. "The Weird, the Posthuman, and the Abjected World-in-Itself: Fidelity to the 'Lovecraft Event' in the Work of Caitlín R. Kiernan and Laird Barron." *Textual Practice,* vol. 31, no. 6, 2017, pp. 1133–1148.
Jennings, Dana. "Masters at Giving People the Creeps of the Kind That Keep on Creeping." *New York Times,* 24 October 2011, C4.
Jeter, K.W. "Letter to the Editor." *Locus: The Newspaper of the Science Fiction Field,* vol. 20, no. 4, 1987, p. 57.
John Hay Library. *Guide to the Caitlín Kiernan Papers 1970–2018.* Brown University, 2018. library.brown.edu/riamco/xml2pdffiles/US-RPB-ms.2017.008.pdf.
Jones, Gwyneth. *Deconstructing the Starships: Science, Fiction and Reality.* Liverpool UP, 1999.
———. "The Icons of Science Fiction." *The Cambridge Companion to Science Fiction,* edited by Edward James and Farah Mendelsohn, Cambridge UP, 2003, pp. 163–173.
Joshi, S.T. "Algernon Blackwood: The Expansion of Consciousness" *The Weird Tale,* by S.T. Joshi, Wildside Press, 1990, pp. 87–132.

Bibliography 181

_____. "Sculptures in Prose." Review of *The Ammonite Violin and Others*, by Caitlín R. Kiernan. *Dead Reckonings*, No. 9, Spring 2001, pp. 3–5.

_____. "A Slow-Moving Tsunami." Review of *Tales of Pain and Wonder*, by Caitlín R. Kiernan. *Dead Reckonings*, No. 4, Fall 2008, pp. 16–19.

_____. *Unutterable Horror: A History of Supernatural Fiction*, 2 vols., Hippocampus Press, 2014.

Jotterand, Fabrice. "At the Roots of Transhumanism: From the Enlightenment to a Post-Human Future." *Journal of Medicine and Philosophy*, vol. 35, no. 6, 2010, pp. 617–621.

Joyce, James. *The Critical Writings of James Joyce*, edited by Ellsworth Mason and Richard Ellmann, Viking, 1959.

_____. *Dubliners*. 1916. The Viking Press, 1961.

_____. *Finnegans Wake*. 1939. The Viking Press, 1955.

_____. *Ulysses*. 1922. Random House, 1946.

Joyce, P.W. *Old Celtic Romances*. C. Kegan Paul & Co. 1879.

Jubainville, H. D'Arbois de. *The Irish Mythological Cycle and Celtic Mythology*. Translated by Richard Irvine Best, Lemma Publishing, 1970.

Jung C.G. *Man and His Symbols*. Anchor, 1964.

_____. *Synchronicity: An Acausal Connecting Principle*. Translated by R.F.C. Hull, Princeton UP, 1973.

Kahneman, Daniel. *Thinking, Fast and Slow*. Farrar, Straus & Giroux, 2011.

Kaku, Michio. "The Moon, Mars and Beyond: It's Time for Your Journey to Begin." *The Globe and Mail*. 3 March 2018, www.theglobeandmail.com/opinion/to-the-moon-mars-and-beyond/article38160646/. Accessed 5 March 2018.

Kaye, Richard, A. "The New Other Victorians: The Success (and Failure) of Queer Theory in Nineteenth-Century British Studies." *Victorian Literature and Culture*, vol. 42, 2014, pp. 755–771.

Kellermann, N.P. "Epigenetic Transmission of Holocaust Trauma: Can Nightmares Be Inherited?" *The Israel Journal of Psychiatry and Related Sciences*, vol. 50, 2013, pp. 33–39.

Kerslake, Patricia. *Science Fiction and Empire*. Liverpool UP, 2007.

Kiberd, Declan. *Inventing Ireland: The Literature of the Modern Nation*. Jonathan Cape, 1995.

_____. *Irish Classics*. Harvard UP, 2001.

Kohlke, Marie-Luise, and Christian Gutleben. "The (Mis)shapes of Neo-Victorian Gothic." *Neo-Victorian Gothic: Horror, Violence, and Degeneration in the Re-Imagined Nineteenth Century*, edited by Marie-Luise Kohlke and Christian Gutleben, Rodopi, 2012, pp. 1–48.

Kotwasińska, Agnieszka Magdalena. *Transformations of the Family in Contemporary American Horror Fiction by Women*. 2016. Uniwersytet Warszawski (University of Warsaw). PhD dissertation. depotuw.ceon.pl/bitstream/handle/item/1898/Rozprawa-DoktorskaAKotwasinska.pdf?sequence=1.

Kovach, Margaret. *Indigenous Methodologies: Characteristics, Conversations, and Contexts*. U of Toronto P, 2009.

krijnen-kemp, rj. "Lilies Among the Thorns: An Overview of American Decadence." *Wormwood*, No. 17, 2011, pp. 48–62.

Kristeva, Julia. *Black Sun: Depression and Melancholia*. Translated by Leon S. Roudiez, Columbia UP, 1989.

_____. *Crisis of the European Subject*. Translated by Susan Fairfield, Other Press, 2000.

_____. "Dialogue with Julia Kristeva." *Parallax*, vol. 4, no. 3, 1998, pp. 5–16.

_____. *Powers of Horror: An Essay on Abjection*. Translated by Leon S. Roudiez, Columbia UP, 1982.

Kuhn, Thomas S. *The Copernican Revolution: Planetary Astronomy in the Developmental Western Thought*. Harvard UP, 1957.

_____. *The Structure of Scientific Revolution*. 2nd ed., U of Chicago P, 1971.

Lakatos, Imre. "Falsification and the Methodology of Scientific Research Programs." *Criticism and the Growth of Knowledge*, edited by Imre Lakatos and Alan Musgrave, Cambridge UP, 1972, pp. 91–196.

Lansdale, Joe R. "The Steam Man of the Prairie and the Dark Rider Get Down: A Dime Novel." *Steampunk*, edited by Ann and Jeff VanderMeer, Tachyon, 2008, pp. 107–145.

Laquer, Walter. "Fin-de-Siècle: Once More with Feeling." *Journal of Contemporary History*, vol. 3, no. 1, 1996, pp. 5–57

Latham, Bethany. "Mosasaurs." *Encyclopedia of Alabama*. 13 Oct. 2016, www.encyclopediaofalabama.org/article/h-2271. Accessed May 23, 2018.

Latham, Rob. "Biotic Invasions: Ecological Imperialism in New Wave Science Fiction." *The Yearbook of English Studies*, vol. 37, no. 2, 2007, pp. 103–119.

Latham, Sean, and Gayle Rogers. *Modernism: Evolution of an Idea*. Bloomsbury Press, 2015.

Lawrence, Jay. "The Perfect Girl." *Carnal Machines: Steampunk Erotica*, edited by D.L. King, Cleis Press, 2011, pp. 71–79.

Le Fanu, Joseph Sheridan. *Carmilla*, edited by Jamieson Ridenhour, Valancourt Books, 2009.

_____. *In a Glass Darkly*, edited by Robert Tracey, Oxford UP, 1993.

_____. *The Purcell Papers*. Arkham House, 1975.

_____. *Uncle Silas*. Dover, 1966.

Le Guin, Ursula K. "Introduction." *The Norton Book of Science Fiction*, edited by Ursula K. Le Guin and Brian Attebery, Norton, 1993, pp. 15–42

_____ "Nine Lives." The *Wind's Twelve Quarters*. Harper and Row, 1975, pp. 129–160.

_____. "A Non-Euclidean View of California as a Cold Place to Be." *Dancing at the Edge of the World: Thoughts on Words, Women and Places*. New York: Grove Press, 1989, pp. 80–100.

Leiber, Fritz. "The Foxholes of Mars." *The Best of Fritz Leiber*. Ballantine Books, 1974, pp. 169–178.

_____. "The Man Who Made Friends with Electricity." *The Black Gondolier and Other Stories*, edited by John Pelan and Steve Savile, e-reads, 2003, pp. 139–47.

_____. "Through Hyperspace with Brown Jenkin." *The Second Book of Fritz Leiber*. DAW, 1975, pp. 182–198.

Levy, Maurice. "'Gothic' and the Critical Idiom." *Gothick Origins and Innovations*, edited by Allan Lloyd-Smith and Victor Sage, Rodopi, 1994, pp. 1–15.

Lewis, Barry. "Postmodernism and Fiction." *The Routledge Companion to Postmodernism*. 3rd ed., edited by Stuart Sim, Routledge, 2011, pp. 169 -181.

Lewis, Simon L., and Mark A. Maslin. "Defining the Anthropocene." *Nature*, vol. 519, 12 March 2015, pp. 171–180.

Liebmann, M.J., et al. "Native American Depopulation, Reforestation, and Fire Regimes in the Southwest United States, 1492–1900 CE." *Proceedings of the National Academy of Sciences*, vol. 113, No. 6, 2016, pp. E696–704. DOI: 10.1073/pnas.1521744113.

Limerick, Patricia Nelson. *The Legacy of Conquest: The Unbroken Past of the American West*. Norton, 1987.

Llamas, B., et al. "Ancient Mitochondrial DNA Provides High-resolution Time Scale of the Peopling of the Americas." *Science Advances*, vol. 2, no. 4, 2016, DOI: 10.1126/sciadv.1501385.

Lloyd-Smith, Alan. *American Gothic Fiction: An Introduction*. Continuum, 2004.

Lorrain, Jean. *Nightmares of an Ether-Drinker*. Translated by Brian Stableford, Tartarus Press, 2002.

Lovecraft, H P. *The Annotated Supernatural Horror in Literature*. Rev. ed., edited by S.T. Joshi, Hippocampus Press, 2012.
_____. *At the Mountains of Madness and Other Novels,* edited by S.T. Joshi, Arkham House, 1985.
_____. *Dagon and Other Macabre Tales,* edited by S.T. Joshi, Arkham House, 1987.
_____. *The Dunwich Horror and Others,* edited by S.T. Joshi, Arkham House, 1984.
_____. "Notes on Writing Weird Fiction." *Collected Essays, Vol. 2: Literary Criticism,* edited by S.T. Joshi, Hippocampus Press, 2004, pp. 175–178.
_____. *Selected Letters,* 5 vols., edited by August Derleth, Donald Wandrei, and James Turner, Arkham House, 1965–76.
MacCormack, Patricia. "Baroque Intensity: Lovecraft, Le Fanu and the Fold." *The Irish Journal of Gothic and Horror Studies,* vol. 2, 2007, irishgothichorror.files.wordpress.com/2018/03/patrica-maccormack.pdf. Accessed 11 August 2019.
Mangan, James Clarence. *Selected Poems of James Clarence Mangan,* edited by Jacques Chuto, Rudolf Patrick Holzapfel, Peter van de Kamp and Ellen Shannon-Mangan, Irish Academic Press, 2003.
Marshall, Nowell. *Romanticism, Gender, and Violence: Blake to George Sodini.* Bucknell UP, 2013.
Masterman, Margaret. "The Nature of Paradigm." *Criticism and the Growth of Knowledge,* edited by Imre Lakatos and Alan Musgrave. Cambridge UP, 1972, pp. 59–90.
Mather, Cotton. *On Witchcraft.* Dover, 2005.
Maxwell, William. "The Actual Thing." *The New Yorker,* 3 Sept. 1938, pp. 16–17.
McCormack, W.J. *Sheridan Le Fanu and Victorian Ireland.* Oxford UP, 1980.
McDowell, Ian. "Caitlín R. Kiernan." *Encyclopedia of Alabama.* 21 Sept. 2016, www.encyclopediaofalabama.org/content/about-eoa. Accessed May 21, 2018.
McGrath, Patrick. "Transgression and Decay." *Gothic: Transmutation of Horror in Late Twentieth Century Art,* edited by Christopher Grunenberg, MIT Press, 1997. 159–153.
McHale, Brian. "What Was Postmodernism?" *Electronic Book Review,* 20 Dec. 2007, www.electronicbookreview.com/thread/fictionspresent/tense. Accessed 10 May 2018.
McKenzie, John M. "Clockwork Counterfactuals: Allohistory and the Steampunk Rhetoric of Inquiry." *Clockwork Rhetoric: The Language and Style of Steampunk,* edited by Barry Brummett, UP of Mississippi, 2014, pp. 135–176.
Melville, Herman. "The Tartarus of the Maids." *In Dreams Awake,* edited by Leslie A. Fiedler, Dell, 1975, pp. 69–82.
Middlebrook, Diane. *Anne Sexton: A Biography.* Houghton Mifflin, 1991.
Midgley, Mary. *Science as Salvation.* Routledge, 1992.
Miéville, China. "Afterword: Cognition as Ideology." *Red Planets: Marxism and Science Fiction,* edited by Mark Bould and China Miéville, Wesleyan UP, 2009, pp. 231–248.
_____. "Having a Higher Bar: Interview with James Carrott." *Vintage Tomorrows: A Historian and a Futurist Journey Through Steampunk Into the Future of Technology,* edited by James H. Carrott and Brian David Johnson, Maker Media, 2013, pp. 173–184.
Miles, Robert. *Gothic Writing 1750–1820.* 2nd ed., Manchester UP, 2002.
Miller, Cynthia J. "Airships East, Zeppelins West: Steampunk's Fantastic Frontiers." *Steaming Into a Victorian Future: A Steampunk Anthology,* edited by Cynthia Miller and Julie Anne Taddeo, Scarecrow Press, 2013, pp. 145–163.
Miller, Cynthia J., and A. Bowdoin Van Riper. "Blending Genres, Blending Times: Steampunk on the Western Frontier." *Journal of Popular Film and Television,* vol. 39, no. 2, 2011, pp. 84–92.
Miller, Cynthia J., and Julie Anne Taddeo. "Introduction." *Steaming Into a Victorian Future: A Steampunk Anthology,* edited by Cynthia Miller and Julie Anne Taddeo, Scarecrow Press, 2013, pp. xv–xxvi.

Miller, Elaine P. *Head Cases: Julia Kristeva on Philosophy and Art in Depressed Times.* Columbia UP, 2014.

Milner, Andrew. "Archaeologies of the Future: Jameson's Utopia or Orwell's Dystopia?" *Historical Materialism,* vol. 17, 2009, pp. 101–119.

Mogen, David. *Wilderness Visions: The Western Theme in Science Fiction Literature.* 2nd ed., Borgo, 1993.

Monaghan, Patricia. *The Encyclopedia of Celtic Mythology and Folklore.* Facts on File, 2004.

Moore, C.L. "No Woman Born." *Two-Handed Engine: The Selected Short Stories of Henry Kuttner and C.L. Moore,* edited by David Curtis, Centipede Press, 2005, pp. 483–532.

Moreland, Sean. "Introduction: Poe After Lovecraft, or Beyond the Flaming Walls of the World." *The Lovecraftian Poe: Essays on Influence, Reception, Interpretation, and Transformation,* edited by Sean Moreland, Leigh UP, 2017, pp. xv–xxiii.

———. "'Not Like Any Thing of Ours': Waking Poe and Lovecraft in Kiernan's *The Drowning Girl.*" *The Lovecraftian Poe: Essays on Influence, Reception, Interpretation, And Transformation,* edited by Sean Moreland, Leigh UP, 2017, pp. 211–234.

Morgan, Jack. *The Biology of Horror: Gothic Literature and Film.* Southern Illinois UP, 2002.

Mori, Masahiro. "The Uncanny Valley," translated by Karl F. MacDorman and Norri Kageki, *IEEE Robotics & Automation Magazine,* June, 2012, pp. 98–100.

Morrow, Bradford, and Patrick McGrath. "Introduction." *The New Gothic,* edited by Bradford Morrow and Patrick McGrath, Random House, 1991, pp. xi–xiv.

Murphy, Gerard. "Saga and Myth in Ancient Irish Literature." *Early Irish Literature,* edited by Eleanor Knott and Gerard Murphy, Barnes and Noble, 1966, pp. 97–142.

Nevins, Jess. "Introduction: The 19th Century Roots of Steampunk." *Steampunk,* edited by Ann and Jeff VanderMeer, Tachyon Publications, 2008, pp. 3–14.

Nicol, Bran. "Introduction: Postmodernism and Postmodernity." *The Cambridge Introduction to Postmodern Fiction,* edited by Bran Nicol, Cambridge UP, 2009, pp. 1–16.

Norris, Joel. *Serial Killers.* Doubleday, 1989.

O'Brien, Jean M. *Dispossession by Degrees: Indian Land and Identity in Natick, Massachusetts, 1650–1790.* Cambridge UP, 1997.

———. *Firstings and Lastings: Writing Indians Out of Existence in New England.* U of Minnesota P, 2010

O'Brien, Paul. "Hibernian Evanescence: Globalisation, Identity and the Virtual Shamrock." *Postcolonial Text,* vol. 3, no. 3, 2007, pp. 1–14.

O'Connor, Frank. *The Lonely Voice.* Macmillan, 1963.

Onions, Oliver. *First Book of Ghost Stories: Widdershins.* Dover, 1978.

O'Riley, Michael, F. "Postcolonial Haunting: Anxiety, Affect, and the Situated Encounter." *Postcolonial Texts,* vol. 3, no. 4, 2007, pp. 1–15.

Osemeobo, G.J. "The Role of Folklore in Environmental Conservation: Evidence from Edo State, Nigeria." *International Journal of Sustainable Development and World Ecology,* vol. 1, 1994, pp. 48–55.

Paglia, Camille. *Sexual Personae: Art & Decadence from Nefertiti to Emily Dickinson.* Yale UP, 1990.

Pagliassotti, Dru. "Technology and Human Relationships in Steampunk Romance." *Steaming Into a Victorian Future: A Steampunk Anthology,* edited by Cynthia Miller and Julie Anne Taddeo, Scarecrow Press, 2013, pp. 65–87.

Palmer, Paulina. *The Queer Uncanny: New Perspectives on the Gothic.* U of Wales P, 2012.

Panken, Shirley. *Virginia Woolf and the Lust of Creation: A Psychoanalytic Exploration.* State U of New York P, 1987.

Papers Relevant to Emigration to the British Provinces in North America: Presented to Both

Houses of Parliament, by Command of Her Majesty, February, 1847. William Clowes and Sons, 1847.
Parry, Benita. "The Institutionalization of Postcolonial Studies." *The Cambridge Companion to Postcolonial Literary Studies*, edited by Neil Lazarus, Cambridge UP, 2004, pp. 66–80.
Perschon, Mike. "Seminal Steampunk: Proper and True." *Like Clockwork: Steampunk Pasts, Presents, and Futures*, edited by Rachel A. Bowser and Brian Croxall, U of Minnesota P, 2016, pp. 153–178.
Peschel, Oscar. *The Races of Man and Their Geographical Distribution*. Appleton, 1894.
Poe, Edgar Allan. *Complete Poems*, edited by Thomas Ollive Mabbott, U of Illinois P, 2000.
Poteat, Tonia, et al. "Managing Uncertainty: A Grounded Theory of Stigma in Transgender Health Care Encounters." *Social Science and Medicine*, vol. 84, May 2013, pp. 22–29.
Powers, Tim. *The Anubis Gate*. Ace Books, 1983
Praz, Mario. "Introductory Essay." *Three Gothic Novels*, edited by Peter Fairclough, Penguin, 1986, pp. 7–34.
Priest, Cherie. "Addison Howell and the Clockroach." *Steampunk III: Steampunk Revolution*, edited by Ann VanderMeer, Tachyon, 2012, pp. 31–36.
_____. *Boneshaker*. Tor, 2009.
Punter, David. "Introduction: The Ghost of a History." *A New Companion to the Gothic*, edited by David Punter, Blackwell, 2012, pp. 1–9.
Pynchon, Thomas. *V*. HarperPerennial, 1999.
Rashkin, Esther. *Family Secrets and the Psychoanalysis of Narrative*. Princeton UP, 1992.
Resnick, Mike. *The Buntline Special*. Pyr, 2010.
_____. *The Doctor and the Kid*. Pyr, 2011.
Ridenhour, Jamieson. "Introduction." *Carmilla*. Valancourt Books, 2009, pp. vii–xxxv.
Rieder, John. *Colonialism and the Emergence of Science Fiction*. Wesleyan UP, 2008.
_____. *Science Fiction and the Mass Cultural Genre System*. Wesleyan UP, 2017.
Ringo, Allegra. "Why Do Some Brains Enjoy Fear." *Atlantic Monthly*. 31 October 2013, www.theatlantic.com/health/archive/2013/10/why-do-some-brains-enjoy-fear/280938/. Accessed 23 October 2016.
Robb, Brian J. *Steampunk: An Illustrated History of Fantastical Fiction, Fanciful Film and Other Victorian Visions*. Voyageur Press, 2012.
Robisch, S.K. *Wolves and the Wolf Myth in American Literature*. UP of Nevada, 2009.
Rose, Margaret. "Extraordinary Pasts: Steampunk as a Mode of Historical Representation." *Journal of the Fantastic in the Arts*, vol. 20, no. 3, 2009, pp. 319–333.
Rousseau, Jean-Jacques. *Confessions*. Translated by Angela Scholar, and edited by Patrick Coleman, Oxford UP, 2000.
Salomon, Roger B. *Mazes of the Serpent: An Anatomy of Horror Narrative*. Cornell UP, 2002.
Scarry, Elaine. *The Body in Pain: The Making and Unmaking of the World*. Oxford UP, 1998.
Schultz, Matthew. "'Arise, Sir Ghostus!': Textual Spectrality and Finnegans Wake." *James Joyce Quarterly*, vol. 49, no. 2, 2012, pp. 281–295.
Sedgwick, Eve Kosofsky. *Epistemology of the Closet*. UP California, 1990.
Sheedy, Alessandro. *Perverted by Language: Weird Fiction and the Semiotic Anomalies of a Genre*. 2016. University of Tasmania. Ph.D. dissertation.
Sellars, Wilfred. *Science, Perception and Reality*. Routledge & Kegan Paul, 1963.
Sexton, Anne. *The Death Notebooks*. Houghton Mifflin, 1974.
Shakespeare, William. *Cymbeline King of Britain*. *The Complete Plays: Romances*, edited by Stanley Wells and Gary Taylor, The Folio Society, 1997.

———. *The Most Excellent and Lamentable Tragedy of Romeo and Juliet*. *The Complete Plays: Tragicomedies*, edited by Stanley Wells and Gary Taylor, Folio Society, 1997.

———. *The Tragedy of Hamlet Prince of Denmark*. *The Complete Plays: Tragedies*, edited by Stanley Wells and Gary Taylor, Folio Society, 1997.

Sharma, Ramen, and Preety Chaudhary. "Common Themes and Techniques of Postmodern Literature of Shakespeare." *International Journal of Educational Planning & Administration* vol. 1, no. 2, 2011, pp. 189–198.

Shawl, Nisi. "Future Alternative Past: Players Gonna Play." *The Seattle Review of Books*. seattlereviewofbooks.com/notes/2019/02/14/future-alternative-past-players-gonna-play/. Accessed 1 May 2019

———. "The Steampunk That Dare Not Speak Its Name." *Tor.com*. 5 Oct. 2011, www.tor.com/2011/10/05/the-steampunk-that-dare-not-speak-its-name/. Accessed 1 May 2018.

Shiel, M.P. *Prince Zaleski and Cummings King Monk*. Mycroft & Moran, 1977.

Showalter, Elaine. *Sexual Anarchy: Gender and Culture at the Fin de Siècle*. Viking, 1990.

Siemann, Catherine. "The Steampunk City in Crisis." *Like Clockwork: Steampunk Pasts, Presents, and Futures*, edited by Rachel A. Bowser and Brian Croxall, U of Minnesota P, 2016, pp. 51–70.

Smith, Andrew, and William Hughes. *EcoGothic*. Manchester UP, 2013

Smith, Clark Ashton. *The City of the Singing Flame*. Timescape, 1981.

———. *The Dark Eidolon and Other Fantasies*, edited by S.T. Joshi, Penguin, 2014.

Smith, John. *The Generall Historie of Virginia, New England and the Summer Isles*, vol. 1, Applewood Books, 2006.

Smith, Susan. "Neither Normal Nor Human: The Cyborg in C.L. Moore's 'No Woman Born.'" *Femspec*, vol. 11, no. 1, 2010, pp. 11–26.

Sokal, Alan, and Jean Bricmont. *Fashionable Nonsense: Postmodern Intellectuals' Abuse of Science*. Picador, 1999.

Spurr, David. *The Rhetoric of Empire: Colonial Discourse in Journalism. Travel Writing, and Imperial Administration*. Duke UP, 1993.

Squire, Charles. *Celtic Myth and Legend Poetry and Romance*. 1905. Bell Publishing, 1979.

Stannard, David, E. *American Holocaust*. Oxford UP, 1992.

"Steampunk." *Brave New Worlds: The Oxford Dictionary of Science Fiction*, edited by Jeff Prucher, Oxford UP, 2007.

Stillman, Peter G. "Dystopian Critiques, Utopian Possibilities, and Human Purposes in Octavia Butler's *Parables*." *Utopian Studies*, vol. 1, no. 1, 2003, pp. 15–35.

Stimpson, Kristin. "Victorians, Machines and Exotic Others: Steampunk and the Aesthetic of Empire." *Clockwork Rhetoric: The Language and Style of Steampunk*, edited by Barry Brummett, UP of Mississippi, 2014, pp. 19–37.

Stock, Amanda. "Battle of the Sexes: How Steampunk Should Be Informed by Feminism. *Gatehouse Gazette* Issue 15, Nov. 2010, Www.ottens.co.uk/gatehouse/Gazette%20-%2015.pdf. Accessed 1 May 2018.

Stoker, Bram. *Dracula*, edited by Nina Auerbach and David J. Skal, Norton, 1997.

———. "Dracula's Guest." *Dracula*, edited by Nina Auerbach and David J. Skal, Norton, 1997, pp. 350–360.

Suggs, George G., Jr. *Colorado's War on Militant Unionism: James H. Peabody and the Western Federation of Miners*. Wayne State UP, 1972.

Sullivan, Jack. *Elegant Nightmares: The English Ghost Story from Le Fanu to Blackwood*. Ohio UP, 1978.

Suvin, Darko. *Metamorphoses of Science Fiction: On the Poetics and History of a Literary Genre*. Yale UP, 1979.

Tabas, Brad. "Dark Places : Ecology, Place, and the Metaphysics of Horror Fiction." *Miranda*, vol. 11, 2015, pp. 1–17. DOI: 10.4000/miranda.7012

Tatar, Maria. *The Hard Facts of the Grimm Fairy Tales*. 2nd ed., Princeton UP, 2019.
———. "Reading the Grimms' *Children's Stories and Household Tales*: Origins and Cultural Effect of the Collection." Grimm, Jacob and Wilhelm. *The Annotated Brothers Grimm*, edited by Maria Tatar, W.W. Norton, 2004, pp. xxvii–xlvii.
Taylor, Mary Anne. "Liberation and a Corset: Examining False Feminism in Steampunk." *Clockwork Rhetoric: The Language and Style of Steampunk*, edited by Barry Brummett, UP of Mississippi, 2014, pp. 38–58.
Tedescui, Victoria. "How 19th Century Fairy Tales Expressed Anxieties About Ecological Devastation." *The Conversation*, March 22, 2017. http://theconversation.com/how-19th-century-fairy-tales-expressed-anxieties-about-ecological-devastation-73137. Accessed 5 November 2019.
Thornton, Russell. *American Indian Holocaust and Survival: A Population History Since 1492*. UP of Oklahoma, 1990.
Tibbetts, John C. *The Gothic Imagination: Conversations on Fantasy, Horror, and Science Fiction in the Media*. Palgrave, 2011.
Toulmin, Stephen. "Does the Distinction Between Normal and Revolutionary Science Hold Water?" *Criticism and the Growth of Knowledge*, edited by Imre Lakatos and Alan Musgrave, Cambridge UP, 1972, pp. 38–48.
Tracey, Robert. "Introduction." *In a Glass Darkly*, edited by Robert Tracey, Oxford UP, 1993, pp. vii–xxviii.
"Transhumanist Declaration." *Humanity+*. humanityplus.org/philosophy/transhumanist-declaration/. Accessed 5 September 2017.
Trexler, Adam, and Adeline Johns-Putra. "Climate Change in Literature and Literary Criticism." *WIREs Climate Change*, vol. 2, 2011, pp. 185–200.
Trussoni, D. "Horror: Nothing Clarifies Your Relationship to Other People Quite Like a Chainsaw Massacre." *The New York Times Book Review*, 31 March 2019, pp. 14–15.
Turner, Frederick Jackson. "The Significance of the Frontier in American Historiography." *Rereading Frederick Jackson Turner*, edited by John Mack Faragher, Yale UP, 1998, pp. 31–60.
U.S. Fish and Wildlife Service. "Natural Resource Damage Assessment and Restoration Program: North Cape Oil Spill, Rhode Island." October 2005. www.fws.gov/newengland/pdfs/North%20Cape.pdf. Accessed 17 March 2015.
VanderMeer, Jeff. *The Steampunk Bible*. Abrams Image: 2011.
Vanderveren, Elien, et al. "The Importance of Memory Specificity and Memory Coherence for the Self: Linking Two Characteristics of Autobiographical Memory." *Frontiers in Psychology*, vol. 8, 2017, pp. 2250.
Veliki, Martina Domines. "Jean-Jacques Rousseau's Dramatization of the Self." *Studia Romanica et Anglica*, vol. LIV, 2009, pp. 307–327.
Villiers de l'Isle-Adam. *L'Ève Future (The Future Eve)*. *The Decadent Reader: Fiction, Fantasy and Perversion from the Fin-de-Siècle*, edited by Asti Hustvedt, Zone Books, 1998, pp. 520–750.
Walpole, Horace. *The Castle of Otranto: A Gothic Story*, edited by Nick Groom, Oxford UP, 2014.
Warner, Michael. "Introduction: Fear of a Queer Planet." *Social Text*, vol. 9, no. 29, 1991, pp. 3–17.
Watkins, John. "Against 'Normal Science.'" *Criticism and the Growth of Knowledge*, edited by Imre Lakatos and Alan Musgrave, Cambridge UP, 1972, pp. 25–38.
Weakland, Joseph, and Shaun Duke. "Out of Control: Disrupting Technological Mastery in Michael Moorcock's the Warlord of the Air and K.W. Jeter's Infernal Devices." *Like Clockwork: Steampunk Pasts, Presents, and Futures*, edited by Rachel A. Bowser and Brian Croxall, U of Minnesota P, 2016, pp. 199–218.
Weida, Jaime. *"I Have Heard the Mermaids Singing, Each to Each": Modernism, Science,*

Mythology, and Feminist Narratives. 2013. City University of New York. Ph.D. dissertation.

Weir, David. *Decadent Culture in the United States: Art and Literature Against the American Grain, 1890–1926*. State U of New York P, 2008.

Westerfeld, Scott. *Goliath*. Simon Pulse, 2011.

Westfall, Aundrea. "Pterosaurs." *Encyclopedia of Alabama*. 21 Nov. 2016, www.encyclopediaofalabama.org/article/h-3664. Accessed 23 May 2018.

Weston, Ruth D. *Gothic Traditions and Narrative Techniques in the Fiction of Eudora Welty*. Louisiana State UP, 1994.

"What Is Folklore?" *American Folklore Society*, www.afsnet.org/page/WhatIsFolklore. Accessed 12 May 2019.

Williams, David. *Confessional Fictions: A Portrait of the Artist in the Canadian Novel*. U of Toronto P, 1991.

Williams J.M.G., et al. "The Specificity of Autobiographical Memory and Imageability of the Future." *Memory & Cognition, Vol.* 24, 1996, pp. 116–125.

Wilson, Sharon Rose. *Margaret Atwood's Fairy Tale Sexual Politics*. ECW Press, 1993.

Wilson, Shawn. *Research Is Ceremony: Indigenous Research Methods*. Fernwood, 2008.

Wilt, Judith. *Ghosts of the Gothic*. Princeton UP, 1980.

Windling, Terri. "The Path of Needles or Pins: Little Red Riding Hood." *CUNY Composers.* cunycomposers.wikifoundry.com/page/%22Path+of+Needles+or+Pins%22+by+Terry+Windling+%28critical+article%29. Accessed 23 May 2018.

Wisker, Gina. "Speaking the Unspeakable: Women, Sex, and the Dismorphmythic in Lovecraft, Angela Carter, Caitlín R. Kiernan, and Beyond." *New Directions in Supernatural Horror Literature, the Critical Influence of H.P. Lovecraft,* edited by Sean Moreland, Palgrave Macmillan, 2018, pp. 209–234.

Wittgenstein, Ludwig. *Tractatus Logico-Philosophicus*. Translated by D.F. Pears and B.F. McGuiness, Routledge Classics, 2001.

Wolf, Leonard. *A Dream of Dracula: In Search of the Living Dead*. Little, Brown and Company, 1972.

Wolfe, Gary K. "Frontiers in Space." *The Frontier Experience and the American Dream,* edited by David Mogen, Mark Busby, and Paul Bryant, Texas A & M UP, 1989, pp. 248–263.

_____. "Review: *The Very Best of Caitlín R. Kiernan.*" *Locus,* 29 April 2019, locusmag.com/2019/04/gary-k-wolfe-reviews-the-very-best-of-caitlin-r-kiernan-by-caitlin-r-kiernan/?fbclid=IwAR04T_NC8bOsU2br8opEu1CZrTqJiCvE7DW4SQMqiDDl6Fqv_CUVdEpBQGw. Accessed 23 June 2019.

Yeats, William Butler. *The Collected Works of W.B. Yeats I: The Poems*. Macmillan, 1989.

_____. *Fairy and Folk Tales of the Irish Peasantry: A Treasury of Irish Myth, Legend and Folklore,* edited by Claire Booss, Gramercy Books, 1986.

_____. *Writings on Irish Folklore, Legend and Myth,* edited by Robert Welch, Penguin, 1993.

Yoder, Don, and Thomas E. Graves. *Hex Signs: Pennsylvania Dutch Barn Symbols and Their Meaning*. 2nd ed., Stackpole Books, 2000.

Youssef, N.A., et al. "The Effects of Trauma, with or Without PTSD, on the Transgenerational DNA Methylation Alterations in Human Offsprings." *Brain Science,* vol. 8, no. 5, 2018, p. 83.

Zipes, Jack. *The Trials and Tribulations of Little Red Riding Hood*. 2nd ed., Routledge, 1993.

Zhu, Liping. *The Road to Chinese Exclusion: The Denver Riot, 1880 Elections, and the Rise of the West*. U of Kansas P, 2013.

Index

A Is for Alien (Kiernan) 13, 35, 54–58, 117, 125–130, 132
À rebours (Huysmans) 36, 39, 41
Abbott, Carl 17, 118, 122
abhuman 70–71, 75; Kelly Hurley on 63, 161*ch*4*n*1
abjection 11, 46–48, 57, 60, 70, 160*ch*3*n*2, 168*n*14
Abraham, Nicolas 73, 113, 165*n*9
"The Actual Thing" (Maxwell) 46
"Addison Howell and the Clockroach" (Priest) 145
The Adventures of Alyx (Russ) 12
"Afterword: Cognition as Ideology" (Miéville) 12
Against Method (Feyerabend) 80
Agents of Dreamland (Kiernan) 6, 8, 152, 169*n*4
Aiken, Conrad 165*n*5
Alabaster: Wolves (Kiernan) 6, 155
Aldana Reyes, Xavier 48, 51
Aldiss, Brian 13, 117
Alexander, Amir 90
"The Ambitious Guest" (Hawthorne) 164*n*10
Ammonite (Griffith) 129
"The Ammonite Violin (Murder Ballad No. 4)" (Kiernan) 56–57, 153, 162*n*17, 166*n*16
Ammons, Elizabeth 124
"Andromeda Among the Stones" (Kiernan) 154–155, 163*n*10
Anthropocene 64, 75, 124–125; *see also* climate change
anthro-technological bodies 48, 57–60
"The Ape-Box Affair" (Blaylock) 136
The Ape's Wife and Other Stories (Kiernan) 7
apocalypse 126–127, 128, 137; and steampunk 146–148
"Apokatastasis" (Kiernan) 20, 162*n*14
Arata, Stephen D. 25, 118–119
Archaeologies of the Future (Jameson) 127, 131
Arendt, Hannah 100, 124
Armstrong, Karen 62, 75
"As Red as Red" (Kiernan) 70, 86, 162*n*14
Atlantic slave trade 127, 168*n*17
Atwood, Margaret 71, 160*n*4, 162*n*13

Avatar (Cameron) 120
Axthelm, Peter 106–107
Azzouni, Jody 163*n*4

Bacchilega, Christina 61–62
Bane, Theresa 73–74
Barry, Tom. J. 165*n*10
Barth, John 148
Là-Bas (Huysmans) 44
Baudelaire, Charles 32–33, 37–38, 44
Beard, David 134, 136, 148
Beauchamp, Tom L. 60
"The Beckoning Fair One" (Onions) 102
"The Bed of Appetite" (Kiernan) 156–157, 162*n*14
Beizer, Janet 35
Belford, Barbara 159*n*5
Bellin, Joshua David 169*n*12
Beneath an Oil-Dark Sea: The Best of Caitlín R. Kiernan, Volume 2 (Kiernan) 7
Benton, Michael J. 82, 84
"Berenice" (Poe) 35
Berlant, Lauren 33
"Between the Flatirons and the Deep Green Sea" (Kiernan) 4, 117
Between Them: Remembering my Parents (Ford) 107–108
biological horror 46, 121, 129, 156; Lovecraft on 42, 46, 150, 160*ch*3*n*1
Birmingham, Kevin 83
"The Birth-mark" (Hawthorne) 87
Black Helicopters (Kiernan) 6, 20, 117–118, 152
"Black Ships Seen South of Heaven" (Kiernan) 120–121
Black Sun (Kristeva) 57
Blackhawk, Ned 118, 168*n*1
Blackwood, Algernon 86, 98, 111, 150, 169*n*2
Blaylock, James P. 134, 136
"Blind Fish" (Kiernan) 59, 82
Blood Oranges (Kiernan) 6
The Bloody Chamber and Other Stories (Carter) 71
"The Bone's Prayer" (Kiernan) 76, 83–84
Boneshaker (Priest) 145
Botting, Fred 10–11

Bowen, Elizabeth 24
Bowser, Rachel A. 134, 136, 141, 147
Bradbury, Ray 120, 122, 167*n*3
Bradbury Weather (Kiernan) 117, 128–130, 132
Bradford, William 169*n*12
Bram Stoker Award 1, 6
"Breakfast in the House of the Rising Sun (Murder Ballad No. 1)" (Kiernan) 36
Brewster, David 78
Bricmont, Jean 15, 78, 164*ch*7*n*4
"Bridle" (Kiernan) 69–70, 162*n*11
Briggs, Katherine 69
Broadmore, Greg 136
Bronner, Simon J. 61
Brooks, Peter 106
Brown, Charles Brockden 11, 111, 150
Brown University 7, 22
Bruhm, Steven 47–49
The Buntline Special (Resnick) 146
Butler, Judith 15; on gender 34, 37, 55; on subjection 50, 60

"The Call of Cthulhu" (Lovecraft) 92
Campbell, Joseph 127–128
Camus, Albert 110, 166*n*20
Canavan, Gerry 118
Candles for Elizabeth (Kiernan) 31
"Canon Alberic's Scrap-Book" (James) 74
"A Canvass for Incoherent Arts" (Kiernan) 50–51
The Captured Bird (Vuckovic) 160*ch*3*n*2
Carriger, Gail 139, 142
Carter, Angela 71, 150
The Castle of Otranto (Walpole) 56, 150
Castricano, Jodey 155
Catlin, George 169*n*12
"The Caves of Death" (Atherton) 88
Chambers, Robert W. 37
"*La chambre double*" (Baudelaire) 43
"*Une charogne*" (Baudelaire) 44
Chenda and the Airship Brofman (Bush) 141–142
Cheng, Vincent J. 25
Cherry Bomb (Kiernan) 6
"The Child That Went with the Fairies" (Le Fanu) 21
Childress, James F. 60
"A Child's Guide to the Hollow Hills" (Kiernan) 21
Churchland, Paul M. 16, 81, 91, 101, 163*n*5
The City of the Singing Flame (Smith) 42
Clayton, Jay 141
climate change 62–65, 73, 78, 84, 124, 127, 132, 155, 163*n*9, 167*n*4; *see also* Anthropocene
"*Le Club des Hachichins*" (Gautier) 42
Clute, John 12, 135
"Cognitive Mapping" (Jameson) 119
"The Collector of Bones" (Kiernan) 36
"The Collier's Venus (1893)" (Kiernan) 137, 139–142

Colonialism and the Emergence of Science Fiction (Rieder) 12, 119
colonization 119, 159*n*9, 166*n*1; of the Americas 16, 25, 118, 134, 136, 146–148; and genocide 133, 145; of Ireland 19–20, 23–24, 28, 30–31, 159*ch*1*n*1; of outer space 58, 130; science fiction glorifying 17, 120; trauma of 121; *see also* imperialism
"Concerning Attrition and Severance" (Kiernan) 49–51, 90, 163*n*14
Confessions (Rousseau) 106
Confessions (St. Augustine) 106
"A Conquest of Two Worlds" (Hamilton) 122, 167*n*6
Cornwell, Neil 10
Craft, Christopher 160*n*5
Crane, Tim 93
The Creature from the Black Lagoon (Arnold) 79
Crisis of the European Subject (Kristeva) 124
The Critical Writings of James Joyce 30
Crosby, Sara, L. 62–63
Crow, Charles L. 11
Crowther, Kathryn 7, 53, 143, 169*n*10
Croxall, Brian 134, 136, 141, 147
"The Cryomancer's Daughter (Murder Ballad No. 3)" 152
Csicsery-Ronay, Istvan, Jr. 120, 169*n*8
cyborg 42, 53, 59, 121, 130–131; Garland-Thomson on 54, 161*ch*3*n*5; Haraway on 54, 161*ch*3*n*5
Cymbeline King of Britain (Shakespeare) 84

"Dark Rosaleen" (Mangan) 26–27
Darwin, Charles 82, 140–141
"Daughter Dear Desmodus" (Kiernan) 51–52
Daughter of Hounds (Kiernan) 5
Davis, Colin 113–115
"The Death of Halpin Frayser" (Bierce) 41
decadence 49, 57, 155; *fin de siècle* 14, 32–44, 138, 139
Deconstructing the Starships (Jones) 13
Dejasu, Barry Lee 8
de la Mare, Walter 90
Dempsey, Aoife 20, 23
"Derma Sutra (1891)" (Kiernan) 36, 43, 137–139, 142, 152
Derrida, Jacques 113–114, 155, 166*n*26
"Dialogue with Julia Kristeva" 123
"The Diamond Lens" (O'Brien) 88
Dickinson, Emily 32, 28
The Difference Engine (Gibson and Sterling) 135–136, 141
Di Filippo, Paul 7–8, 139
Dillard, Annie 82
Dillon, Grace L. 120
Dimitriadis, Greg 9
Discipline and Punish (Foucault) 125
The Doctor and the Kid (Resnick) 146
"Dr. Heidegger's Experiment" (Hawthorne) 87
Dorney, John 24

Index

Dracula (Stoker) 20, 24–30, 159n5, 160n5
"Dracula's Guest" (Stoker) 26–28
"Drawing from Life" (Kiernan) 73–74
"The Dreams in the Witch House" (Lovecraft) 94
The Drowning Girl: A Memoir (Kiernan) 6, 16, 104, 105–116, 153, 155, 164n11, 165n12, 166n21, 166n24
"The Dry Salvages" (Eliot) 83
The Dry Salvages (Kiernan) 117, 121–125
Dubliners (Joyce) 150
Duhem, Pierre 16, 104
Duke, Shaun 145–146.
Dumbrava, Gabriela 65–66, 162n7
Dundes, Alan 61
Dvorak, Ken 135
dystopia 14, 17, 58, 117, 119, 124–128, 134, 146–147, 156, 168n10

ecocriticism 62–63, 65
ecoGothic 15, 61–65, 105, 161ch4n5
Edgar Huntly (Brown) 11, 150
Einstein, Albert 91–92, 95
Eliot, George 151
Eliot, T.S. 83, 152
Ellerby, Janet M. 112
Ellis, Edward S. 135
Ellul, Jacques 168n11
"Emptiness Spoke Eloquent" (Kiernan) 28–30
The Encyclopedia of Science Fiction (Clute and Nicholls) 135
Epistemology of the Closet (Sedgwick) 33
"Estate" (Kiernan) 39
L'Ève future (Villiers de l'Isle-Adam) 139
"Ex Libris" (Kiernan) 41, 93, 99
extraordinary bodies 48, 51–54
Extraordinary Engines: The Definitive Steampunk Anthology (Gevers) 135

"Faces in Revolving Souls" (Kiernan) 54–55, 59, 161ch3n6
"The Facts in the Case of M. Valdemar" (Poe) 88
Fairhall, James 25
Fairy and Folk Tales of the Irish Peasantry (Yeats) 27
"Fairy Tale of Wood Street" (Kiernan) 74
fairy tales 15, 21, 71–74, 109, 162n17; definition of 61–62; *see also* folklore
The Fall (Camus) 166n20
"The Familiar" (Le Fanu) 92, 94
Ferguson, Christine 134
Feyerabend, Paul K. 16, 80–81, 91
Fiedler, Leslie 9, 13; on science fiction 148; on the tyranny of the normal 52, 131, 161ch3n4
fin de siècle 14, 30, 32–34, 39, 41, 43–44, 138
Finnegans Wake (Joyce) 19
"Fish Bride (1970)" (Kiernan) 70–71
The Five of Cups (Kiernan) 4–5, 14, 24–26
Les Fleurs du mal (Baudelaire) 38, 42, 44

"*Les Fleurs Empoisonnées: or, Dans le Jardin des Fleurs Toxiques*" (Kiernan) 40
"Flotsam" (Kiernan) 101–102
folklore 13–15, 17, 63, 65, 67, 75, 152, 156, 157; definition of 61–62; Dineh folklore 162n8; Irish folklore 19, 21, 26–28, 30, 159ch1n3; Norwegian folklore 74; Romanian folklore 65, 67; Swedish folklore 73; *see also* fairy tales
"For One Who Has Lost Herself" (Kiernan) 68–69
Ford, Jeffrey 143
Ford, Richard 107–108
Forster, E.M. 168n10
Foucault, Michel 125, 165n7
Four Quartets (Eliot) 83
Fowler, Karen Joy 13
"The Foxholes of Mars" (Leiber) 167ch8n3
"A Fragment of Life" (Machen) 97–98
Frank Reade and His Steam Man of the Plains (Enton) 145
Frankenstein (Shelley) 13–14
Freaks: Myths and Images of the Secret Self (Fiedler) 52
Freneau, Philip 169n12
Freud, Sigmund 107
"From Cabinet 34, Drawer 6" (Kiernan) 79–81
From Weird and Distant Shores (Kiernan) 24
"Frontiers in Space" (Wolfe) 120, 167n3
"Further Notes on Edgar Poe" Baudelaire 32

"Galápagos" (Kiernan) 118, 152
Ganz, Shoshannah 65
Garland-Thomson, Rosemarie 15, 37, 51–52, 60, 160ch3n3, 161ch3n5
Gautier, Theophile 36–37, 41–42, 44
Gender Trouble (Butler) 34, 37
genocide 120, 121, 133
Gibson, William 135
Gill, Jo 106
Gilman, Felix 146
"Glass Coffin" (Kiernan) 38–39
Glotfelty, Cheryll 62–63
Goddu, Teresa A. 11, 48, 151
"Goggles (c. 1910)" (Kiernan) 137, 146–148
Goliath (Westerfeld) 136
Gomolka, C.J. 161n8
The Gothic Imagination (Tibbetts) 151
Gould, Stephen Jay 141
Graves, Robert 161ch4n4
Graves, Thomas E. 64
"The Great God Pan" (Machen) 88
"Green Tea" (Le Fanu) 22–23
Grewell, Greg 120
Gutleben, Christian 136

Hager, Lisa 135
Haggerty, George E. 33; on the figure of loss 56–57; on "Gothic" and "gothic" 12, 48
Halberstam, Judith 55

hallucination 73, 74, 86, 95–96, 98, 100, 109, 114; definition of 93; *see also* illusion
Hamilton, Edmond 122, 167*n*6
Haraway, Donna 54
Harris, Jason Marc 21, 23, 75
Harrison, Harry 136
"The Hashish Eater; or, The Apocalypse of Evil" (Smith) 42
"The Haunter of the Dark" (Lovecraft) 99
The Haunting of Hill House (Jackson) 90, 163*n*15
Hawthorne, Nathaniel 87, 111, 126–127, 150, 164*n*10
Hillard, Tom, J. 62, 65
The History of Sexuality (Foucault) 165*n*7
"The Hole with a Girl in Its Heart" (Kiernan) 96
Hollinger, Veronica 13
Holmes, Richard 104
"L'Homme aux têtes de cire" (Lorrain) 34
"The Hound" (Lovecraft) 42
"Houses Under the Sea" (Kiernan) 44, 46, 152
"Houston, Houston, Do You Read?" (Tiptree, Jr.) 129
The Huge Hunter; Or, The Steam Man of the Prairies (Ellis) 135
Hurley, Kelly 33, 97; on the abhuman 63, 161*n*2; on the New Woman 30, 140
Hutton, James 67
Huysmans, Joris-Karl 36, 42, 44
"Hydrarguros" (Kiernan) 92–93, 117

"I Am the Abyss and I Am the Light" (Kiernan) 130–131
"The Icons of Science Fiction" (Jones) 58–59
illusion 94, 100, 115–116, 144, 156; definition of 93; *see also* hallucination
imperialism 19, 20, 31, 146, 148; and science fiction 119–120; *see also* colonization
In a Glass Darkly (Le Fanu) 27
"In the Dreamtime of Lady Resurrection" (Kiernan) 87–88
"In the Water Works (Birmingham Alabama 1888)" (Kiernan) 5, 65–66, 76, 78–79, 152, 167*n*7
"In View of Nothing" (Kiernan) 118
Indigenous peoples 11, 168*n*1; colonial attitudes toward 25, 122; demonization of 135, 168*n*2; devastation of 19, 136–137, 138, 145–146, 167*n*2; incarceration of 147; racist attitudes toward 143–144, 145; research methods of 164*ch*7*n*4; resisting colonization 123; science fiction as non-fiction 120; writing out of history 148
"The Inmost Light" (Machen) 88
intergenerational haunting 73, 113, 154–155, 166*n*25
"Introduction: The 19th Century Roots of Steampunk" (Nevins) 135
Invasion of the Body Snatchers (Finney) 120
Inventing Ireland (Kiberd) 19–20, 25, 159*n*4

Irish Classics (Kiberd) 27, 30
Irwin, W.R. 91

Jackson, Rosemary 11; on fantastic literature 96, 102; on fear 95, 130–131
Jackson, Shirley 90, 150, 163*n*15
Jagoda, Patrick 135
James, M.R. 74, 76, 77, 164*ch*6*n*4
Jameson, Elizabeth 141
Jameson, Frederic 82, 119, 127, 131
Jamieson, H.E. 66
Jarvis, Timothy 7
Jennings, Dana 7
Jeter, K.W. 134, 136, 141
"John Four" (Kiernan) 126–127, 152, 168*n*13
John Hay Library 7
Johns-Putra, Adeline 73
Jones, Gwyneth 13, 58–59
Joshi, S.T. 1, 10, on Kiernan 7, 79, 104, 170*n*10
Jotterand, Fabrice 57
Joyce, James 19, 29, 30, 105, 117, 150, 152
Joyce, P.W. 21
Jung C.G. 93–94, 102–103

Kahneman, Daniel 99–100
Kaku, Michio 167*n*4
Kerslake, Patricia 119
"A Key to the Castleblakeney Key" (Kiernan) 22–23
Kiberd, Declan 27, 30; on the colonization of Ireland 19–20, 25, 159*n*4
Kincaid, Paul 12
The King in Yellow (Chambers) 37
"The King of Birds" (Kiernan) 23–24
"The King of Nodland and His Dwarf" (O'Brien) 41
Kohlke, Marie-Luise 136
Kotwasińska, Agnieszka Magdalena 7, 108, 114–115
krijnen-kemp, rj 42–43
Kristeva, Julia 11, 15, 16; on abjection 46–47, 70, 161*n*2; on melancholia 57; on writing one's life 106, 110, 112, 123–124, 166*n*22
Kuhn, Thomas S. 16; on science 80; on scientific paradigms 162*n*3

The Lair of the White Worm (Stoker) 28
Lansdale, Joe R. 145
Laquer, Walter 43
"The Last Child of Lir" (Kiernan) 21–22, 31
The Last Man (Shelley) 128–129
The Last September (Bowen) 24
Latham, Bethany 4
Latham, Rob 119
Latham, Sean 164*ch*7*n*3
Latour, Bruno 16, 78, 162*n*1
Lawrence, Jay 139
Le Fanu, Joseph Sheridan 14, 19, 94; and colonization 23; influence on Kiernan 21, 22–25, 27
Le Guin, Ursula K. 13, 120, 167*n*3

Index

Leiber, Fritz 162*n*9, 164*ch*6*n*3, 167*n*3
Lem, Stanislaw 123
Levy, Maurice 10
Lewis, Barry 105
Lewis, Simon, L. 64
LGBTTQ+ 14, 32, 33–34, 44–45, 156
Liebmann, M.J. 167*n*2
Limerick, Patricia Nelson. 140, 168*n*4
"The Literature of Exhaustion" (Barth) 148
"Little Red Riding Hood" 152, 162*n*16; in Kiernan's work 13, 62, 71–73, 162*n*14
Lloyd-Smith, Alan 83
"The Long Hall on the Top Floor" (Kiernan) 93, 97–98, 164*n*5
Lorrain, Jean 34
Lovecraft, H.P. 91–92, 100, 123; on biological terror 160*ch*3*n*1; and decadence 5, 6, 41, 42; influence on Kiernan 46, 71, 77, 80, 94, 99, 108, 120, 150, 154, 162*n*18
"The Lovesong of Lady Ratteanrufer" (Kiernan) 162*n*10
Low Red Moon (Kiernan) 5, 162*n*10, 164*n*5
"Lullaby of Partition and Reunion" (Kiernan) 36
Lyell, Charles 67, 82, 140

MacCormack, Patricia 95
"Madonna Littoralis" (Kiernan) 40–41, 152
Man and His Symbols (Jung) 94
"The Man of Adamant" (Hawthorne) 126–127
"The Man Who Made Friends with Electricity" (Leiber) 162*n*9
Mangan, James Clarence 26, 134
Margaret Atwood's Fairy Tale Sexual Politic (Wilson) 160*n*4
Marshall, Nowell 47–48
The Martian Chronicles (Bradbury) 120, 167*n*3
Maslin, Mark A. 64
"The Masque of the Red Death" (Poe) 43
Masterman, Margaret 162*n*3
Mather, Cotton 168*n*2
Maxwell, William 46
McCormack, W.J. 23
McDowell, Ian 3
McGrath, Patrick 109, 130, 161*ch*4*n*6
McHale, Brian 105
"The Melusine (1898)" (Kiernan) 13, 93, 137, 144–146
Melville, Herman 167*n*9
Memoirs of the Life, Writings, and Discoveries of Sir Isaac Newton (Brewster) 78
"The Mermaid of the Concrete Ocean" (Kiernan) 47, 161*n*10, 166*n*14
Middlemarch (Eliot, George) 151
Midgley, Mary 148–149
Miéville, China 12, 136
Miles, Robert 11
Miller, Cynthia J. 135, 144, 147
Miller, Elaine P. 112, 121, 124
Milner, Andrew 12, 127
Moby Dick (Melville) 123–124

Modernism: Evolution of an Idea (Latham and Rogers) 164*ch*7*n*3
Moers, Ellen 13, 169*n*1
Mogen, David 120, 167*n*3
Monaghan, Patricia 68
Monsieur Vénus (Rachilde) 35
The Moon Is a Harsh Mistress (Heinlein) 122
Moore, C.L. 53, 168*n*16
Moreland, Sean 7, 108, 111
Morgan, Jack 46, 160*ch*3*n*1
Mori, Masahiro 161*n*2
Morrow, Bradford 161*ch*4*n*6
"Murder Ballad No. 7" (Kiernan) 20
Murder of Angels (Kiernan) 5, 38, 47
The Myth of Sisyphus and Other Essays (Camus) 110

La Nausée (Sartre) 165*n*13
Nevins, Jess 135
The New Gothic (Morrow and McGrath) 161*ch*4*n*6
Nicholls, Peter 12
Nicol, Bran 164*ch*7*n*3
"A Non-Euclidean View of California as a Cold Place to Be" (Le Guin) 120
"Nor the Demons Down Under the Sea" (Kiernan) 84–85
Norris, Joel 57
The Norton Book of Science Fiction (Le Guin) 13
Notes from the Underground (Dostoyevsky) 165*n*13
"Notes on the Phantom" (Abraham) 73, 113, 165*n*9

O'Brien, Fitz-James 41, 88
O'Brien, Jean M. 169*n*12
O'Brien, Paul 159*n*10
O'Connor, Frank 156
"Ode to Katan Amano" (Kiernan) 59
"One Tree Hill (The World as Cataclysm)" (Kiernan) 77, 85–86, 152
"Onion" (Kiernan) 6, 16, 93, 96–97, 162*n*2
Onions, Oliver 102
O'Riley, Michael F. 23
Osemeobo, G.J. 74

"Paedomorphosis" (Kiernan) 71, 162*n*12
Paglia, Camille 50
Pagliassotti, Dru 169*n*6
paleontology 79, 82, 89; Kiernan's work in 1, 3–4, 7, 9, 13, 15, 76, 81, 92, 141
Palmer, Paulina 33; on hostility toward non-normative people 33, 55, 161
Papers Relevant to Emigration to the British Provinces in North America 26
Parry, Benita 19–20
"The Pearl Diver" (Kiernan) 124–126
"*La Peau Verte*" (Kiernan) 6, 34–35
"The Perfect Girl" (Lawrence) 139
Perschon, Mike 141

194 Index

"Persephone" (Kiernan) 4
Peschel, Oscar 138
Peshawar Lancers (Sterling) 136
the phantom 73, 113
"Pickman's Model" (Lovecraft) 41, 77,
The Picture of Dorian Gray (Wilde) 41
"*Le pied de la momie*" ["The Mummy's Foot"] (Gautier) 36
Poe, Edgar Allan 35, 163n13; and decadence 32, 42, 43; influence on Kiernan 84–85, 88, 108, 150, 164n1, 169n3
The Political Unconscious (Jameson) 82
"The Politics of Staring" (Garland-Thomson) 37, 52, 54
"Pony" (Kiernan) 94, 108, 116, 166n16
postcolonial theory 1, 14, 19–20, 23
postmodernism 16, 45, 105, 108, 116, 164$ch7n$4, 166n21
Poteat, Tonia 55
Powers, Tim 134
Powers of Horror (Kristeva) 11, 47, 168n14
"The Prayer of Ninety Cats" (Kiernan) 6, 41, 152
Praz, Mario 10–11, 151
Priest, Cherie 145
Prince Zaleski and Cummings King Monk (Shiel) 42
Problems of Empiricism (Feyerabend) 91
Prudence (Carriger) 139
"Pterosaurs" (Westfall) 3
Punter, David 10; on gothic trauma 11, 20, 48, 109
The Psychic Life of Power: Theories in Subjection (Butler) 50, 55
Pynchon, Thomas 129, 168n19

"Quatrains and Aphorisms" (Yeats) 21
Queer Gothic (Haggerty) 33
Queer theory 1, 14, 33, 48, 60, 160$ch2n$1
The Queer Uncanny (Palmer) 33, 161n7

"Random Thoughts Before a Fatal Crash" (Kiernan) 37–38
"Rappaccini's Daughter" (Hawthorne) 87
"Rappaccini's Dragon (Murder Ballad No. 5)" (Kiernan) 87–88, 162n17
"Rats Live on No Evil Star" (Kiernan) 77, 88–89
"Reading the Grimms' *Children's Stories and Household Tales*" (Tatar) 62
Red Delicious (Kiernan) 6
The Red Tree (Kiernan) 6, 16, 62–65, 70, 93, 104, 105–116, 153, 161$ch4n$3, 164$ch7n$2, 165n11, 169n2
"A Redress for Andromeda" (Kiernan) 163n10
Resnick, Mike 146
reverse colonization 29, 118–119, 123
Ridenhour, Jamieson 23, 25
"Riding the White Bull" (Kiernan) 59, 121, 124
Rieder, John 12, 17; definition of "colonialism" 166n1; on science fiction and empire 119; on science fiction as social criticism 132, 149
The Rise of Ransom City (Gilman) 146
"The Road of Needles" (Kiernan) 6, 13, 72–73
"The Road of Pins" (Kiernan) 72
Robb, Brian J. 134
Robisch, S.K. 162n8
Rose, Margaret 135, 169$ch9n$5
Rousseau, Jean-Jacques 106
Russ, Joanna 12

St. Augustine 106
"Salammbô" (Kiernan) 39, 42, 43, 44
"Salammbô Redux (2007)" (Kiernan) 39, 47
"Salmagundi (New York City 1981)" (Kiernan) 39–40, 160n6
Salomé (Bryant) 41
Salomé (Wilde) 35–36, 160$ch2n$3
Salomon, Roger B. 11, 48, 83
"Sanderlings" (Kiernan) 84
Scarry, Elaine 48; on the body in pain 15, 49, 51, 60
Schultz, Matthew 113–114
Science Fiction and the Mass Cultural Genre System (Rieder) 12, 132, 149
science studies 15; critique of 15–16, 78, 164$ch7n$4
Scientific Realism and the Plasticity of Mind (Churchland) 91
"Sculptures in Prose" (Joshi) 7
"A Season of Broken Dolls" (Kiernan) 34–35, 59–60
"The Second Coming" (Yeats) 127, 160n11
Sedgwick, Eve Kosofsky 33, 160n5
Seetee Ship (Williamson) 122
Sellars, Wilfred 97
Seshagiri, Urmila 164$ch7n$3
"The Seventh Expression of the Robot General" (Ford) 143
Sexton, Anne 88–89, 110, 166n18
"The Shadow Over Innsmouth" (Lovecraft) 80
Shakespeare, William 84
"Shambleau" (Moore) 168n16
Shawl, Nisi 8, 139
Sheedy, Alessandro 7
Shiel, M.P. 42
Showalter, Elaine 36; on Victorian gender roles 138–140
sídhe 6, 19, 20, 21, 25–29, 159$ch1n$3
Siemann, Catherine 135
Silk (Kiernan) 4–5, 22
"Skin Game" (Kiernan) 36
"Slouching Towards the House of Glass Coffins" (Kiernan) 117, 127–128, 152
Smith, Andrew 161$ch4n$5
Smith, Clark Ashton 42–43
Smith, John 168n2
Smith, Susan 53
Sokal, Alan 15–16, 78, 164$ch7n$4
Solaris (Lem) 123
Soulless (Carriger) 142

Index **195**

specters 16, 31, 106, 110, 151; Derrida on 113–115, 155, 166n26
"The Sphinx" (Wilde) 35
"The Sphinx's Kiss" (Kiernan) 35–36
"Spindleshanks (New Orleans, 1956)" (Kiernan) 94, 100–101
Le spleen de Paris (Baudelaire) 32, 38
Spurr, David 25, 122, 148; on surveillance 137
"Standing Water" (Kiernan) 16, 93, 98–99
Stannard, David, E. 168n17
"The Steam Dancer (1896)" (Kiernan) 53, 137, 142–143
"The Steam Man of the Prairie and the Dark Rider Get Down" (Lansdale) 135, 115
Steamboy (Otomo) 143
"The Steampunk That Dare not Speak Its Name" (Shawl) 139
Sterling, Bruce 135
Sterling, S.M. 136
Stillman, Peter G. 132
Stimpson, Kristin 135–136, 139, 168n4
Stock, Amanda 135
Stoker, Bram 10, 14, 19, 20, 24–30, 90, 159n5, 159n7, 160n5
"Stoker's Mistress" (Kiernan) 20, 26–28, 159n6
"The Street of the Four Winds" (Chambers) 37
"The Striding Place" (Atherton) 88
Suggs, George G., Jr. 141
Supernatural Horror in Literature (Lovecraft) 46
Suvin, Darko 12
Synchronicity (Jung) 102–103

Tabas, Brad 63–64, 67, 74
"*Tableaux Parisiens*" (Baudelaire) 38
Taddeo, Julie Anne 135, 178
Tales of Pain and Wonder (Kiernan) 6, 38
"Tall Bodies" (Kiernan) 93, 98
"The Tartarus of the Maids" (Melville) 167n9
Tatar, Maria 62
Taylor, Mary Anne 135, 140
Teaching a Stone to Talk (Dillard) 82
"Tears Seven Times Salt" (Kiernan) 42, 55–56, 161n9
Tedescui, Victoria 62
"The Third Expedition" (Bradbury) 122
Thornton, Russell 138, 167n2
"The Thousand-and-Third Tale of Scheherazade" (Kiernan) 159ch1n3
Threshold: A Novel of Deep Time (Kiernan) 5, 66–67, 78–79, 81
Tibbetts, John C. 151
"Tidal Forces" (Kiernan) 93–95, 102–103, 118, 152
The Time Machine (Wells) 149
Tiptree, James, Jr. [Alice Bradley Sheldon] 1, 6, 129
"To This Water (Johnstown, Pennsylvania 1889)" (Kiernan) 93, 103
Torok, Maria 113

Tracey, Robert 21, 27
A Transatlantic Tunnel, Hurrah! (Harrison) 136
transgender 14, 38, 48, 161n8; bias against 54–55, 131
"Transhumanist Declaration" 58
"The Treasure of Abbot Thomas" (James) 164ch6n4
Trexler, Adam 73
Trussoni, Danielle 8
Turner, Frederick Jackson 168n4
Two Worlds and In Between: The Best of Caitlín R. Kiernan, Volume 1 (Kiernan) 7
the tyranny of the normal 14, 52, 60, 119, 131, 145, 156
Tyranny of the Normal (Fiedler) 52, 161ch3n4

"Ulalume" (Poe) 88
Ulysses (Joyce) 105, 117
Uncle Silas (Le Fanu) 24
"Unter den Augen des Mondes" (Kiernan) 67–68
"Untitled Grotesque" (Kiernan) 36–37
Unutterable Horror (Joshi) 10, 104, 169n3

V (Pynchon) 168n19
"Valentia" (Kiernan) 76, 81–82, 86, 152, 163n7
VanderMeer, Jeff 134
Van Riper, A. Bowdoin 144
Veliki, Martina Domines 106
"Victoria" (Di Filippo) 139
Villiers de l'Isle-Adam 139
"A Voyage in My Bed" (O'Brien) 41

Walpole, Horace 10, 56, 150
The War of the Worlds (Wells) 120
Warlord of the Air (Moorcock) 120
Warner, Michael 33, 160ch2n1
Weakland, Joseph 145–146
Weida, Jaime 7, 116
Weir, David 32
"The Wendigo" (Blackwood) 111
"Werewolf Smile" (Kiernan) 108
Westerfeld, Scott 136
Westfall, Aundrea 3
Weston, Ruth D. 69, 86, 125
"What I Didn't See" (Fowler) 13
"When It Changed" (Russ) 129
When Life Nearly Died (Benton) 84
"Whilst the Night Rejoices Profound and Still" (Kiernan) 13, 20
"Why Has Critique Run out of Steam?" (Latour) 78
The Wild Wild West (CBS) 145
Wild Wild West (Sonnenfeld) 143
Wilson, Sharon Rose 72, 160n4, 163n13
Wilt, Judith 151
Windling, Terri 162n16
Wisker, Gina 7
Wittgenstein, Ludwig 83
Wolf, Leonard 90

"The Wolf Who Cried Girl" (Kiernan) 67
Wolfe, Gary K. 1, 120, 152, 167n3
"The Wood of the Dead" (Blackwood) 86, 98
Woolf, Virginia 110, 164n11, 166n19, 166n23
The Word for World Is Forest (Le Guin) 120
Wormwood: A Drama of Paris (Corelli) 34
Writings on Irish Folklore, Legend and Myth (Yeats) 27
Wrong Things (Brite and Kiernan) 38

Yeats, William Butler 19, 30, 46, 152; influence on Kiernan 21, 23, 27, 127, 128, 159n6
The Yellow Book (Kiernan) 41
Yoder, Don 64

"Zero Summer" (Kiernan) 131–132
Zhu, Liping 169n9
Zipes, Jack 62